NICKOS
The Young Greek Immigrant

The remarkable story of a thirteen-year-old
Greek boy who went from peeling potatoes
at the Trocadero Cafe in Trangie, NSW – to becoming
one of Australia's most successful businessmen.

First published in 2019

Published by
A.K.A. Publishing Pty Limited
24/2–14 Bayswater Road, Kings Cross NSW 2011
PO Box 2135, Strawberry Hills NSW 2012 Australia
Phone: +1300 69 78 67
Fax: +1300 55 44 61
Email: admin@akapublishing.com.au
Web: www.akapublishing.com.au

ISBN 9780646996011

Cover design and typesetting by Nikki M Group Pty Ltd
Printed by Ligare

NICKOS

The Young Greek Immigrant

NICK ANDREWS

Contents

Dedicated to Maria Andrews,
the woman who is there,
through thick and thin.

BOOK ONE

Growing up in Greece

Chapter One

My father was a policeman living in the village of Porovitsa, some 150 kilometres from Athens. There were only forty-six houses and forty-six families in Porovitsa in the 1940s. And if you imagine my father as being something like a 'country cop', nothing could be further from the truth. Unfortunately, being a policeman anywhere in Greece at that time was a dangerous occupation, as you will learn from my story. I was born on 16 August 1933, the oldest child of Harry and Maria Androutsopoulos. Almost all of my childhood took place against the backdrop of war.

When World War II began on 3 September 1939, the Italians joined the Axis alliance with Germany and invaded Albania, Egypt and Somalia. They then invaded Greece on 28 October 1940. Benito Mussolini, the Italian Prime Minister, had dreams that once more the Romans would have another empire, but to everyone's surprise the Italian forces was no match for the Greek army. Within four months, the Italians had been driven back to Albania.

Left: With my mother, myself, my three younger brothers, and cousin Peter.

Above: My father in the early days of his marriage
Left: My father, Harry Androutsopoulos, in uniform, 1941.

This was a humiliating situation for Mussolini and an intolerable one for Hitler. German troops invaded on 6 April 1941. People with long memories remember Greece being invaded in World War II, but not many know about the brutal civil war that took place after that. This broke out after the Germans were defeated and continued on until 1949. But I am getting ahead of my story. I was seven and a half years old when the Germans invaded and at that moment became the head of my family.

Every man in the village aged between twenty and forty had to go into the army. I can remember the men forming up in the village square before they marched off. My father pulled me aside and we talked. "When I am away, you are the man of the house. You have to look after your younger brothers and your mother." I was very proud of my father and although I was only a boy, I took very seriously the responsibility he had given me. I have many memories of the war, and because they are the memories of a child, they are things that come into my head without any set order or logic. But that moment in the village when the men, including my father, marched off to war was the beginning of a chapter in our lives when we all lived in fear.

This was a story which was being repeated all over Europe at this time – young men being marched off to war – and women and children left behind to somehow make ends meet. My mother couldn't understand how life could possibly go on without the men being in the village to do their work.

In the early days of the war, school lessons continued but this became increasingly difficult. There were no teachers available – they were all in the army. Some ladies in the village tried to continue

Left: My grandfather Nicholas Androutsopoulos.

the classes, with limited success. And as the government wasn't paying them, we used to bring to school a few eggs or a lettuce, and sometimes even a chook that had been killed. We also sent food – boxes of fruit, corn and eggs – to Uncle Milton, who was a solicitor in Athens. During the war, there was no work for him and food was scarce in the cities. When we killed a chook or a goat, we would send him a bit of meat.

Our school classes would be held for a few weeks and then we would have a break of three weeks. Obtaining an education was not a priority in our village and there were plenty of distractions to keep me busy. Straight after school, I would pick olives or work in the garden with my mother. Often, I would do a full day's work after school.

One day a mother from the village with two boys around about five and seven years old knocked on our door. She was crying and she lay the boys down on the floor.

They were going blue in the face – their stomachs were swollen from hunger. She asked my mother for something to eat. My mother grabbed a bottle of olive oil, rushed in – and I went with her – she put two soup spoons of olive oil in the kids' mouths and made sure they swallowed. After five or ten minutes they opened their eyes and the colour in their face came back. The way that food could be so comforting and healing and pain alleviating stuck with me for a long time.

Before he left for the war, my father showed me how to do various things including how to make wine. This was very important for our family because it was our only source of cash revenue. We used to sell bottles of wine to the holiday-makers from Athens. And although we also sold them olive oil, wine was the main cash product. We had three of these five-hundred-litre kegs and at least one, and sometimes two of them, had wine in them which was being aged from previous years.

He taught me how to prepare the wine. My father gave me a little thermometer to put into the wine and told me it had to come up to the number twelve. He said, "If it goes above the number twelve, put water in it." If instead it was too low – then it needed sugar. After testing it, I had to seal the top of the keg with resin from a pine tree. I had to heat it up in the fire on the saucepan and then melt it. "Be careful you don't burn yourself when you do this," he warned, "but you need to make the seal 100% airproof when it's full." As my father gave these instructions in the art of winemaking, I wrote them down very carefully. Even as a boy, my father instilled in me a sense of pride in the things that I did. It was important to me, even as a boy, that I did not let him down.

Above: My grandmother Sophia with her four children. She was widowed at the age of twenty-seven.

Chapter Two

I was born in Porovitsa, which is a little town up in the mountains of Western Greece. The Krathis River comes down from the mountains and passes on to Porovitsiana, which is the beach-side area of the town. They call it Porovitsiana because it's down low, near the sea, while the rest of the town is up in the mountains. The distance would be about six kilometres from one end to the other. In between these two locations is the village of Akrata, which is where all the villagers go and do their shopping. The saying goes that Porovitsa is the main town and Porovitsiana is the weekender. The townspeople who lived by the seaside in Porovitsiana would go back up to the mountains in the summer because the mosquitos and moisture were unbearable. Also, tuberculosis was still a common health problem when I was growing up, so escaping the damp summer air swarming with mosquitos could really be a life changer. The fresh mountain air was also better for one's health. Today it's the opposite – everyone lives near the beach in the summer, because the mosquitos are no longer a problem.

My family lived in the mountains year-round. We had wine, sheep, goats and figs. Although my father was a policeman, the salary he received was very small – certainly not enough to support a family with. This was how it was with anyone so employed – teachers or public servants – people always had to have other means of income, such as having a few sheep or goats. Back then there were no cars in the village – people had to commute on horseback or by foot. Summers were glorious, but winters were harsh and it was not unusual for two feet of snow to fall in our village. Many decided they would go back and live by the sea during the winter and return to their rustic roots in the summer. Because of this, there was consistent migration from Porovitsa to Porovitsiana between the seasons, and my family was no exception.

Our house in the mountains was bought by my great-grandfather and was three hundred years old. Down by the seaside at Porovitsiana we had a smaller house, because the main town was closer to the mountainside. It's where all the celebrations and events happened in the spring and summer time. A lot of tourists and relatives would come down from Athens to have long weekends there. In Australia the farmer lives on the property and goes into town to get supplies.

In Greece, and in most places in Europe, the farmer lives in the village and walks out to the farm every day. I don't know why this is, but to me the difference is that in places like Greece farmers are much more part of the community – they live in it – and see their neighbours every day.

Every morning I would wake up and milk our goats and collect our chooks' eggs. Usually, this was what I had for breakfast – goat's milk and eggs. My favourite goat had black and white stripes, so we called him *Liara*, which means 'zebra' in Greek. Even during the war time I would come back from school and take Liara and the other goats out into the paddock to feed so that there would be enough milk for me and my younger brothers in the morning.

The village had a local shepherd whose name was Tsekenis. He would come down to the little square between the houses every morning and let out a whistle that was heard by the entire town. In response, everybody would open their doors and their sheep would hurry on out because they recognised the shepherd's whistle. They would gather on the square and when the shepherd had about three hundred sheep – basically all the sheep in town – he would take them out to feed them in various paddocks and locations in the district. At about four o'clock each afternoon the shepherd would return to the square with his flock. Then as soon as they came into town, all of the sheep would separate of their own accord and wait by the gates of their various owners. One person had two sheep, another might have only had one and another ten, but each one knew their homes. The lambs would be inside – it was springtime when they were born – and they would often bleat for their milk. The mothers would be outside and the lambs would be at the gate with their little tails wagging excitedly. Then my mother would open the door and they would race in and feed the lambs. Sometimes the little lambs didn't have a mother and they would go to another for milk. The mother would reject it, until their lamb had a feed first, and then after that they would accept them. This was a daily ritual in our village, and as you may have guessed, the lambs lived under the house with us. It does amuse me today when we all take it for granted that our children should have their own bedroom – there I was in a small house with my father, mother and brothers, and our sheep, horse and four goats downstairs.

Previous page: Porovitsa – a small village up in the mountains. The house where I was born and lived in until I was thirteen is the one in front with the windows and a balcony on the left.

Our goats were not given to the shepherd because he had his own goats to look after and also because they feed differently to sheep. Whereas sheep like to forage over pastures, goats tend to take care of themselves and are famous for eating virtually anything. After I came home from school, the first thing I did was collect our two goats, Liara and Zonari, who was white with brown stripes. I would take the goats out to feed after school every day.

We used to kill a goat and put it in the oven. Sometimes, there was too much meat for one family, so we used to give half to our relatives and when they killed a goat they would give us half of theirs. One of my many roles was to be the messenger and delivery boy. I would take meat left over from one of our goats to our relatives and sometimes exchange this for goat's milk. To make cheese, you do need more milk than that produced by our own goats. So we would go around the village and people who had milk would give us gallons of goat's milk to make cheese. When the cheese was made, I would then go back to these people and distribute to them portions of the cheese. The same applied with the chickens, the eggs, the meat and everything else. In some villages in Greece that is still going on now. As you can imagine, it creates a strong bond between all the villagers as what we had was shared for the benefit of everyone. It was very rare for money to change hands.

My grandmother used to knit jumpers for us from the wool shorn from the half-dozen sheep we had. On celebration days my father would kill one of the little goats. He would give half to my uncle and then cook the rest of it – beautiful baked goat.

We used to also produce wheat, but not in any great quantities. I still remember how when it was time to harvest the wheat, the whole family, young and old, would be out there because my father couldn't pay wages for this. We would do it all together and sing songs as we worked. The stalks of wheat would be about a metre high and there we would all be cutting and binding up the harvest in the sun while people sang and whistled and celebrated life. It doesn't get more beautiful than that. My mother would fix a meal for the harvesters – perhaps ten people – and she would sometimes kill a rooster, or we would have spaghetti, or even baked beans. One of my tasks was to carry the dishes from the house out to the fields, which would have been one to three kilometres away. To make sure that the food didn't get cold, I would run the whole way.

The wheat would be bound into bundles, tied and put on the horse – two bundles on either side – and taken into town. It would then be stacked up on the side of the threshing floor which was a large flat area in the village with a big post in the middle. The horses were tied to this post and then walked around and around in a circle, stomping on the wheat which had been packed in. They would hook up about four horses which would walk around the threshing floor crushing it down, so that all the straw would break and the wheat would go to the ground while the straw stayed up. When this was happening, I walked behind the horses with a whip to make sure they weren't running, and that they all pulled their weight and walked in a straight line. The horses needed to go at a fast pace without running, and without nodding off, which they sometimes tended to do. My father used to take over and wake them up because the horses knew whenever I was behind them and would go slower, not worried about the whip in the arm of a ten year old. Then my father would come over, and just hearing his voice they would brighten up and starting walking faster.

After the straw broke from one metre down to about thirty centimetres, the horses would be taken away. It would usually take two to three hours to do each lot of wheat. We would then rake up all the straw and put it into bags. The straw was compressed and used to make bricks. Then the family would get in and sweep the wheat that was still there on the ground. It would be swept into a corner and then picked up with a big shovel and thrown up into the air. The wheat would then separate from the small pieces of straw and then we would put the wheat into a canvas bag. Our animals survived on that wheat during the winter as the paddocks were too frosty to graze on.

I was so pleased to be able to help with the harvest because I was the oldest son in the family and really the only help my father had. I was always competing, always trying to do the best I could because he didn't have anyone else. Other people had older sons and they were producing much more and so I was trying to work hard to be as useful as them.

The vineyards we owned were blocks of land about a hectare in size. They were a few kilometres away. My father inherited the vineyard from his parents. It was inherited by them from their parents and they inherited it from their parents and so on. Every time someone got married, they would have children and had to divide their block of lands between each of them. Because of this the blocks would get smaller and smaller. Our vineyard produced a beautiful rose. At harvest time the grapes would be picked and placed in these great baskets which were on the horse's back – one basket on either side. When the baskets on the horse were full, the pickers would take a break in the shade and have something to eat. As a youngster, my father would lift me and put me on the horse and tell me to take it back to the house which was about a half an hour's walk on the horse. At the house, other members of the family would unload the baskets brimming with grapes and put them into a huge timber vat. It was just like you have seen in the movies – people wearing shorts and no shoes would stand in the vat and crush the grapes with their feet. The wine was drained off, fermented, then later put into kegs.

We also had a few fig trees and these trees produced the most beautiful figs – big, brown and juicy – the honey would just run out. And so this picture of village life that I have described was put under a lot of stress when the war started. And although our little village had no strategic importance to any army, the Italian and German soldiers were a daily presence in our lives.

Above: Porovitsa Church.

Chapter Three

The Greek army was no match for the Wehrmacht, and after a series of defeats we surrendered. The country was then occupied by both German and Italian troops. And so the men who had proudly marched off to war returned, in dribs and drabs, and took up where things had left off. Sadly, some men from our village never came home, and their families were devastated. My father was one of the lucky ones, and one day he appeared and we were overjoyed. He was pleased with the things that I had done to help my mother and my younger brothers. When he tasted the wine I had made, he told me it was the best wine that had ever been made in the village. I suspect he said this to me just to make me feel good about all the hard work I'd done while he was away in the army. Even so, it did make me proud to hear him say such things.

When the Italians and Germans came in to occupy the country, they imposed a 7 pm curfew. All armies do this in wartime – it means that they have better control of the situation at night. We weren't even allowed to take our goats out to feed them – if you were seen outside after that time you could be shot on sight. Also, we weren't allowed to have lights on inside the house. The windows had to be blocked in the night time. Mind you, we never had electricity in our town in all the years I lived there. We used kerosene or olive oil lamps. At night, the animals were kept downstairs, and when the goats had little ones, there was always the risk that they would accidently tip over a kerosene lamp and start a fire.

My father resumed his role as a policeman and now was expected to work with the Italian and German occupying forces to maintain law and order. As time went on, his work became increasingly difficult because a hard core of Greek soldiers refused to lay down their arms. They took to bases in the mountains and began guerrilla attacks against the occupying soldiers. Our village was in the mountains and so we were on the front line of this new conflict. This situation makes life very difficult for the ordinary person: if you help the guerrillas, the Germans will punish you; if you obey the Germans, the guerrillas will attack you for being a traitor. But for a policeman it is ten times worse. My father's major responsibility was to keep the peace and to make sure the German soldiers and officers were safe from attacks by the guerrillas.

Because he was a Greek, he was always suspected by the Germans of being sympathetic to the guerrilla's cause. And because he had to work with the Germans, the guerrillas suspected that he was a collaborator. So my father had to walk this fine line: one false move, one atrocity too many – and he would be as good as dead.

I remember that the German officers liked coming for lunch or dinner in our village. No doubt they found the food and wine delicious and cheap. My father and three other policemen would then be there to protect them while they dined and drank. He and the other policemen had to make sure the German officers were safe from attacks by the guerrillas. Often, these officers would have lunch or dinner in a village, drink too much and then take a long walk. The Germans had made it clear that if they were attacked by guerrillas they would blame the police and their lives would be kaput! I also thought it was very cunning of the Germans to have Greek police protect them, because they knew the guerrillas would think twice before attacking their own. Guarding these German officers during their lunch was one thing, but after lunch they insisted on going on a long walk. I can remember my father saying how he could not understand why anyone would want to go for a walk in such dangerous conditions, but that is what they did. And so the officers would finish their lunch and go for an afternoon stroll while my father and his fellow officers went with them – all the while terrified they would be attacked. Whilst they might survive an attack from the guerrillas, they would not survive their 'punishment' at the hands of the Germans.

As the German occupation dragged on, life became harder. All these soldiers had to be fed and so food became scarce. And the attacks by the guerrillas intensified and they became more daring. The British encouraged the guerrillas and parachuted guns and ammunition in to them.

Chapter Four

War is an ugly business, and often the consequences can be catastrophic. One day two prostitutes from the town of Kalavrita arrived and started flirting with the German soldiers – showing off their legs and so forth. Then they let it slip that there was going to be a wild party up in Kalavrita in a few night's time – lots of girls, lots of wine, lots of fun to be had. Word of this then spread like wildfire among the soldiers and on the night about seventy soldiers sneaked off in the middle of the night. When they arrived in Kalavrita for the party, the guerrillas were waiting for them. They shot them all. Then they decapitated them, took all their clothes off and left them in nothing but their underpants. Some kids even played with the decapitated heads.

For five days the Germans searched for their missing soldiers and finally found them at Kalavrita. It was quite a large town with a population of about 3,000. The bodies of these seventy headless corpses had been left lying out in the open in one of the public squares. The German officer in charge called for the town priest and two came up, a young one and an old one. The officer turned to the old priest. "How many years have you been a priest?"

The priest said, "All my life. Sixty years."

"Why didn't you bury them?" the German asked. "Why did you leave them here to rot?"

The priest replied, "Because the guerrillas told me if I went near them they would kill me. They told me to stay away. They said, 'Let the people come and see these dead Germans.'"

To this the officer said, "But when you were sworn in as a priest to serve the Lord's wishes, they didn't ask you to listen to the instructions from the Greek guerrillas. These men are human beings – they could be German, Italian or Greek. They could be anyone, but they are certainly human beings. So why didn't you act as you have sworn when you were ordained as a priest?"

"I was scared they were going to kill me."

"Well, you are not worth living." The German officer raised his pistol and shot him on the spot.

When this happened, the young priest went down on his knees, "Please, please don't kill me." The German looked at him and said, "No, stand up. I am not going to kill you. I'm going to let you live so you can go around and tell people about this terrible thing that has happened to tell all the Greeks around that this is never to happen again. This is not an act of war, this is the work of barbarians. It is inhuman." He then ordered the young priest to gather all the children from the local high school to come to the square. When this happened, the officer stood up on a large stone by the local creek and announced, "I want you all to know that this is not to be repeated. It is inhuman." The officer then drew his pistol and started shooting the children. People panicked and started to run away, but the German soldiers fired their machine guns and soon there were dead children everywhere.

A few days later I was feeding our goats about a kilometre from town when I saw Germans soldiers coming through the vineyard.

There were lots of them and they were spaced about ten metres apart. Quickly, I ran home. When I told my father, I could see from his reaction that he had been expecting this. He knew the Germans were now determined to wipe out the guerrillas once and for all. As he didn't want to upset my mother, he dressed up in his suit, mounted his horse and told her he was going off on some police business. On his way he collected one of his cousin's sons, who was only about nineteen years old. They went off to a place where my father knew there was a little cave where they could hide. There they waited, and the German patrol went past them and did not see them. After a few days this cousin's mother took food to the cave so they would not starve. For about three weeks the German soldiers scoured the countryside looking for the guerrillas. The villagers were able to see the German patrols as they came and went. Then, this cousin's mother said to my father, "Harry, you can go home now. They have gone."

Instead my father replied to her, "Bring the food for another two days. We are not coming home."

"But they are gone. They are not around!" She insisted.

My father, who had experience in the army and as a policeman, replied, "They are not fools, the Germans. They have left other people behind playing ghost." The cousin's mother did as she was told and brought more food. After a few more days she lost patience. She could see that there were no longer any German patrols anywhere and that my father was being unnecessarily cautious.

She went back to the cave and said to my father, "The Germans have gone. There's nobody around. I am taking my son." He tried to talk her out of it, but she would not listen.

As soon as they walked into town the Germans appeared out of nowhere and seized her son. They sent him to a concentration camp in Germany and she never saw her son again. That woman died not long after this happened – overwhelmed by grief and remorse for her own lack of patience.

While all this was happening, there was no sign of my father. Three weeks had passed and we began to believe that he had not survived. I remember playing soccer with some boys and overheard someone say, "Harry is a smart policeman, but he didn't get away." My mother and a cousin searched the grounds for Harry's body because there was still no sign of him and the Germans had well and truly gone.

There was this beautiful flat area in the village where we used to play soccer, but we didn't have a proper ball. The 'ball' we used was made from clothes, stitched together to make it look like a ball. I was playing soccer with my friends when I looked across the road and saw this man in a torn, blue suit walking beside a very skinny horse. I knew it wasn't our horse because he didn't look like this at all. But the more I looked the more I realised this was my father and that was our horse. My father was determined that the Germans would not take the horse for their own use. So he had tied up its legs and hidden it in the high grass of the paddock. After many weeks like this, the horse had almost starved to death. It was just skin and bones. And instead of running up to my father and welcoming him, I turned on my heels and ran back to tell my mother. I don't think I could believe what I was seeing. And my mother – she couldn't believe it either. While we were discussing this, my father arrived at the house with his horse. He had survived. Soon everyone was crying with happiness. My father was riddled with lice. My mother hung up a few sheets in the yard and handed him a razor to shave himself. After that she used methylated spirits to kill the lice, but because he had been living in a cave for weeks his skin was broken in many places and he was soon screaming from the methylated spirits. "Don't do that!" he screamed, but she had to do it to get rid of the lice.

Chapter Five

My grandmother, Sophia, played a big role in my life as a child. She was left a widow with four children when she was about thirty years old. Her husband, Nikos, developed pneumonia when working in the fields and died at the age of thirty-three. Sophia used to go out into the paddocks and do all the manual work. That woman managed to raise those children on her own. Her oldest child, my uncle Milton, became one of the top lawyers in Athens. The second son, my father, Harry, joined the police force. Sam, who was Sophia's third child, immigrated to Australia after the First World War, and had a cafe in the country town of Trangie, New South Wales. I wasn't to know then as a boy that this little, insignificant town of Trangie was to change the course of my life. Effie, the fourth child of Sophia and Nikos, was both beautiful and rich. When she was sixteen, she married a wealthy man from America.

My father's nickname was cognacki (pronounced 'con-yaki'). When I was growing up I used to wonder why they called him that. Then, one day at a cafe in the village, I heard him order, "One cognac, please." The cafe owner brought over to him a glass of cognac. He would have one after work when he could afford it. Most of the time he didn't have the money to buy one. And us, his sons, they used to call us cognac-cakia – meaning 'small cognacs'.

As I grew up, I used to help my mother and father because I was the eldest in the family. But if I did something wrong, my mother would give me a couple of hits with the cane or the stick on the backside. When this happened, I used to burst into tears and then run into my grandmother's arms. She always protected us when we were kids. My mother and grandmother used to live most of the time on their own down at our place by the seaside because it was a flat area near the ocean and she didn't have to climb stairs or put up with snow in the winter time. My grandmother didn't swim, but there were a lot of grandmothers who lived down there, and they used to get together to talk about the past and how they brought their kids up and the rest of it. If it was winter time, and we were around the fire, and I was trying to do my homework, I used to listen to them and listen to the family gossip. It is worth remembering that this was a time when there was no such thing as television or radio, never mind the internet. People talked and for entertainment we drank and sang and danced.

My grandmother was very important to me and to my brothers, but more so to me because she was still very young when I was born. She was always there for advice even though she wasn't well educated and couldn't help me with the simple problems I had with school homework. My mother was even worse – she couldn't help me with my homework – and my father was never there – he was always busy either with the police or with the farm. I had to study on my own and solve any problems I encountered myself. Our family finances were such that we didn't have the money to buy the books I required for class. This meant that I had to borrow textbooks from my friends and read them on the way to school at

Akrata or ask schoolmates what the homework was and they'd help me out. Sometimes I had to improvise. If a schoolmate didn't seem to know what he was talking about, or it wasn't quite making sense to me, I would go and ask someone else.

Sometimes after school I would go to help my mother in the fields and she would find that I was really not that much help. On those occasions she would tell me to go and visit my grandfather Peter, who lived with his two brothers, George and John. In the winter they used to take some coals from the fire and put them to one side. Then they'd put a piece of greaseproof paper down, put some feta cheese on it and cook it. While it was cooling down, they'd open a bottle of wine and quickly finish that off. One of them couldn't hear well, and as they became drunker they started to talk very loudly. I used to wait there for my mother while they got drunk and teased each other. And whenever there were any mishaps, such as spilling the wine or burning the cheese, they blamed each other. "You did it," one of them would complain.

"No I didn't!" would be the reply. "You did!"

"No, I didn't. You did." "I didn't say that."

Every time I was there, they would end up having this conversation over and over again while they were having a few walnuts, cheese, bread and wine. Even though they argued, they were always laughing, always enjoying themselves.

Grandfather Peter used to put these blocks of cheese inside a sheepskin to improve the flavour. When they skinned a lamb, they would pull the skin off like peeling a banana, salt it and leave it out to dry in the sun. Then they would wet the lamb's skin, turn it inside out, then tie the legs tight, both sides and the neck, and then add salty water and these big blocks of white, homemade cheese. Somehow, it improved the flavour of the cheese. They would put all this in the lamb's skin and seal it up. There was no refrigeration in those days.

One day I went there and to my surprise Peter and George seemed quite sad. They didn't laugh or argue or say anything much. Finally, the third brother arrived and looked around and then asked, "What's the matter, has somebody died?" Grandfather Peter replied, "No, nobody has died. I can't find the bloody cheese. I put it away somewhere and can't find it."

I was just a young boy, but I looked around and spotted one of these lamb skins of cheese up high near the ceiling. I called out excitedly, "Hey, Papou – look, the cheese is up there!" Peter turned around and looked to where I was pointing. "My God," he said. "I was waiting to see Barros." In Greek 'Barros' means when somebody dies, their soul is taken away and only their body remains. Grandfather Peter said, "I waited for me to see somebody come to take me away because I died, but I didn't expect to see the cheese on the roof."

He stood up, picked up his walking stick, went over and hooked it to the lamb's skin and pulled it down. It fell to the floor. The skin burst and there was salty water and cheese all over the floor everywhere. They did not bother cleaning up and started cooking and eating. When my uncle John, my mother's brother, came in from the fields with his wife, they were disgusted with the mess on the floor and the two old men cooking this cheese. My grandfather said, "You can say what you like. Just as well I'm deaf, I can't hear a thing." He didn't care. He was quite drunk and laughing and covered from head to toe in cheese. Those were the sorts of things that life was about in those little villages.

Grandfather George was a funny man. He once loaned his coat to a relative whose daughter was getting married. After the wedding, this relative moved further west to be with his daughter and took the coat with him. Not long after the wedding this fellow died. When he was told that he had passed away, Grandfather George said, "Yes, it's a shame he's died, that old mad dog. But I hope they didn't bury him in my coat! Someone please go and find my coat!"

Chapter Six

Word spread that the Germans were determined, once and for all, to follow the guerrillas into the mountains and destroy them. The concern in our village was that along the way these soldiers might be tempted to take our sheep and goats. After a discussion among the village elders, it was decided that everyone in the town would gather their goats together and move them further north as it was thought that the Germans would not go that far. They believed that if we lost everything else, our houses, our crops and our village, at least we would still have our goats. I took our four goats and with other boys from the village made our way up to a place called Valimi. This was the next village up from Porovitsa. There were other boys, most of them older than me, with their family's goats, and we were told to stay off the road and instead go via the paddocks. We put all our goats together and fed them, gave them water and milked them – the goat's milk we drank for ourselves. There wasn't much food. My mother had given me some cheese and bread and told me not to eat more than one piece of bread a day, otherwise it would run out and I'd starve. The other boys and I slept under the stars – we each had a blanket and pillow.

Day after day we looked after our goats. Often, we moved from place to place to avoid being found. Being the youngest, I followed where the others went. It was an experience and a half with few laughs. After about a week there was no food left and we were all very hungry. Finally, after we had survived three days without food, someone from the village came and told us that the Germans had come and gone. We could go back home. When we arrived back in Porovitsa, I was so glad. I felt like I had lived for a lifetime because of that experience – we were away for ten days and for a young boy that is an eternity. It turned out that the German patrols did not interfere with our livestock. The biggest stress was on the parents because they didn't know where we were!

Nothing the Germans did to destroy the guerrillas worked and they grew stronger. One band of guerrillas established themselves up in the mountains in a town called Valimi, which was a little bit bigger than Porovitsa and about an hour away by horse. This is where they set up their headquarters. The guerrillas would come down to the villages and set up an ambush on one of the roads. When some German vehicles went past, they would open fire with their machine guns and kill all the Germans.

Unfortunately, there were times when the guerrillas mutilated the bodies of their victims – pulling their eyes out and worse. Then they would get back on their horses and escape once more up into the mountains. This kind of thing was completely unacceptable to Hitler and his generals. An order was issued, and it was announced in our village that for every German soldier the guerrillas killed, they would hang ten civilians.

The Germans were as good as their word and when another of their soldiers died, they started hanging people. When I walked to school, my mother gave me a handkerchief to put over my mouth because of the smell of the bodies hanging from gallows. After they hung people, the Germans wanted the bodies left up as a constant reminder. This created friction between ordinary Greek civilians and the guerrillas. It hadn't been like this since the Peloponnesian War of 400 BC. Villagers argued with the guerrillas, "If you come down and shoot the Germans, they are going to hang me and my wife and my kids. Stop it." To this the guerrillas would respond, "You are not with us. You are not fighting for your country. You are all Germans." If anyone continued to complain about the guerrillas, they would deal with them ruthlessly. And over time this town of Valimi developed a terrible reputation – anyone who was asked to go up there never ever came back. If anybody appeared to be giving information to the Germans, or suspected of not supporting the guerrillas, they were taken up there and put on trial. A hearing would be held under the trees – that was the court – then judgement would be passed and they would take them up into the mountains and cut their throats. It is estimated that some 25,000 civilians were killed by Greek guerrillas during the war.

Every town had a guerrilla leader and ours was Leonidis Tsekenis, who happened to be an old school friend of my father. Because we didn't have things such as telephones or telegrams, the only way to deliver messages was to write it down, put it in an envelope and deliver this by hand. The guerrillas would ask boys like me to run messages for them. Sometimes, it would take one or two hours to walk or run barefooted to the next village and hand over a message. Also, I suspected one of the reasons the guerrillas used me was because they did not trust my father, and this was a way to see what he would do.

I remember one day Capitano Tsekenis asked me to take a message to the village of Arfara, which was up in the hills about eight kilometres away in the direction of Athens. Normally, it was an hour and a half round trip. But as it was starting to get dark

I knew I would have to do it in half the time – otherwise it would be too dark for me to find the path.

I took off running barefoot. As it was summertime there was a lot of dust on the path and as I ran along I could hear this 'foomp, foomp, foomp' sound behind me, which was the sound of my feet on the powder of the dust. It was becoming darker and darker and the 'foomp, foomp, foomp' echoed behind me and I started to imagine it was someone running after me. My little heart started thumping and I was scared. Every now and then I would stop running and look behind me to see who was following me – but of course there was no one there. Then I'd start running again and straight away hear the 'foomp, foomp, foomp' of my feet in the dust. Eventually, I reached the village of Arfara, delivered the message and then turned around and headed back for Porovitsa.

It was with great relief that I arrived home and my mother gave me something to eat and drink. Then, there was a knock on the door. It was Capitano Tsekenis again with another message. "I want Nick to take this to Voutsimo," he ordered. This was a village down on the other side which would be another two-hour round trip. My mother wasn't putting up with this. "That boy's feet are bleeding," she explained. "He has only just come back now from delivering another message."

"Bring him out," Tsekenis ordered.

"It's late now. He can't do it. Send somebody else."

Tasso was determined. "He has to do this."

My father overheard this conversation and started talking to Tsekenis, and within a few seconds they were having an argument. Mother pulled me aside and said, "Nick, for your father's sake don't let him do this. They will take him to Valimi and we won't see him again. So please go and do it." Meanwhile, I could hear Tsekenis saying, "You're telling me you refuse to help us. What do you call fighting together – being allies – you are trying to be the opposite and you refuse to send your son?"

My father was talking calmly. He was a very well-spoken man and had good self-presentation. For years, on and off, he was elected the president of the town. "I don't think it's fair," he was saying. "Nick's already run a message for you tonight." I could see that my mother was really worried about what might happen. She whispered to me, "Help him Nick, or there'll be trouble."

Tsekenis had the message in an envelope in his hand. I went up to him, took the message and ran off. My father called out, "Come back here," but it was too late. I ran and ran and delivered the message to Voutsimo. Had I not done this, my father would have been sent to his fate in Valimi. I didn't care about my swollen, shoe-less, bleeding feet.

Sometime after this, Capitano Tsekenis approached my father in the village and said, "I want to talk to you." So my father invited him home for dinner. The guerrilla agreed, but then added, "I don't want anyone to see me coming to your house. Make sure no one knows." When they were having dinner, my father was very critical of the guerrillas. He said that the way they behaved by killing people made them no better than goat thieves. The Capitano did not like this at all. He said to my father, "Listen, you talk too much. Shut your mouth." Then he told him that if he continued to criticise the guerrillas they would come for him and all of us. "They will kill all your family," he warned. "They will nail the house shut so no one can get out and then pour petrol on it and set it on fire. You will all burn together. Think about what you're saying because it would be a shame to kill the other people in your family with your big mouth."

My father believed him and that this threat was real. After that meeting, he never said another thing against the guerrillas.

Chapter Seven

One day, I was out looking after a couple of goats near the village of Valkouvina when I saw some German soldiers off in the distance. Then, out of nowhere, a guerrilla appeared and said to me, "I want you to run into town for me." He saw me look at the goats and said, "Forget about your goats. Run into town and tell the leader of the Communist party in town to meet us in the church." I did as he asked and ran off as fast as I could. When they arrived for the meeting, I stayed there and listened to what they were saying. The guerrillas wanted to know what the best way to Valkouvina was. Me and my friend – we must have been eleven years old – went after them. We stayed a distance away from them and when we were close to Valkouvina my friend and I climbed to the top of this olive tree. It was a huge tree – the trunk was as wide as a table. We hid inside the branches and could hear the sound of machine guns in the distance.

About a hundred metres away was a spring with water coming out, and there was a stone cistern with a tap where the horses drank. A German soldier who had been wounded dragged himself to the water tap for a drink. As I was watching this, two guerrillas quickly appeared and bayonetted him on the spot. The guerrillas then took the German's boots off and the rest of his clothes. I used to have bad dreams about what I saw. Sometimes, in the middle of the night, I would wake up screaming.

After the fighting stopped, the guerrillas took the three remaining men as prisoners. It turned out that two of them were Italians and one was a German. My friend and I came down from the tree and went into the town where the guerrillas were celebrating their victory and mocking their prisoners. Then they took them away. While all of this was going on, I happened to overhear one of the guerrillas talking and my father's name came up. One of them complained that my father was uncooperative. Another agreed. "Androutsopoulos is not with us." The leader of the guerrillas was sitting on his horse as this conversation was happening. Then the names of another two men came up. He said, "Get the message out to the others and bring them up to Valimi." Even though I was a child, I knew that once men were taken there they never came back.

Of course, no one noticed me there amongst the crowd – men never give children any credit. After I heard them talking, I quickly ran home. I opened the door and said to my father, "They are talking about you. They are going to come and get you." However, it seemed it was already too late as we could hear their footsteps coming up the steps. Then my father lifted a rug from the floor which revealed a secret passage. He disappeared through the floor and the rug was put back. By this time they were banging on the front door. My mother opened it and one of the men asked, "Where's Harry?" Cleverly, she invited them into the house knowing this would prevent them from seeing him leaving the property and also making it look like she was being helpful. "I don't know where he is," Mother said. "He has disappeared."

They looked around, but our house was not large and they could see that she was telling the truth. The one in charge said, "Let us know when he gets back. We want to talk to him." They then left and we all breathed a sigh of relief.

My father went to another town and didn't come back for seven days. That was often the best way of surviving in these times – by not being in the wrong place at the wrong time.

Chapter Eight

The Germans surrendered in May 1945, but sadly for us Greeks, the war was not over. Within days of the Germans leaving, fighting broke out between the Greek Government forces and the communist guerrillas. They were tough years. Being a policeman, my father had managed to survive dealing with the Germans and the guerrillas. Now, he had to try and keep his head during this conflict between the government and the Communists. Just to give you some idea of how bad it was, about 135,000 Greeks died in the Second World War and over 150,000 died in the Civil War.

Obtaining an education in the middle of a war was a haphazard affair. Sometimes I went to school one day a week, and sometimes not at all. I did not do 4th, 5th or 6th class at all. And it didn't help that one of my primary school teachers was a relative of ours. He used to send me out to look after his goats during class. Despite the lack of importance given to education, I was determined that I should go to high school when I turned twelve. I remember a funny moment when I was discussing this with a friend in front of our fathers. Dad pointed out that I could hardly expect to get into high school when I had missed so much primary school. My friend's father said that the pair of us were too stupid for high school. When we protested about this, my friend's dad said, "Okay. Let me ask you geniuses this: 'Where were you boys born?'"

With one voice both of us shot back, "Porovitsa."

"And how do you spell Porovitsa?"

My friend looked at me with a smile and said, "You spell it."

"P-o-r-r-v-i-t-s-a," I replied confidently.

"Bravo," said my friend's father. "Bravo, but wrong." "Why is it wrong?" I wanted to know.

"Because there is one 'R' and one 'O' in Porovitsa."

He then said to my father, "Harry, let's go. Our kids are idiots – blind as well as stupid. They can't even spell the town where they were born and they want to go to high school." Off the pair of them went. My friend and I were embarrassed and humiliated. I felt so small and have never forgotten that feeling. As it turned out, that was the least of our problems.

There were also fees to be paid for attending high school and my father could not afford this.

After that I walked down to the timber mill at Akrata and spoke to the man in charge. "Can you give me a job? Like I could sweep up, or load trucks, even cut the timber on the saw."

"You are too young," he replied. "Can't I do something?" I pleaded.

He looked at me and he asked, "Why are you desperate?"

I said, "I want to put myself into school so I can do the exams."

"You'll be wasting your time." Then he recognised me and added, "You must be Harry's son?"

At that moment I wished that there was a hole in the ground that I could fall into. "Please don't tell my father, because I didn't ask him if I could come here."

The mill man said, "We will keep it a secret. How much money do you need?" I explained how much was required for enrolment and he said, "Go and book yourself in, then come here every afternoon after school and we'll work something out."

I did what he suggested. I went and booked myself into First Form in high school. Then after school I would go down to the sawmill and do various jobs around the place. The money I earned there paid for my high school fees. However, being at school was one thing – and doing well quite another thing altogether.

Two days before the exam results came out I was with my father and we were going from Porovitsiana up to the other village with both our horses fully packed. As we were going past the Maths teacher's house, a single-storey house up on the hill, the teacher stood up and opened his window for some fresh air. My father, who grew up in the same village as the teacher, asked him how he was. "I have just finished marking everyone's Maths exam," the teacher remarked.

"How did my boy go?" Dad asked.

The teacher explained that a cover was put over the name on the exam paper, so he marked them not knowing whose paper it was. Then he said, "I can't tell you the name, but if you recognise the handwriting I can tell you what your result was." With that we went into the teacher's house and Dad looked through the various exam papers and then said, "There it is. That's Nick's."

The teacher smiled and then whispered the result to my father. My father then put his arm around me and said, "Let's go back to the shops. I forgot something." We turned the horses around and walked back a couple of hundred metres to where the square was with the shops. He took me inside the cake shop and gesturing to all the sweets said, "Pick whatever you want," I looked at him with surprise and commented, "Gee, it must have been good news from the teacher."

My father leaned over and whispered, "Congratulations, you topped the class in the Maths – 95%." In the shop I picked out a sweet called coc, which is round, with cream in the centre and chocolate on the top.

My joy in obtaining a high mark was short-lived. I failed, and failed miserably, every other subject. History – 45%, Geography – 50%, Greek – 40%. All my exam papers, apart from the Maths paper, were a sea of red ink. However, because of my excellent result in Maths, I was given a pass. If it had not been for that, I would not have been able to go to high school.

Chapter Nine

Our fig trees produced the most beautiful figs, but all we ever did with the figs was eat them. One day it occurred to me that I could sell the figs and make money out of it. I used to place some leaves from the grapevines down on the bottom of a basket. Then I'd cut these figs and put them gently in the basket and lay them down so they didn't touch each other because they were very soft and ripe and easily bruised. I would put down more vine leaves and some little sticks that I cut from cane to support the weight and then put the next layer of figs on it – then the next one and the next one. A basketful of figs weighed about five kilograms and although I was a little fellow, I would carry them all the way down to Akrata, to the railway station.

There was no platform at Akrata station – people would just step off the train onto the ground. I would carry the baskets of figs down to the station and wait for the train. When the train came in, I would knock on the top window of the carriages! I had a broomstick with a little basket attached, holding a couple of figs. Passengers would open the window and take the figs that I offered. Most of the time they gave me small change for them but occasionally I was given nothing at all – they would take the figs and then close the window. I would knock again, but they wouldn't open the window because they thought I was a good Samaritan.

My father didn't know about my little enterprise with the figs and I wasn't game enough to tell him because I really wasn't supposed to do anything without his approval. I used to bring the money back to Porovitsa and hide it. Our toilet was positioned out in the yard. It was not much more than a curtain around the side of the tree and a brick wall with a timber floor and a hole. I would pull a brick out from the toilet wall and hide a small pouch with a string in the cavity and put the brick back. Even though everybody was using the toilet, they didn't know there was money hidden there by me.

My mother was very religious and she never missed church on Sunday. One Sunday she realised she didn't have any money for the collection. As everyone knows, this is an important part of any church service – giving money to the poor and unfortunate. Despite our very humble circumstances, we never considered ourselves as being poor.

She asked my father, who told her he didn't have any money. I heard her say, "You have enough money to have your cognac and to go and have a coffee, but no money for me to go to church!"

"You go to the church too much," he replied. "Forget about the church." I could see that my mother was getting very hot under the collar. She was dressed ready to go to church, but there was no way that she would attend without being able to put money into the collection plate. My father walked away.

When this happened I went out to the brick wall where the outhouse was, pulled the money out and went inside and handed it to Mum. She couldn't believe what she was seeing. There was a lot of money there. "Where did this come from?" I explained about the figs I sold at Akrata station. She said, "I will go to the church, but we will have to talk to your father when we have lunch today."

"He's going to pull my ears because I didn't ask his permission," I said.

"We do not do anything behind his back. He must be told," my mother insisted. "Do we have to?" I pleaded.

"Don't worry about him. I will handle it," she said.

Mother went off to church, much to my father's surprise. When she returned she said to him, "Do you know where I got the money for the collection today?" He shook his head. "Nick gave it to me." My father turned and looked at me. Mother continued, "Nick wants to tell you something. Nick, tell your father what you have been doing."

I put all the money I had on the table and I said, "This is yours, Dad." Then I told him what I had been doing, waiting for him to give me a clip over the ears. He looked at the money, then looked at me and said, "That is your money. Where you spend it is your decision. But never do anything before we talk about it. We are a family and we have no secrets from each other." He then walked off to the cafe for his cognac.

In retrospect I guess the idea I had for selling the figs at Akrata station was my first business venture. I was really only a boy, but this idea came naturally to me. After my father told me I could spend the money how I liked, I bought a few things – braces for my short trousers, some sandals – and even a pair of sunglasses.

Chapter Ten

When you tell people you lived through a war, they imagine all sorts of horrible and violent things happening. But in almost every war the biggest danger you face is not being shot or blown up, but hunger and starvation. Everything changes when the fighting starts. For one thing, there are suddenly hundreds of thousands of enemy soldiers who need to be fed. And they take first priority – often getting the food they need at the point of a gun. In the meantime, food had to be there for our own soldiers. Yet a lot of these soldiers were from villages where they were involved in producing food. So there are many more people who need to be fed, less people involved in producing it and less food available all round. Luckily, rural Greece in the 1940s was able to feed its own people – food might have been scarce, but there was no famine.

The situation was a lot worse in the cities, and during the war a lot of people in Athens were desperate for food. People used to go out to the farmers in the country towns to find it. We were very fortunate, living in the country where we produced all our own food. Because we had our own chooks, we had eggs. Also, we could kill a chook and eat it, or kill a little goat. We grew our own wheat, our own corn and our own olive oil. The only thing we didn't have was money to pay a doctor if we needed one, or to buy clothes. This meant that we owned very few items of clothing, and everything we had was patched and mended. My mother would cut pieces from the old clothes and mend a hole. Because my clothes had so many patches, it was often hard to tell what the original colour of my trousers was!

As the situation with food became more desperate in the cities, people there started to trade their homes and units in return for food. Some farmers had legal agreements where they had a deal to supply people with a certain amount of food in return for the title to their house or unit. Depending on the value of the property they would, for example, reach an agreement to supply food for two years – so many eggs, so many litres of olive oil and so on. I only learned about such things through my uncle, Milton, who was a lawyer in Athens.

He was a clever man, and after the war he had clients who came to him who had surrendered title to their properties in these circumstances. Milton noted that although these documents were all legal – that is, signed, witnessed and stamped – there was on the face of it no way to dispute the transaction. However, being the brilliant lawyer that he was, he argued that in Greece we had Roman law and not the Anglo-Saxon law. Because there was no value mentioned in any of these agreements, he considered the situation unfair for his clients because they gave far more by way of property for very little. Even though that very little, which was food, would have saved lives – the house wouldn't have saved the life of anyone starving. That was where the difference was. My uncle challenged one of these agreements and won the case. His clients didn't get their property back, but the farmers who had been given the title had to pay the full value. Eventually because of his success, Milton had about thirty solicitors working for him and made a lot of money.

I recall visiting my uncle one time with my father, who was amazed to see the number of people he had employed. "How the hell are you paying all these lawyers?" my father wanted to know. Milton explained his business strategy. "I have given them all a desk," he explained, "but they don't receive any wages. All the jobs that come into this office are assigned to them in rotation. I set the fees. Each lawyer on a case receives half the fee and I get the other half. They don't pay rent. They don't pay electricity. They don't pay cleaners, or wear and tear, or phone bills etc." Milton was able to capitalise on the fact that he won the first case of this type and he was in all the newspapers. After that, everybody wanted him to be their lawyer. He made a lot of money, but he later lost it through a business deal that went sour. Milton gave financial backing to his best friend who came up with a proposal to open a company in Belgium and export goods from there and Germany into Greece. Unfortunately, Milton was too busy in his legal practice and did not check on his friend, who stabbed him in the back and he lost everything. He trusted somebody he shouldn't have. That is how I learnt my favourite business tip, and it is something I use almost every day: "Trusting is good, checking is better."

Chapter Eleven

As the fighting between the government forces and the Communists continued, my father tried to work out what to do. All through the war with the Germans he had worried that his family could be wiped out. We had come through that, and now we faced the same risks. In the end, he decided that it would be safer – and smarter – to send his oldest son away. Then, a couple of things happened that decided my future for me.

My father's brother, Sam, was forty-two years old and still a single man. He had moved to Australia and had done well. In the aftermath of World War II, Australia had opened its arms to refugees from war-ravaged Europe and the country was thriving. Uncle Sam was looking for a wife. He wrote to my father and explained that there had been a young woman in his class at school whom he had liked. This was before the war and obviously before he went to Australia. "Find out if she is still there and if she is free. If she is, I will marry her." Arranging marriages this way was not at all unusual in Greece. So my father went off to find this woman who, it turned out, was still single, and working as a school teacher. My father said to her, "My brother in Australia wants to marry you." She remembered Sam, and replied like a real Greek woman, "You must ask my father."

My father then went to see Maria's father and explained the situation. There had been another man interested in marrying his daughter, but this fellow had been demanding a large dowry. This is what traditionally happened in Greece, and sometimes with serious consequences. I have known many instances where a family have surrendered possession of their home as a dowry for their daughter and then found themselves living as guests with their married daughter and her new husband. This is why, when it was announced that a man's wife had given birth to a daughter, instead of playing happy music they played sad music. The parents knew they would have to have a dowry to make their daughter marriageable, and this could cause huge financial problems as women had no other form of income or financial means.

When my father approached this young woman's father, he said that his brother Sam in Australia did not require a dowry. The father's eyes lit up immediately. Not only that, he would also pay for her journey to Australia. This was too attractive a proposition for the father to turn down and so it was agreed that Maria and my uncle Sam would marry.

Then my father decided that I should go to Australia. I could travel there with Sam's fiancée and live and work in Sam's business. Everyone was happy: Maria's father was marrying off a daughter without having to pay a dowry; Sam had found a wife; and my father felt he had protected his family's future – grandmother, himself, my mother, my three younger brothers (Peter, John and Bill) and myself – by sending me to Australia.

After I learned that I was going to Australia and would be travelling with a young woman my uncle had asked to become his wife, I lost all interest in my schoolwork and stopped doing my homework. Eventually, my teacher noticed what was happening and said to me, “You aren’t doing very well. You’re missing classes and falling behind.”

I replied to the teacher, “I’m going to Australia, so I don’t have to go to school. Why would I want to go to school in Greece? I’m going to Australia.”

“I will have to speak to your father,” he said.

He was a very good teacher and the three of us had a meeting. “It doesn’t matter where you go, Australia or any country, you still need a good education.”

“But they don’t speak Greek in Australia,” I said. This was the way I thought – what was the point of learning anything now. The teacher thought this was a ridiculous argument and again repeated that it was very important to obtain a good education. He pointed out that because I had neglected my studies I was a long way behind the other students. My father agreed with the teacher and told me to concentrate on my studies until I left. I wasn’t to know it then, but this was to be the end of my education and I was only thirteen years old. It is something I now deeply regret.

Chapter Twelve

I almost didn't make it to Australia. It seemed that the Civil War was being won by the government troops and the Communists withdrew into Serbia and Macedonia. My father continued to worry that the Communists would launch a counterattack and be back. The plan was for me to go to Australia, and then as so often happens with plans, things started to fall apart.

An uncle of mine, my mother's brother, by the name of Dino, entered the picture. Like Sam, he also was a single man. One day my father suggested to him, "Why don't you go to Australia?" Dino thought that was a good idea. My father then checked with Sam and he agreed to sponsor us both – and this meant that I would be travelling with Maria and my uncle Dino. For my father, this gave him great peace of mind as he now knew that his boy would be safe on such a long journey. After all, I was only thirteen and could not speak a word of English. My uncle Sam paid for the air tickets for the three of us.

Left: This photograph of me was taken for my passport in 1946 before I left Greece.

Thomas Cook was the travel agent, and it was set up with them that we could have access to £50 each in case we needed money on the way.

Everyone was happy, but no one more than my father. "Okay," he said, "let's have a party to celebrate!" Lots of people came to our house. A goat was killed and there was plenty of wine to drink. Someone brought a gramophone which you had to wind up and it would play records. Everyone was enjoying themselves. It was the first time I wore long trousers and new shoes and the first time I had danced with a grown-up girl. The girls were my cousins and friends of the family – they pulled me up and all wanted to dance with me. I must admit I was shy because my face was right at the same altitude as their chests, so I had to stare straight down, attempting a bit of chivalry. Eventually though I found this too difficult to do and would lean my head on their chests. All my friends were laughing at me because the girls had well-developed breasts while my little head was wedged in between and out of sight.

Everybody was upset about me leaving, but I was looking forward to it. I wanted to go as soon as possible. I couldn't wait to go to Australia. I really knew nothing about the country, but it seemed obvious from the way my relatives acted that it was a place where life was full of promise.

After the party my father pulled me aside and said, "We are going to miss you a lot, but your mother and I want to tell you something." My father was a man of few words, but what he had to say spoke volumes. He pulled me aside and said, "When you go to Australia you will make mistakes. Of course you make mistakes when you make decisions. The only one who doesn't make mistakes is the one who doesn't make decisions."

"I understand father," I said.

"But," he continued, "don't make more than two mistakes out of every ten decisions you make. And learn from these mistakes; every disadvantage, turn to your advantage."

It was very good advice. His last comment to me on that occasion was important. "You are the oldest. Never forget that. In the years to come, you might be able to take your brothers and give them the opportunity of a better life."

Then, all hell broke loose. The day before we were due to leave, my uncle's intended, Maria, announced that she had changed her mind. She wasn't going to go to Australia anymore. The reason for the sudden change of heart was that she had met someone, a Greek man, who also did not want a dowry from her father, and they would marry and stay in Greece. Uncle Sam in Australia had sent her lots of presents – jewellery, dresses, lots of things – but it made no difference in the end. Everyone was shocked at this news and my father was extremely upset that she had waited until the last minute to do this. But that wasn't all.

As we were dealing with all this drama, my mother's brother, Uncle Dino, arrived. "I am very happy! I am very happy!" he announced. Obviously, he had been drinking and soon blurted out his news. "I'm going to get married!" His bride to be was Nicoletta, a general's daughter. "She has a dowry," he said, very pleased with himself, "and I've got nothing."

I had never seen my father so angry and started arguing with my mother, "Your brother is a snake! You are all the same!"

She started crying. "What the hell have I done?"

This changed everything. My father turned to me and said, "You're not going to Australia." The two adults I was supposed to travel with had both pulled out. However, no matter what, my mind was made up. "Dad, I'm going."

"No, you're not," he insisted.

I looked into his eyes and said firmly, "I am going."

My father realised that there was no turning back. He headed off to town and in one of the local clubs he was told that there was an Australian lady who had come to Akrata on her holidays to visit her Greek relatives. She was a Sydney girl and by coincidence would be leaving on the same flight to Australia as me. After my father spoke to her and told her the story she said, "I will take care of the boy. I will take him with me."

Chapter Thirteen

One of my chores had been to help my father take everything we needed from Akrata to Porovitsa. Our horse would be loaded up with goods and vegetables and we would walk from the flat area of that town up a hill called Vigla. This hill is a couple of hundred metres high and from there you can look down to the beach at Akrata and all the houses there. One day, after my father and I had worked all day we climbed to the top of Vigla hill. It was tough going and he was out of breath. We had a break and as we were standing there I said to my father, "When I get to Australia, I will send you money so you can buy a pushbike. Then you will be able to ride the pushbike, at least here where it is flat." This was my dream – to be rich enough to buy my father a pushbike. Owning something like a car was beyond my imagination. After all, there was one taxi in the entire town of Akrata. My father put his arm around me and together we looked down to the beach. "When you grow up Nick, I would love to have a house down there so I don't have to walk up this damned hill, because you know I am getting old." That moment stuck in my mind because I decided there and then that I would do this. Someday,

I would come back and buy my father a house on the beach at Akrata.

The Civil War continued on for a few more years, and after almost ten years of war, the Communists were defeated. Some of the communist guerrillas left the country and made their way to Russia where they were welcomed with open arms. However, what happened to those people was cruel. Being committed communists, they felt that life for them in Russia would be everything that they had ever dreamed about. Instead they became victims of Stalin's brutal repression and many of them ended up in labour camps in Siberia.

This happened to the uncle of a friend of mine. All his hopes for a better life were shattered when he worked as a virtual slave labourer in Siberia for years and years. I met this man many years later in the 1970s and it was an experience which taught me a lot about human nature. During the time that Gough Whitlam was Prime Minister of Australia, some of this man's relatives in Australia asked the government to try and get permission for him to leave Russia. The government diplomats were successful and my friend flew to Russia and brought his uncle back to Australia.

I met him at a lunch and could not believe what I was hearing. It is very rare to find someone, anyone, who comes to this country and does not like what they see. But this is not what happened with my friend's uncle. Despite the terrible things he endured under the Communists in Russia, he remained a hardline, committed communist. He told me that the wealth and prosperity of Australia disgusted him – it represented everything that he despised about the capitalist system. His relatives were really embarrassed by this and didn't know what to do. They had expected that he would have enjoyed the welcome that he was given and that perhaps he would find some happiness here.

However, he was a communist through and through, and could not accept that it was a much-discredited ideology. His family tried to change his attitude, or at least stop him from being so critical of everything that he saw, but nothing could change this man's mind. In the end the family took him back to Greece where he continued to speak about his faith in communism. There were still at that time many people in Greece with very strong memories of the appalling things the Communists had done when they tried to take over the country, and no one would talk to him. About three years later he was dead. Sometimes, I think it would have been more humane to have left him in Siberia.

And so this chapter of my story, my early years growing up in war-ravaged Greece, came to a close. During the war I had seen many things that a human being, never mind a young boy, should never see. But the terrible things I witnessed never made me bitter or traumatised me. I survived thanks to the love and protection of my family. The experience instilled in me the belief that family is more important than anything. And I always remained hopeful that the best years of my life were ahead of me.

BOOK TWO

Journey to Australia

Chapter One

My mother took my hand and stood me under the icons, which were in a small room of our house. Hanging in front of the icons were *kandili.* There were icons of Saint Nicholas, Jesus Christ, Mary and others. Being placed in front of the icons was very important. Before we went to bed at night, mother would make us kneel before the icons, cross ourselves, and if we did something bad we had to ask for forgiveness and promise never to do it again. My mother was very religious. She had never been to school and grew up during the Turkish occupation. The Turks were brutal and tried to suppress religious observance. My mother told me that they used to worship in the basement and if they were discovered the Turks would drag them out and punish them. Greece was under Turkish rule for 400 years.

My mother told me to kneel down before the icons and said, "Now, I want you to make a promise to me, in front of God, that you will come back no later than in eight years' time."

"I promise," I replied.

"And you will not marry, but stay single."

Because I was only thirteen years old, marriage was the furthest thing from my mind. Even so, I did ask her, "Why not?"

"If you get married, she might be a wife who won't let you come back home. Then you will have another family, and we will be far away from you."

She thought eight years would be enough time for the aftershocks of the war to settle and enough time to make something of myself in Australia. Also, in eight years, I would be twenty-one years old, and would return to Greece a man. And although nothing was said of my responsibilities to my family, I knew that it was important that I return to Greece a success. Whatever happened to me, I vowed that I must come back a success. Naturally, I was too young to know what success would look like, but I guess I felt that my mother would be pleased if I returned with enough money to buy a house in our village. I could then marry, settle down and have a family at the ripe old age of twenty-one.

When the time came to leave, I had to catch a train from Akrata station, the same place where I used to sell my figs. My schoolmates were there to see me off because I was the first one to leave from the district. My father and I sat in the back carriage and as the train pulled out my school friends ran behind the train. That picture is still in my mind – us sitting there, and the boys running after us – and as the train gathered speed they became smaller and smaller in the distance.

We stayed a couple of days in Athens at my uncle's house and then went to the airport. Air travel was very different in those days – there were only eleven passengers on the aeroplane. My ticket had been purchased through Thomas Cook, the famous travel company. They explained that it was a seven-day journey to Australia, and no guarantee that it would not take longer.

At the airport in Athens, my uncle Milton, the lawyer, gave me some advice. "When you go to Australia, be careful to be a good man. You're only young, but you will have to grow up quickly. Don't steal. Don't tell lies. Don't mix with bad company because people will say, 'Show me your friend and I will tell you who you are.' And don't mix with bad women." How fortunate was I to receive such wisdom from this man. As he was saying this my father stayed silent. After he said what he had to say, my uncle started crying. It was the first time in my life I had seen a man cry. Despite all the terrible things that had gone on through the wars – this had never happened.

As only one person was allowed to take me out to the plane, my uncle stayed in the terminal and my father walked with me. He said, "Your uncle means well, and I know you will follow his advice. But I'm your father, and I'm telling you, everything in moderation."

"Yes, Dad."

Then he reminded me of the advice he had given me before. "Of course you will make mistakes. We all do. But learn from them. People who say they don't make mistakes, don't make decisions either. Don't ever do anything to another person that you wouldn't want others to do to you. To respect yourself you have to do the right thing. You are a young boy, but when you reach twenty-one years of age you should know what is right or wrong. If I ever hear you took the wrong road, then I will make it my business to go to Australia and put you on the right road. So watch out." Then he handed me two British sovereigns. "Good luck!" Those were his last words to me before I climbed the steps into the aircraft.

Chapter Two

The main passenger aircraft of that time was the Douglas DC-3. It had twin propellers and room for about twelve passengers. Our plane landed in Cyprus where it refuelled and then we flew on to Cairo. After we landed in Cairo, everything started to go wrong. We walked down the steps and onto the tarmac and then I became confused about what to do – where to go. This was the first time I had been on an aeroplane and I became a bit disorientated after the flight. People took off in this direction and in that direction and the woman I was travelling with vanished into thin air. I didn't know what to do. All I had was my little suitcase with all my belongings. In the airport terminal I found a place where I could sit down and keep an eye on 'our' aeroplane – one thing was certain – that plane would not take off without me being on it. No one seemed to notice me and no one seemed to care. So I stayed in the airport. As the hours went by and it became darker as night fell, I started to become a bit worried. It seemed like I would have to sleep at the airport.

Then, a car pulled up, and a man who said he was from Thomas Cook Travel came into the terminal looking for me. It turned out

that his name was Nick, and he was either a Greek, or at least spoke Greek. He looked at me and asked, "What are you stupid – you didn't get on the bus?"

"What bus? I didn't see a bus."

"The bus that took everyone from the airport into town. We've been looking for you everywhere." Nick was in a bad mood and let me know it.

"I've been watching our plane because I knew it would take me to Australia."

Nick was unimpressed. "That's a complete waste of time as that aircraft will return to Athens. Now, get in the car."

The man from Thomas Cook Travel drove me into the city and dropped me off at a hostel called Luna Park Hotel. Today, you'd probably call it a dive; but to me, a boy from the village of Porovitsa, this was luxury on a grand scale. The owner of this establishment was Greek, which was not an uncommon situation in Egypt; after all, one of the most famous Egyptians of all time – Cleopatra – was a Greek.

Although the owner was kind to me, he was a fearsome little man who ruled by terror. Not long after I arrived, there was an incident where a large flower pot fell from a window ledge and onto the footpath. It smashed to pieces and if it had struck anyone in the street it would almost certainly have killed them. Somehow, it was established that one of the staff was to blame, but none of them would own up to being at fault. So the owner lined the five staff up, made them face the wall and then whipped them. It was a horrible thing to see. These proud Egyptian men were wearing the traditional long white robe as a uniform, and they stood there

Left: A photo sent to me, many years after leaving Akrata, of my brother Bill (fifteen years younger than me) as an officer in the army.

as this man flogged them in public. He was yelling at them as he did this and the men screamed out in agony and were distressed and crying. I stood there not understanding why these grown men did not turn around, grab hold of that nasty little man and break his neck.

It was a strange situation that I found myself in. The lady who had reassured my father that she would look after me had disappeared and I never ever saw her again. I had no interest in exploring Cairo because I had very little money – only the two sovereigns my father had given me – and there seemed to be no point because I would be flying to Australia either tomorrow, or the day after. Well, the days came and went and I wasn't going anywhere. When I asked the hostel owner if he knew about when my plane was leaving, he just shrugged his shoulders. Nick, the man from Thomas Cook Travel was nowhere to be seen.

Little by little I ventured out onto the streets and then started going for walks. One day during my stay at Cairo, crowds appeared on the street clapping and cheering. I was keen to see what was going on and made my way through the crowd and to the front. I couldn't understand what all the fuss was about. Off in the distance was a man in a car, and as it drove towards us I could see this very fat man wearing a fez and waving to the crowds. Thousands of people were clapping and waving and cheering. And then I made out the words, "Farouk, Farouk!" It was King Farouk. I couldn't believe how many thousands there were admiring this one man.

Then Nick from Thomas Cook appeared one day and explained to me that he was having difficulty getting me onto a flight. Because of soldiers coming back from the war and refugees moving to new countries, there was a drastic shortage of transportation. Nick told me he would look after me, but it might take a few more days.

I used some of the money my father had given me to buy cakes, and also to hire a pushbike. However, when I got on the bike I had a lot of difficulty riding it – I was going backwards and forwards and all over the place. There was this middle-aged Arab man walking along in front of me. The wheel of my bike caught the back of his sandal heel and he fell face down. When he stood back up he smacked me hard. I left the bike where it was and ran back to the hostel. I told one of the Greek fellows there what had happened and he came back with me. We picked up the bike and took it back to the place where I had hired it. He said to me, "We had better go away in case it is damaged. We will leave it here, but don't say anything – and don't come back and get another bike tomorrow."

One week passed, then another, and I was still in Cairo. After about a month, Nick from Thomas Cook came to see me. He said that he had been in touch with my father, and that he had asked him to return me to Athens. I've often thought about what happened next, because my life would have turned out very differently had I gone back to Greece. After all this time away on my own I missed my family and was homesick, but instinctively I knew that the past was there, and my future was in the opposite direction. Also, I think Nick expected me to be in favour of this as he looked shocked when I said, "I don't want to go back home. I want to go forward." Nick thought about this for a moment and then said, "There is a ship, the *Queen Mary*, coming in from England in about a week. It's taking 3,000 British troops to Singapore. I might be able to get you a berth on that ship." He said that the *Queen Mary* was the biggest passenger ship in the world.

"And it goes to Australia?" I asked. "No, it goes to Singapore."

"Where is Singapore?" I wanted to know.

"It's only a stone's throw to Australia," Nick explained. "Once you're in Singapore, you're more or less in Australia."

Obviously, this was not true, but I had no idea as I had never studied geography and imagined from what Nick told me that Singapore was as close to Australia as Porovitsa was to Akrata. "Fantastic!" I said. "What do I have to do?" Nick told me he would come and collect me when the ship came in.

And so after six weeks in Cairo, Nick dropped by the hostel. I put my suitcase in his car and he drove me to the railway station. He explained that I had to catch a train to Port Said. I was a bit embarrassed to tell him that I had no money at all – he paid for my train ticket out of his own pocket. "Now," he explained, keep a lookout on the train until you get to the Suez Canal. You'll see the water and then this big ship. Don't get off the train until you see that. Then get off and go to the Thomas Cook office and they'll look after you.

There was only one flaw in his plan – the train was delayed for some reason. By the time we came into Port Said it was getting dark, and I could not see the water or the ship. I left the train and then walked along looking for the port and the Thomas Cook office. Eventually I found myself in a park where I approached an old fellow sitting on a seat. I sat alongside him and asked him in Greek: "Thomas Cook – his office – where is it?" After all, I did assume that Thomas Cook was a real person rather than the name of a company hundreds of years old. The old man on the seat did not understand me and told me to get lost in Arabic. However, I didn't understand him. He had a walking stick and he stood up and before I realised what was happening he hit me with his walking stick on the back of the neck, twice. I took off and kept on walking until in the distance before me appeared the brightest lights I had ever seen. The closer I came, the more I realised these were the lights of the *Queen Mary*. It was without doubt the most amazing thing I could have imagined. I followed the lights and soon found the office of Thomas Cook Travel, but it was closed.

I put my suitcase down in the doorway and sat on it. By this time I was exhausted and fell asleep on my suitcase. At about seven the next morning, I felt a hand on my shoulder shaking me awake. It was the office girl from Thomas Cook. I showed her my passport and she looked after me. She gave me bacon and eggs and coffee – it was the best breakfast I had had in a long time. Then the woman from Thomas Cook took me to the ship and I was given a bunk in one of the few berths reserved for civilians, as there were 3,000 soldiers on board. At last I was on my way to Australia, or so I thought.

Chapter Three

Much of my memory of that voyage is lost now. I was not seasick, and like a little, scared boy I saw the whole thing as an adventure. But I do recall that every morning, without fail, the British soldiers ran around the decks to keep fit. It seemed like a great thing to do and so I started running with them and was soon 'adopted' by the soldiers as one of them. From the soldiers and the crew, I started to pick up my first words of English – 'yes', 'no', 'hello', 'good morning', 'good day', 'good afternoon' and 'goodbye'. I thought this would help me when I arrived in Australia only to learn later that Australians speak with an accent so broad that nothing I learned from those British soldiers was much help at all.

And of course as anyone who has been on a ship knows, the food is unbelievable. They had buffet-style breakfasts, lunch and dinner, and it would be true to say that I had never in my life seen so much food in one place. Everything was there, and I assumed that this was only because we had soldiers on board. I remember thinking to myself, "Being in the British Army is paradise." Had someone asked me to join up at that moment, I would not have hesitated to enlist.

Everything was looking good for me until one day I found myself in conversation with a soldier who spoke some Greek. He asked me if I had family in Singapore and I explained that I was going to live in Australia with my uncle. "Oh," he said, "and how are you getting to Australia?"

"Well," I answered, repeating the words of the man from Thomas Cook Travel, "it's only a stone's throw from Singapore, so I'll catch a bus or a train." It was then I learned, to my horror, that it was over 6,000 kilometres from Singapore to Sydney.

When the *Queen Mary* berthed in Singapore harbour, it was the first time I saw someone playing the bagpipes. As the soldiers made their way down the gangplank, the piper played his bagpipes – it was to my ears terrible music – but I found the ceremonial part of it really impressive. I had no idea what I was supposed to do and was one of the last to leave the ship.

As I was walking down the gangplank, I saw out of the corner of my eye a man notice me and then come walking towards me. He came over and shook my hand. As he spoke English, I had no idea what he was saying, although I did recognise the two words I had learned very well in Cairo: "Thomas Cook". Once he said those two words, I knew he was there to look after me. This fellow then then took my suitcase from me and escorted me to a truck parked out on the street.

Men who had obviously just come off the ship were sitting in the back of the truck. There wasn't much room, but I climbed up and found a bit of space – I remember I rested one leg on the tailgate of the truck. The man from Thomas Cook passed me my suitcase and then banged the side of the truck. With that signal, the truck roared off, and for the next thirty minutes or so I prayed to God I would survive this part of the journey. The driver drove like a maniac and I was desperately hanging on to a bar worried that at any moment I would fall out the back and onto the road.

We arrived at a hostel where I was given a room. Quite a few of the men at this hostel were Greeks, and so that was reassuring for me. At least I could communicate with people and also get some sense of what was going on. No one from Thomas Cook or from the hostel ever explained to me what was supposed to happen to me. I was the only child in the hostel and I guess none of them were used to dealing with a child passenger. But what I learned from the men there over my first few days in Singapore was that we all had to wait until our travel arrangements to Australia were finalised.

I was fed and looked after but had no money. Some of the Greek men would play poker after lunch. I noticed they played with British currency. When I ran little errands for the card players – such as getting cigarettes or buying them cakes from the bakery – they used to let me keep the change. In this way I was able to accumulate a few shillings. This is what I did most days – watch the men play cards and run errands for them. After many weeks of nothing happening, an obvious thought popped into my head. I was quite friendly with a man called Con, who was about twenty-two years old and the youngest player. I asked Con, "Where do you get the money to play cards?" Obviously, they had no form of income. He replied without a moment's hesitation, "Thomas Cook." When he saw that this was news to me he added, "You go up to the office and they will give you money." I couldn't believe what I was hearing. Con explained that Thomas Cook paid their living expenses while they were waiting for their flight to Australia.

After Con gave me the directions, I caught a tram to the offices of Thomas Cook which was right on the port. I took my passport with me and said in Greek to the person behind the desk, "I want money." They took my passport and then pulled out this huge green coloured accounts book. In my mind I can still see it. The clerk ran a finger down the page and there was my name. One of the girls in the Thomas Cook office was very friendly and came over and explained the situation to me with a mixture of English, one or two words of Greek, and sign language. When there was a delay to a passenger's travel arrangements, Thomas Cook was required by law to give each passenger £50 for their expenses. "You are entitled to claim up to £50," the girl informed me. "How much do you want?"

I said, "The lot."

She was shocked, "The lot? What are you going to do with it all?"

I replied, "What I spend, I spend. And when you put me on the plane to go to Australia, what's left, is all yours. My uncle is very rich and I don't need it." As we talked, she asked about my situation and was amazed that I was travelling on my own. Then the girl handed me £50 from the till and instructed me to go back to my room at the hostel and wait. "Stay there," she said. "Wait for my phone call." I did what she told me and caught a tram back to the hostel and waited in my room. Sure enough, a couple of hours later I was told there was a phone call for me. It was the girl from Thomas Cook. "I have a seat for you on a plane. Pack your bag and get all your things and come back to our office." She said I was not to tell anyone I was leaving, just pack up and go to her office.

I packed up and then snuck down the stairs. They were old, timber stairs which creaked as I went down them. I tiptoed past the room where the men played cards and as I did so, I heard Con call out, "Is that you Nick?" I put my head in the door and didn't think to try and hide my suitcase. "Where are you off to?" Con wanted to know. "Nowhere," I replied. I was so naive. Then I took off. I could imagine that they would have been thinking that only this morning

I was asking about money and here I was going somewhere with a packed suitcase.

Again, I caught the tram and when I arrived back at Thomas Cook the girl was waiting for me. "I have a plane flying to Indonesia," she said. I told her I had no idea where Indonesia was. "It's just next to Australia," she replied in a reassuring manner. "From there, no problem. You are almost in Australia." In the back of mind I thought to myself that I had heard this before, and it was far from being true. But what choice did I have? "All right," I said.

We then left the office and she took me to the seaport where there was a small seaplane. There were only about thirty passengers in total. As we were about to take our seats, two of the card players from the hostel arrived. They could see that I was about to fly out and they were very angry. "Why is this fellow leaving? He came here last and is going first. We have been here the whole time and have waited for months!" My friend from Thomas Cook replied, "Because he is the youngest, and the lightest, and I only have one seat."

"But we have been waiting longer than him – we should be going first."

"Yes, but he is the youngest," the girl answered. Being Greeks, they started to argue with her and raised their voices and cursed and complained. She was accused of favouritism and then one of the men turned to me and asked me whether I had given the girl any money for my seat on the seaplane. I hesitated too long. They suspected something was going on and before long the manager was called.

They separated me from the girl. She looked at me in tears as the manager questioned me. "You went this morning and got some money from our office? Is this the girl who looked after you?"

"Yes," I said.

"How much did she give you?" "£50."

"£50?" the manager repeated. "Yes. I asked for the lot?"

"How much did she ask you to pay her?"

I said, "Nothing."

"Well, why did you take the whole fifty pounds?"

"Well," I explained. "She said I could have the lot if I wanted it. So I said give me the lot."

"And you were going to give her the money?"

"No."

I saw in her face that she was relieved. The manager asked, "What did you do with the money?"

"It's in my pocket," I replied. "Can I have a look at it?"

I pulled out the £50, and then added, "I didn't get a chance to spend any of it. I would have been in the cake shop first thing, but I didn't have time."

The manager nodded and then said, "Okay."

With that I was ushered onto the seaplane despite the fact that the two Greek men were continuing to complain. What sort of men were they, I wondered, who would demand that they take the place of a child. The girl from Thomas Cook was now smiling – when I thought about it she came very close to losing her job because of her generosity. When I think back I can't believe that I offered to give her what was left of my £50. It was quite a considerable amount of money, but at that time I believed that Uncle Sam was one of the richest men in Australia.

The seaplane took off and once more I found myself heading east and south. Eventually, I said to myself, this journey has to come to an end.

Chapter Four

The girl in the office at Thomas Cook Singapore who made friends with me must have done something or said something after I left. Because I don't know how else to explain what happened when our plane landed in Surabaya, Indonesia. After going through customs, I was ushered into a taxi and sent to the Hotel Majapahit. It is a historic hotel and famous as being the place where the Indonesian revolutionaries tore down the Dutch flag and replaced it with a red and white Indonesian flag in the lead up to the Battle of Surabaya.

The thing I remember most about Indonesia is the pushbikes. I had never seen so many bikes, there seemed to be millions of them. With every move I made on my journey to Australia, I tried to learn from what I saw and digest everything I was seeing. In Egypt I had seen and heard Arabs, and then the Singaporeans, and now the Indonesians. All their faces were so different and to me so interesting.

The Hotel Majapahit was luxurious and I was put into a room with a four-poster bed. Little Indonesian girls served me tea and coffee using what seemed to be expensive cups and saucers and solid silver trays. I had everything I wanted. I was like a king in there. My room was on the ground floor and my window had a view of the hotel's massive garden. Gardeners used to come every morning to look after the gardens and these very pretty young girls would appear with baskets and cut the roses. One morning I went out to see these girls cutting the roses up close and offered to hold their baskets while they cut the flowers. They laughed and teased me, and we chatted as only people can who don't speak the same language. I might have only been thirteen years old, but I was starting to notice pretty young girls.

My time in paradise came to an abrupt halt one day when I heard for the first time in a while the sound of Greek being spoken. Instinctively, I was attracted to this sound and then turned and saw two men sitting having a coffee. They were the same two men who had complained about me being put on a flight before them. One of them saw me and yelled out, "Here's that little bastard!" I took off and ran and ran, but they were faster than me.

Not knowing where to go, I ran straight back to the hotel. Once we were in the foyer, one of the managers intervened and asked what was going on. These two men called me a bastard in Greek, but had no real complaint about me. This manager kept wanting to know what the problem was and I think because of that these men started to feel a little bit foolish – here they were still complaining about a boy who had jumped the queue – and yet was no closer to Australia than they were. The manager ordered coffee to be brought out and then we were all sitting there talking about how we had arrived in Indonesia and when we expected to fly the last leg to Australia.

Within a few days of that incident I was put on a Catalina seaplane bound for Australia. We flew to Darwin where we refuelled and then from there on to Sydney. This was another long journey and I remember it was freezing on that plane. It was winter in Australia and I only had a silk shirt which my aunt in Athens had given to me – it was her shirt. Then I saw this fellow coming down from upstairs. The seaplane had a couple of bunks upstairs and when he came downstairs to go to the bathroom I snuck up the stairs and saw these bunks with warm blankets. I could not help myself and climbed into the bunk. When this bloke came back from the toilet he saw me sleeping there and pulled my leg. “Hey you! Get off my bed.” As there was no response from me he went to one of the air hostesses and told her that there was someone in his bed. They came back to the bunk and he again tried to grab my foot. But when he did this I kicked back and hit him in the eye. Because of the way the bunks were set up, his face was at the level of the bunk where my foot was. I went boom! and hit him in the eye. When this happened he cried out, and then the hostess was running around trying to put a bandage on his eye and I was worried that if I moved from the bunk he would then try and bash me up. So I lay there until we arrived in Sydney.

The Catalina flew into Rose Bay, which is on Sydney Harbour, and what I saw below struck me as being perhaps the most beautiful sight I had ever seen. There is still a seaplane which operates from Rose Bay today and a very smart restaurant there, Catalina, named after the type of seaplane which once operated from there.

My uncle Sam was there to pick me up. Then the man on the plane who I had accidentally kicked came over and started talking to Sam. He told him what had happened – that I had taken his bunk and kicked him in the face.

I shifted nervously in front of my uncle as all this was being said. Sam put his hands on my shoulders and asked why I did it. I told him the truth – that I was freezing cold on the plane, that I had got under the blanket to get warm and was so tired had fallen asleep, and when the man had pulled my leg I did not know what was happening and kicked him by accident. I apologised to the man for what had happened. This fellow then extended his hand and we shook hands. He said to my uncle, "This boy is going to make a good Australian, a good Aussie. That is all we want here. You look after him." Uncle Sam was pleased when he heard this. We left Rose Bay and caught a taxi to the city.

Our taxi dropped us at the Ritz Hotel in Elizabeth Street, which was in the centre of Sydney. It is odd how things turn out, but I was not to know then that in later years I would come to know this street very well as I bought property in Elizabeth Street about three buildings down. The *Ritz Hotel* was an old brick building which had seen better days. My uncle and I got into the lift where I had an experience which had a real effect on me, on my ambitions and on how I was to operate as a businessman in the future.

The lift had a steel cage/gate and was an old-fashioned one which required an operator. The lift driver was an old Greek fellow. He said hello to us and then he controlled this wheel device which operated the lift. I noticed he was unshaven and untidy. His trousers were so old they were shiny. I had seen grape pickers in my village with trousers that looked like that. Then I saw that his shoes were grubby and one shoe had no laces at all. I realised that this old Greek fellow was doing it tough and of course I felt sorry for him. He was talking in English and Greek with my uncle – using both languages – but I really didn't listen. Then we arrived at our floor and went to our room.

As we walked along the corridor, Uncle Sam pointed back to the lift driver and said to me, "This is his place." When he saw the look of disbelief on my face, Sam added, "He owns this hotel." My uncle told me that this old man came from the little Greek island of Kythira in the south of Greece.

I knew at that moment that my life in this new country would be a success. "If an old man like that can own a building like this, a hotel in the heart of Sydney," I thought, "I also I will buy a building like that." I said to myself, "One day I will buy a hotel just like this." And so I went to sleep on my first night in Australia, where I had at long last arrived after so many months of delay.

That old man, the lift driver who was the hotel owner, also taught me that there is a way to behave when you are fortunate enough to have money. Whilst I admit I was never unshaven or untidy, or wore old trousers, I did think that it was important not to be a show-off with money; that if you were blessed with success, you should thank your lucky stars and never flaunt it in front of people.

Of course, the city I arrived in was very different to the Sydney of today. Its population in 1947 was a bit over a million people and there were virtually no Asian faces anywhere – the infamous White Australia policy was still in place. Considering that the Japanese had tried to invade the place and had torpedoed ships in Sydney Harbour, it's hardly surprising that Australians were wary of Asians. But the country had thrown open its doors to immigrants from Europe, to people like me, who were thankful that they had survived the war and wanted nothing more than to live a life of peace and get another start in life. People were sick of war, fed up with rationing, and there was this sense that this country wanted to do things, build things and make things happen. However, the temptations of Sydney would have to wait. Home for me was going to be a room at the back of my uncle's cafe in the country town of Trangie.

BOOK THREE

Life in Trangie

CIRCUS
AND
ANIMALS.

Chapter One

The next morning my uncle and I caught a plane to Dubbo and from there a train to Trangie, New South Wales. Most Australians have never heard of Trangie. It is a small, country town located nearly five hundred kilometres north-west of Sydney. The population has never grown above about a thousand people, and arriving there for the first time I felt that a terrible mistake had been made. Gone were the mountains of Greece and before me were these vast, flat, empty open plains. I could not imagine how a human being could scratch a living from this place.

Over the past twenty or thirty years there has been a noticeable decline in the prosperity of country towns. There are many reasons for this, but on the whole farmers will tell you prices have been depressed for decades, droughts have taken their toll and the young people of the community leave and go to places like Sydney in search of work. Looking back, I can now see that it was my luck that I arrived at the right time. Although small, Trangie was

Left: Me standing on the street outside the Trocadero Cafe, Trangie, when I arrived from Greece on 3 August 1947.

a prosperous place owing to strong wool, cattle and wheat prices which surged in the aftermath of the war. The place was booming, and the farmers were enjoying their best prices in years.

It was lunchtime when we arrived. My uncle pulled up outside the Trocadero Cafe, and I climbed out of the passenger seat dressed in my suit and tie. There I was, a little Greek boy arriving with my name Nicholas Androutsopoulos, now given a new name to use – Nick Androutsos, as that was the surname my uncle used. Standing in the roasting sun, people walked past, looked at me and started laughing. After that day I never wore a suit and tie in Trangie. My uncle disappeared and no one showed me where my room was, so I couldn't go and get changed.

As well as the Trocadero Cafe, my uncle Sam also owned the small fruit shop next door. It was full of kids from the school because their parents used to pay my uncle to give them lunch. The kids were from all the classes from the primary school – and I remember the older ones from about Years 5 and 6 were riding pushbikes. There I was – standing on the footpath, in my suit and tie – feeling quite foolish. People assume that my uncle took me under his wing and introduced me to some of the locals and people working in the shop, but there was none of that.

When we had pulled up in his car he didn't say, "Welcome to Trangie" or anything like it. He just walked into the shop and left me where I was. It might have been thoughtless of him, but he wasn't mean. This is how children were treated then – you were left to sort things out for yourself. And it was lunchtime, so the place was busy.

There I stood on the footpath trying not to look conspicuous. I was admiring the pushbikes when a young girl wearing shorts, who was well built, came out of the shop and saw me standing there admiring her bike. She had finished her lunch and started talking to me. Naturally I couldn't understand a single thing she was saying. Apart from "yes" and "no", the only English I knew was the three greetings, "Good day", "Good morning" and "Good night". Despite the fact that I could not understand her, it was unmistakable to me that this girl was being genuinely friendly. And when you are a stranger in a strange place, nothing is more valuable than that hand of friendship.

Someone explained to her that I was Sam's nephew and I had just arrived from Greece. She was saying, "Sit, sit here." She pushed me to sit on the seat of the bike, and so I sat on it. I was thinking she did this just so I could see what it was like to sit on a bike. I had only once ridden a bike before, and that was when I hired a bike in Cairo and crashed it. Then the girl signalled me to make room and then she got on – grabbed my hands and put them around her waist. I couldn't believe I was putting my hands around a girl! Do I have to? What will they think? "Hang on," she said, and then she started pedalling. "Don't be scared, take it easy," the girl said trying to reassure me.

And so off we went, riding slowly at first. I made the mistake of trying to put my foot down to balance and it looked like we were going to fall over any minute. She tried to get me to relax, and with her movements and the way she was saying it I began to understand. She took me for a ride down the other end of the Dandaloo Street and back again.

The girl's name was Helen. A lovely Greek name. I thanked her profusely for the ride on her bike. I was so proud when I told my aunt and uncle. By coincidence someone took a photograph of me on Helen's bike that day – it's a black and white photo – and for many years we talked about my ride on her bike that day. A few years later, when Helen was a married woman, she would come into the cafe with her kids and tell them about the day she

TRANGI
CRAFT
CENTR

Jeanettes coffee stop
meals drinks
coffee snacks
health bar

'doubled' me down Dandaloo Street. It was as good a way as any to say to someone, "Welcome to Trangie."

That is what I remember of my first day in my new home. I had been under the impression from what people had said in Greece that Uncle Sam was one of the richest men in Australia. Looking around me I knew that couldn't be true and could not imagine how I was ever going to make a success of my life here. The Trocadero appeared to be a good business, but at the end of the day it was just a cafe in a small country town. However, I thought of the promise I had made to my mother and resolved to make the most of it. Eight years I had to stay, and for a boy of thirteen, that seemed like an awful long time. What I could not have imagined then, and what still amazes me today, is that this little unassuming town was the place that made me a man and set me on the road to riches.

Above: Riding a bicycle on my first day in Trangie, 1947. The only person in three hundred miles wearing a suit.

Previous page: The Trocadero Cafe, Trangie – where it all started for me.

Chapter Two

After my uncle had arrived with me that day, he completely forgot about me. He was newly married and went off to see his wife, Maria, who he hadn't seen in a few days. He left me with the chef, Ernie Andrews, who was from the same Greek family as ours, but was not a close relation. Ernie was about twelve years older than me. I was very happy to be talking to someone younger who spoke Greek. At least I had someone to communicate with. His Greek was broken because he had come out to Australia when he was young as well, but I could understand him. He must have said to the other cafe workers, "We will have a bit of fun with young Nick." Ernie walked up to me and asked in Greek, "So, you have come out to Australia to make some money, hey?" He then turned to the others and translated what he had said. I nodded my head. "Are you looking for work?" Ernie asked.

"Yes, yes," I replied.

He said, "Are you ready to start?"

Being very eager I repeated, "Yes. Yes."

He took me out the back to this iron shed and showed me a bag of potatoes, a bucket of clean water and another bucket to place the peeled potatoes in. It was incredibly hot in this shed. Ernie explained, "You have to dig out the black spots." There I was, still in my suit and tie, sitting on a stool and peeling potatoes. The ladies who worked in the cafe would come out to the shed, watch me working and smile. Then they'd go back into the cafe and soon after I would hear a roar of laughter. I didn't catch on straight away, but after a few people came out and looked at me and then started laughing I got the message. This sort of thing didn't bother me. It only made me grow up faster, to become a man. And to me it seemed that Ernie was just having a bit of harmless fun.

My next job was washing dishes. The immediate problem was that I was too small to reach the sink. In those days bananas came in wooden boxes. Ernie handed me this empty banana box and told me to turn it upside down in front of the sink. So, I stood on the banana box and washed the plates. On that day, there had been about a hundred people to lunch at the cafe so I was kept very busy washing all those dishes.

The next job Ernie taught me was how to make sandwiches. After that we did toasted sandwiches and then how to cook fish and chips. The stove in the kitchen was woodfired and it generated a lot of heat. I used to wear a big canvas apron and the heat from the stove was so intense that I would put the apron under the tap and soak it with water. I would hang it on the front of me to stop the heat corning through to my stomach, the fire was that strong.

We used to cook the fish and chips – we had to slice the fish, salt it, butter it, put it through flour and then dip it into the hot dripping, as there was no oil in those days – and finally cook it. When the fish came to the surface, we used to rake it and put it on the side, on top of the greaseproof paper with a newspaper underneath to cool off and then stack it nicely on the tray before putting it in the refrigerator. We didn't have a coolroom, it was just a refrigerator.

After a few weeks I was 'promoted' to go inside and help serve behind the counter of the cafe even though I didn't speak English. I soon learnt the important English words "this" and "that". Customers would come in and say something like, "Give us a quarter pound of Cadbury's chocolate, Nick." Not understanding a thing that they said, I would turn around to the display behind me, put my finger on something, like a packet of cigarettes, and say, "This?"

The customer would roll their eyes and repeat, "Nah, nah, a quarter pound of chocolate." "This?" I would say, pointing to some cakes in the display.

They realised that I didn't understand what they were saying and so they would then start doing the pointing. The customer would point to the chocolate and explain, "Not this, that. That is Cadbury chocolate."

I would say, "That. Thank you, thank you."

Then I would lift up a block of chocolate, turn to my uncle who was sitting at the other end of the cafe drinking coffee, and ask him in Greek, "How much?"

"Two shillings, Nick."

I would ring up two shillings and the customer would leave with their chocolate. Most of the customers used to help me. They would talk with my uncle and teach me at the same time. Sometimes, they would walk around behind the counter to show me what they were looking for. Also, usually the locals knew what the price was, so they would be able to tell me this as well. That is how I learnt English – from our customers.

I was then asked to serve tables and when I was waiting tables I learnt a bit more English. For example, the girls would take an order of coffee, or sandwiches, or toast, or bacon and eggs. The waitress would say to me, "This is for that table; pick it up and take it to them."

I would take the order to the customer sitting at a table and they'd say, "Hello. Thank you." Then they would ask, "Can we have a bit more bread please?"

Having no idea what they had said I would turn to my uncle, lift up my hand and ask, "What does he say?"

Uncle Sam would reply in Greek, "He says he wants more bread." "Oh, *psomi*," I would say to myself and repeat it: "*psomi* – bread."

Afterwards, I would go and write it down. I used to have a little notebook and in this I would write words in English and alongside them the Greek equivalent. Bread – *psomi*; butter – *voutiro* and so on. There were about four girls working in the cafe and about three boys. There was one girl, called Dawn, who was there for many years with my uncle. God bless her, she was a fantastic worker. She wanted to help me with my English. She used to go to the paper shop and buy me a comic book and because I could see the illustration and the block letters underneath, she would tell me what it meant. Sometimes, I would see something in these comics, and if Dawn was not around, I would ask my uncle or my aunt, or whoever was going past me, "What does that mean?"

The Trocadero was more than a cafe; with the fruit shop next door it was more like a mixed business. We sold cigarettes, tobacco, peanuts, jam, smallgoods and things like Bex powders. I quickly learnt these English words and sometimes I would put it all together and make a sentence. I had to learn English this way because I didn't go to school at all after I arrived. In fact, my uncle nearly got into trouble for not sending me to school. He didn't want to send me to school because he needed someone to peel potatoes!

Chapter Three

My room was behind the cafe – my uncle built three rooms with timber walls, an iron roof, no insulation and one fan in the middle. In summer the temperature would be 40 degrees or more. There were always two beds, one for me and one for another fellow. The end room was a little bit better and it belonged to Sam and his wife. It had a double bed in it and it was a little bit bigger – but there was still no air conditioning in that room either. To keep the mosquitos away I used to spray this chemical, known as DDT, around the room. Years later it was banned because of its toxicity. There was a large box on the verandah which we threw our dirty clothes into. Sam paid a lady to come in and do the washing, although there were not many dirty clothes. Things like underpants and singlets we would wash when we had a shower and hang them up to dry. In a way we lived like Spartans!

In the wintertime it was very cold, as there was no heating. I used to put broken empty boxes under the mattress because the mattress was only a thin one. Then I would put a blanket over the top of the mattress and two or three blankets on the top, to keep the cold out. Sometimes I had a pillow-fight with the other bloke in

the room and everything would be thrown up in the air. That was part of the fun we had, because in a town like Trangie there was not much in the way of entertainment. It was a routine of work, eat, sleep, repeat.

We had a roster, and once a month in the summertime each one of us would go to the movies to the open-air picture show. There were no movies in the wintertime. Sometimes we used to go and watch a football game, or a tennis match if there was one on in town. That was the only thing we used to do.

The cafe cook, Ernie, was very popular because he was a fine singer and a good-looking chap. He used to broadcast the horses at the small race meetings. He was also a gambler. As race day approached, everyone would ask him, "Ernie, what's the favourite?" Most of the time he could tell them. He was very close with the racehorse owners and the jockeys.

He knew everything about the horses: the dam (mother), the sire (father), how old it was, who owned it, when it stopped racing and went to the paddock for a spell, when it came back, how it ran on a wet or a dry track, and so on.

Also, Ernie had an incredible horseracing memory. In the cafe he would walk past some tables and one of the customers would say to him, "Hey Ernie, can you give us the Melbourne Cup of 1952?" Ernie would then sit down in a cubicle in the cafe – the tables were all partitioned into cubicles – he'd sit in the corner, with his feet on the seat, his eyes closed and with an upside-down coffee cup or glass for a microphone, he would 'broadcast' the Melbourne Cup from the year they requested. It was the most amazing performance.

Left: At the back of the Trocadero Cafe in 1952 practising playing the accordion. It was here that I built five small flats for my workers who were newly arrived from overseas.

He would start with the advertising, as everything starts, then talk about the preparation of the horses, every one of them and bring them out onto the track and then boom! When the gates opened, off he would go with them. When he finished his broadcast, people would applaud. It was comforting to see someone as popular as that and know that they had come from the same humble place that I did.

Ernie was well known all around the district. He was very good-looking and had beautiful wavy black hair. To me he looked like the film star Clarke Gable. We used to say he could talk to the King and Queen if they came to visit. He claimed that when he'd gone to the Melbourne Cup he'd worn a hat, a long black coat and white gloves. He claimed that a chauffeur in a Rolls Royce drove him to the races. I was proud of Ernie and very entertained by him. Sometimes, we would stand out the front of the shop watching the people going by. Ernie was always looking at the girls, nothing else.

I remember once we were standing there and this young woman walked out from the newsagents across the street. I recognised her and said to Ernie, "Didn't you take her out the other night?"

"Yes," he replied, "but just keep it between us." This woman then walked towards the bakery. Ernie turned to me and said with a smile on his face, "Before she goes inside the door, she's going to stop. Then she's going to look this way because she knows I am standing here in front of the shop." I could not see how he would know such a thing. The next minute she was walking, taking beautiful steps, in high heels. She was a well dressed woman and looked straight ahead in the direction of the bakery. Then, she opened the door to the bakery, stopped in her tracks, turned and looked straight at Ernie. He didn't do anything – just stood there.

"Wave," I suggested.

"No, no, no, my young friend," he whispered. "You don't show them that you noticed." To me it was all experience of life, watching Ernie. He spoke beautifully, and never swore. He was polite and well-mannered although I think now in hindsight he probably only told people what they wanted to hear. Ernie was very popular and for me very good company.

Although he might have been a great entertainer, unfortunately Ernie was always a hopeless worker. He'd often disappear from the kitchen. He'd say to me, "Be back in half an hour." Then he'd head over to the pub and talk about the races. The half-hour would be well and truly over and still there would be no sign of Ernie. He'd 'forget' to come back, and I'd have to do all the cooking and serving. Once, I made the mistake of complaining to my uncle about Ernie disappearing. When Ernie found out, he was furious. He called me a squealer and the next minute we were in a punch-up. He tried to hit me, and I hit back. But we were mates, and I would have been lost without him. I liked him, and he was at that time the only friend I had.

I remember the first time I met his wife, Edith. I hadn't realised he was married because she lived in a house with her mother and father. One day when I was at their house, I couldn't see Ernie anywhere. "Where is Ernie?" I asked.

"Can't you hear him?' Edith asked.

"No."

"Come here, Nick."

I was in the dining room and sat down. Then I heard Ernie's voice outside the window saying, "Listen to me Cleopatra, you have cost me a lot of money up to now. Now either you are going to start earning money for me or you are going to be dead, I tell you." "Who the hell is Cleopatra?" I wondered.

I went outside and there was Ernie sitting on the bench with his racing dog. He had his face up to its face and he was talking to it, staring directly into its eyes. His wife said he had been out there for an hour talking to it. He was going to do this and going to do that. She said, "That isn't the first time I've heard that. Tomorrow he's going to put his money on it and he's going to lose it again."

Ernie's wife was what we then called a 'half-caste' – being half white and half Aboriginal. She didn't talk much, but she was a nice lady. And they had two young girls – who were beautiful, little blondes. He loved them so much. Ernie brought them up to Sydney a couple of times. Everyone wanted to be with Ernie, wherever Ernie was – no one could take that away from him.

Eventually, Ernie's gambling caught up with him and a few years after I arrived he lost everything. He left Trangie and went to Warren, which is about fifty kilometres away. Although he was broke, at the time Ernie was only about thirty so he still had his whole life ahead of him. At one stage he worked for the post office, going out to the poles, getting up a ladder and fixing the wires on the telephone lines. A couple of times we spoke on the phone. Then, one Christmas, he called me. I asked, "How is it going?"

"Nick, I don't have a job."

"How are you managing mate?" "Well, I have to do something."

As you always knew with Ernie, there was a story. Apparently, he and some of the other workers started playing cards on the job. They'd be out fixing telephone lines and end up spending most of the job time sitting in the shade under a tree playing cards and gambling. So then he got the sack and didn't have any money. I helped him a little bit. I sent him a box of meat, with hams and everything, for Christmas. I did that every Christmas, for many years to come, even though he never asked.

Chapter Four

The success of the cafe was built on a couple of things: it provided good food at affordable prices, sold practically everything and seemed to be open all the time. The official opening hours were 7.00 am to 11.00 pm, seven days a week – although as Church was on Sunday, we didn't open until after 10.00 am. The reality was we were always open. Today's generation take the flexibility of trading hours for granted, but in 1950 it was a very different story. There were strict government regulations about trading hours and most retail businesses traded according to the rules – not when it might have suited the customers. You can still see this today with the opening hours of the major banks – it still amazes me that apart from some major metropolitan branches – not one of the major banks trades on a Saturday.

Emigrants like my uncle knew instinctively that customers loved being able to turn up early in the morning or late at night and find they were made welcome. We were always up very early, and if for instance someone arrived at the cafe at 6.00 am, they were never told, "We don't open until 7.00 am," but instead asked, "What would you like?"

On a normal day we served at least one hundred people, and as many as one hundred and fifty. There were a few reasons why the cafe was so popular – the fact that it seemed to be always open, and because my uncle was very popular with the lady customers. The women used to be drawn to him; he had this way about him that everyone liked. He was open about things that no one else would talk about. They would ask him to sit at their table while they were having a meal or a coffee and would love to listen to his stories. Sam was a storyteller – he was a bigger storyteller than me. He usually didn't like sitting down, he could just stand up for hours on end, and talk. He was tireless.

One day in Trangie he was talking to these women and I overheard one of them ask, "Sam, you've just gotten married. Are you going to have a family?"

"Yes, I am going to have five children."

"Five!" And the ladies laughed.

"Yes, five."

"What would you prefer to have – boys or girls?"

"The first one is going to be a boy to carry the name. A year after we will have a girl to help the mother in the household – and then boy, boy, boy. Five children."

Again, they laughed. But over the next few years Sam did just that – his first child was a boy, then they had a girl; and then three boys after that.

Those women never forgot Sam telling them this was what was going to happen and because of this a lady who had four girls came to see him. I can't remember her name now, but her husband's name was Mervyn. And Mervyn never liked my uncle. He always called him names or accused Sam of robbing him because of the prices we charged. But Mervyn's wife liked Sam, and even more so because of his success at producing boys. As I said, she had four girls and she asked Sam what she had to do to have a boy. "What do you do Sam? Can you tell my husband Mervyn the secret?"

"Tell him to come and see me and I will tell him what to do," Sam replied confidently.

This lady went back to her husband and in the end this fellow had to bite the bullet and swallow his pride. He hated Sam and hated being in this position, but really, he had no choice. He came to see Sam and said to him, "What is this bullshit you're talking to the women about; that you know how to punch out a girl or a boy? What do you know about it?"

My uncle ignored the hostility and said, "If you didn't think I knew, why are you coming and asking me?"

"Cut out the bullshit now," Mervyn said. "What are you telling my wife? We would like to have a son, but what do we do?"

Sam took Mervyn to one side and then revealed to him his secret. "You go next door to the stock and station agent and you buy a pair of docking pliers – you know, the thing they use for castrating lambs."

Mervyn nodded his head. He knew farmers used these pliers to put a rubber ring around the testicles of a lamb – the rubber band stopped the supply of blood, the testicles of the lamb dried up and that was it. "If you want to have a boy," said Sam conspiratorially, "you put one of those rubber rings on your left testicle while you are having sex." Poor Mervyn was grimacing as he listened, and my uncle added, "It's painful, very painful, but it works. Put a rubber on your left ball and your right ball will give you a boy. If you want a girl, then switch it." As he stood there, Mervyn memorised what Sam was telling him.

A couple of days later Mervyn's wife came down to the cafe and reported that her husband had done as Sam suggested, but had almost passed out from the pain. "I know," replied Sam, "it's bad, but it works." And remember he has to do this every time you do it. And so this situation went on for some time until Mervyn's wife revealed that she was pregnant. This made her very happy because thanks to Sam's advice, they were going to, at long last, have a boy. Her husband had been through hell, but it would be worth it.

Finally, the day arrived when the wife went into labour. We were busy in the cafe one morning when one of the local girls ran in and screamed, "Sam! Get out of town!" Everyone was shocked. "It's bloody Mervyn," the girl explained. "His wife had a girl and he's going to kill you!" Mervyn had walked home from the hospital, picked up his shotgun and was heading our way. My uncle knew this was serious. "Ring up Ray!" he told us. Ray was the only taxi driver in town. He used to take people out to the farms off the train and bring people back in. "Tell Ray to pick me up around the back. I'll be waiting on the next corner." Just as Sam was about to bolt, someone asked, "I thought you gave Mervyn the formula for having a boy? What happened?"

Without a moment's hesitation, Sam said, "Obviously that idiot put the rubber ring on the wrong ball." He then escaped out the back.

A few minutes later a very angry Mervyn stormed into the cafe foaming at the mouth, "Where is that bloody Greek bastard?"

"He's in Sydney," one of the waitresses lied. Mervyn didn't quite know whether to believe this or not and didn't quite know what to do. He headed for the kitchen and the rooms out the back and no one tried to stop him. Soon he was back, still angry, but feeling helpless. I asked if he would like a cup of coffee. He looked at me like I was mad. One of the girls congratulated him on the birth of another baby. Mervyn stood there fuming, but powerless to do anything. Then he stormed off with his shotgun over his shoulder and was gone. Neither he nor his wife set foot in the Trocadero again.

Uncle Sam spent the week in Dubbo and came back after things had calmed down. He was always adamant that his technique worked, and that Mervyn should have written down the instructions he had given him. After that, no one took advice from Uncle Sam on his foolproof method for having boys and girls.

Chapter Five

One day terrible news arrived from Greece that my mother had been in an accident and was in a coma. She had been walking on the street when a big truck full of sand hit her from behind and threw her five or six metres. This happened inside the paddock with the olive trees. Mother was in a coma and there were fears she may not live. My father desperately needed money for her medical treatment. The hospital where she was needed £75 and he didn't have that sort of money. He asked if I could borrow some money from my uncle and pay him back. I went to my uncle and I said, "Look at this letter from my father. My mother is in the hospital." There were tears in my eyes as I said to Sam, "Can you lend me £75 and I will pay it off?" At that time, I still owed Sam money for my airfares and was only getting paid £4 a week. However, Sam said to me, "I am sorry about your mother. But I am not a bank and I don't lend money. Only the banks lend money."

As I knew the bank manager, because he came into the shop, I decided at the grand old age of sixteen to approach him. I went to see the bank manager I knew who was in Dandaloo Street, Trangie. I explained about what had happened to my mother, in my broken English because my English wasn't the best at that stage. "Can you lend me £75 please?" I asked.

The bank manager shook his head. "I'm sorry to hear that about your mother, Nick, but you are underage and the banks don't lend money to people when they are underage. I think you should ask your uncle."

"I did ask him," I explained, "and he said he doesn't lend money, but that the banks do. That is why I have come to you."

To this day I can never forget the expression that appeared on that bank manager's face. He looked at me and this smile broke out on his face. Then he pulled out a chequebook from his pocket and wrote out a cheque for £75. He said, "The bank won't lend you, Nick. But I will lend you the money personally. You owe me the money, not the bank. But because you are working for your uncle, and you are a good boy. I can understand what you are doing for your mother. I'm going to lend you the money myself."

He called a teller from behind the counter, gave them the cheque and said, "Make a draft cheque." Then, he turned to me and said, "Write down your mother's name."

I wrote it down, handed it to the teller, and I was given a cheque for £75. I thanked the bank manager again and again. I think he was slightly embarrassed because I was so grateful.

I made my way back and ran into the cafe waving the cheque. "Look at it!" I said to Uncle Sam. "I got it. The bank gave me the cheque." He could not believe his eyes. It was then I saw from his reaction that he didn't mean to help me. He did it to test me to see what I would do. All these things were going through my head. Sam looked at the cheque. There were people having a meal in the cafe and he said to them, "You wouldn't believe it. If I went to the bank manager and asked him to lend me money he probably wouldn't do it. This kid here, my nephew, he goes down there and he gets a bank draft cheque for £75. How do you work that out? He's underage."

These customers were then asking questions, and when I heard the way my uncle spoke to me, my thoughts were moving so fast it was just like going to university for ten years. I thought to myself, "Why did he say he wouldn't do it? Did he really mean it? Would he have given it to me in the end? Or, was he testing me straight up, not to make it easy for me, that anytime I want money to ask for it? I was sure he didn't believe that I would run to the bank, take initiative and come back with a cheque." All these thoughts went through my mind.

Sam invited the bank manager over for dinner and they talked about it and laughed. My uncle said to him, "If I had come and asked you, you would have put me through everything and made me sign a security and the kid comes down there and he gets the money straightaway!"

"Nick is a good boy," the bank manager replied. "I trust him. I lent it to him myself, not through the bank."

This made a huge impression on me. I thought, "This man is almost a complete stranger and yet he trusts me." That made me feel good about myself. And this has been something which has followed me to this day. People trust me with money. Bills are paid, debts are honoured and loans paid out. The bank manager then said to me, "Keep doing what you are doing, Nick. You'll go a long way."

I did wonder if Uncle Sam had given me the loan when I asked whether I would have become more and more dependent upon him. While £75 doesn't seem like a lot of money, in today's dollars it would probably be the equivalent of $4,000. But it's no different today – how many bank managers today would loan $4,000 to a teenager? This was one of those pivotal moments in life when

I realised that other people, like that bank manager, could see that I had potential. It had an immense impact on me. I sent the money to Greece, my mother received good medical treatment and recovered. Over time, I saved up the money and paid back the bank manager.

Chapter Six

My uncle used to work us hard. Whenever there was a quiet moment in the cafe, he would tell us to get down and wipe everything clean. I remember one time when it was really wet, and we had not a single customer. As we had nothing to do, the eight of us working there were mucking around playing cards. When Sam saw us doing this he was not happy. "You, you and you," he pointed, "polish the floor. On your knees." We often had to clean the windows at the front, even when we had cleaned them the day before. I would say, "But they are clean."

"Clean them again."

"But why?"

"Don't ask questions, just do what I tell you." He said, "Do it early in the morning, do it at about eight o'clock in the morning."

"Why?" I wanted to know.

Sam's answer was clever. "When people are driving or walking to work they'll see you cleaning the windows. They see that the

Left: A photo I received after leaving Greece. It shows my Mum, Dad, Uncle John and Uncle Constantine with my two younger brothers John and Bill.

front of the shop is beautiful and clean all the time. Because of that they know the kitchen where the food is prepared is also beautiful and clean. That's why you always hose every morning. You are telling your customers, 'I'm proud of this cafe – that is why I clean it.'" Those were his rules and if anybody didn't do that, they didn't last long with him. The floors were often so well polished that when dogs came in they would slip all over the place on their claws.

We used to wear leather-soled shoes in those days, and we'd run around the slippery lino floor frantically taking food everywhere, skidding past tables and sliding towards the kitchen. It was a bit of a show for the customers. They would say to my uncle, "Where do you get all these young boys? They work so hard." We were all friends and we were hungry for money, and with my uncle around, it was good pay.

One of my uncle's friends, who owned an abattoir in Bourke called Tancred Brothers Meat Industries, saw us in action sliding along the floor with orders and asked Sam, "Why can't I get some young men to come to Bourke to work? What do I have to do?" My uncle set him up with a Greek newspaper to advertise with some organisation from Greece, hoping they could send him young people to work in Bourke in the abattoirs. I also sent a letter to all my cousins in Greece about this work. This friend of Sam's finished up with about thirty Greek boys as workers. When they arrived in Bourke, they asked him a lot of questions about where they were going to live and what he was going to pay them and things like that.

This man told them if they signed a contract to work for him for five years, he would build every one of them a house. At the end of the five years they would own that house. Most of those young men stayed there for five years. After that they started looking for better jobs. By then most of them were only thirty years old. They now spoke good English and they put their heads together and combined their money to buy little farms. They became cattle station owners instead of living on unemployment benefits. My uncle's friend came to the cafe and said, "Thank you Sam. You made my life easier because I couldn't find people prepared to work." This all came about because of the Greek boys of the Trocadero Cafe sliding about enthusiastically on their leather-soled shoes. I guess even a show of hard work can help the reputation of your countrymen.

I can say that I was blessed to have an uncle like Sam. I learnt so much from him. He arrived in Australia in 1920. He had no one here for him like I did and had a tough time of it. He worked in Mackay doing things like cutting sugarcane. I used to listen to his stories for hours every night in my bedroom until I went to sleep. He would just stand there talking to me in the bedroom and when he saw me fall asleep he would then go to his own room.

Sam tried to tell me never to gamble because the chef was a gambler and never had any money. He always stressed to me that quality was important in running a business. He used to always go and argue with the butcher or the baker. Sam would ask me to have a look and see what I thought. I learnt not to take short cuts for the sake of lower prices which in turn could affect the quality. He said, "Stick to the quality and charge – not too much, as long as you make a profit. People understand, and they will come back. But if you charge half the price and the people can't eat it, then you won't see them again." That was the sort of attitude he had. Unfortunately, he didn't have much more business knowledge than that. I learnt a lot from Sam, but over time I began to realise that he could have done more and made the business a lot more profitable if he had charged more for his services. Even so, Uncle Sam was more or less satisfied with the way things were.

He was also very traditional when it came to his family. When it came to his sons he made most of their important life decisions for them – that was the Greek way. If his sons wanted to do something they had to ask their father first. He was even involved in decisions about what girls they would marry. Even though I was younger, I disagreed with some of these things and I felt the quicker I could get out on my own, the better off I would be. Then I remembered what my father had told me when I was working with him on the farm in Greece – we would grow things together, go and sell things together, and build our lives together.

I used to think Uncle Sam was a bit harsh on me. After all, I was just a teenager living thousands of kilometres from my parents. Every now and then I'd overhear Sam saying something nice about me; like once I heard him saying to a customer, "This boy is going to go to high places one day." He wouldn't tell me this of course,

Above: The staff of the Trocadero Cafe 13 November 1949 – my Uncle Sam in centre and that's me on the end on the right.

just say it to others. When I learnt what he thought about me, I felt an inner pride. And I respected Sam. He was popular with the customers and the people who worked for him. Some of the girls there were with him for many years. There were times though when I felt that Sam should have shown more respect for his wife. He was from that generation of Greek men who felt it was their right to tell their wives what to do. I didn't think that was right. Sometimes, my aunt would come and talk to me about things that were going on or had happened. Maria felt isolated in Trangie.

There was no Greek community in the town and no other Greek women of her age. Like all emigrants, she missed her family a lot. There were times when she told me something that Sam had done, and I would say, "He shouldn't have done that Aunty." She never said a word – she would just turn up her eyes and walk away.

During these years there were many days when I was not very happy. Whilst my uncle was not cruel to me, sometimes he seemed indifferent to me. There were many times when I felt desperately lonely and would cry by myself. I would wonder what was to become of me. I missed my mother and father and brothers. But I had promised my mother that I would return to Greece at the age of twenty-one, and in my mind I was determined not to come back as a failure.

In the first couple of years I didn't have money because I was paying my uncle back for my airfare to Australia. My trousers were about six inches short and they used to split on the back. I'd give them to a lady who used to come and do the washing up for us. She had a sewing machine and would open them up from the back and let them down as much as she could – if they were too short, it didn't matter. For the ones who had bigger bums, she would put in some more material and stitch them. We used to wear an apron as our uniform and it used to cover up to the knees, so we didn't care what our cheap pants looked like because no one could ever see them properly – so long as they were clean, that's all that mattered.

After three years in Australia, I had saved about £100 – today the equivalent of about $5,000. It might seem like a lot, but to me, this was a pitiful result. After so much hard work, day and night, as well as scrimping and saving, I had managed to put aside £100. I felt there was no hope for me. All I could see in the future was more of the same – more loneliness, more work – and probably after eight years I would have saved £200 to £300. I would go back to Greece a failure and this weighed on me, as I was the oldest son. Although I was disappointed, I reminded myself that things change. All you must do is be patient and wait for opportunities.

Chapter Seven

There was another factor in Aunty Maria wanting to get out of Trangie. She didn't want her kids to be in the same school as the Aboriginal kids. You must remember this was the 1950s, and at that time Aboriginals didn't even have citizenship. Obviously, there was discrimination against Aboriginals – and against newcomers like me. People called us 'wogs' and 'dagos' behind our backs – and sometimes to our faces. But that sort of thing never bothered me. I knew that there was only one way to gain respect – and that was by hard work and earning money.

I found the local Aboriginals to be good people, quiet people. In those days they were forbidden to buy or drink alcohol and so there was not the level of drunkenness you see in some country towns today. I learnt a lot from the Aboriginals and listened to their advice whenever we went shooting. On Sundays, we were not allowed to open before 10.00 am so that people could go to church. Many in the community attended church every Sunday. My uncle was not a religious person, nor was I, and on Sunday mornings we often went shooting. We'd come back at about 10.30 am and then open up for lunch.

A couple of times when I went shooting, I got lost. One time I was with a friend and after a couple of hours we realised we didn't know where we were. I climbed a tree and looked for our tent. It was a blue colour and easily spotted. We saw the tent and then set off. But the Macquarie River breaks into lots of different little streams and then we became confused as to which branch of the river we were on. Then I climbed a tree again, but our blue tent was nowhere to be seen. All I could see was more trees, more scrub and more branches of the river. We had no water left and so I had to take my singlet off, push into the mud and lick the water to survive. And that mud wasn't just mud, it was cow shit and everything else you can think of – dead cats, dead snakes and so on. You learn from your mistakes, so after that we used to take some Aboriginals with us. They were very ingenious fellows. We never got lost again.

After a morning's shooting we would go back to the cafe and start work. Like all country towns, there wasn't a lot to do in Trangie. People went to the pub, or our cafe, or both. There was a rugby league club which I joined, and I went to the Police Boys Club to learn boxing. Apart from that, there was nowhere else to go and not much else to do.

Not long before my arrival in the town, there had been a tragedy involving a young Greek boy from the local high school. An older Greek couple had a shop with one or two people working there. Their son was an incredible sportsman, best at cricket, best at football, the best at schoolwork – basically, the best at everything. He was a big boy and a health and fitness fanatic. Apparently, the local boys were jealous of him and used to call him 'dago' and things

Left: Me in 1952. People sometimes told me I looked a lot like Elvis Presley.

like that. One day this Greek boy went swimming in a waterhole at the river with his friends. Something happened, and the boy drowned. It seemed impossible that this could have happened to someone so fit and strong and such a fantastic swimmer. At the time, there were about ten other boys at the waterhole and they all told the same story – the Greek boy had dived in and hit his head on a rock, lost consciousness and drowned. The only problem with this account was that the police autopsy revealed that the boy had been hit by a blow to the back of the head. The suspicion was that someone had hit him, and he had then drowned, but it could never be proved. According to my uncle, the whole town covered up this crime.

Above: A terrible change in the weather in 1951 where the sky turned blood red! We all left the cafe and stood on the footpath when the earthquake hit. Luckily, no one was inside the Trocadero Cafe at the time.

Left: Me doing boxing training at the Police Boys' Club, 1951.

The parents of this boy were devastated. He was their only son. They had a girl who was much younger, but nothing could make up for the loss of their precious son. After that they didn't give a damn about their shop. I used to stop by the store and say hello, but you could see in his eyes that the father had nothing to live for. Because of this tragedy, Sam's wife believed that it was not safe for Greeks in Trangie. Personally, I thought this was ridiculous, but this is what she believed. In all the years I lived in Trangie, I never felt unsafe. But it was true that Maria was lonely. She had Greek friends in Dubbo, which was a much bigger town and, as she pointed out, had many more business opportunities for Sam. She started to put pressure on Sam to sell the Trocadero and buy another cafe in Dubbo.

Chapter Eight

One day in about 1950, my uncle asked me to go outside. Sam said to me, "Get out the back in the little garden and dig it out where I have got my fruit trees. I want to plant tomatoes and cucumbers." He had cucumbers, tomatoes and a couple of small fig trees, they were only about a metre high. He said, "It's an important operation and when I leave it too long it needs to be stretched, when it is stretched it is good."

I said to him, "Uncle, you know why the tomatoes go red?" "What do you mean?"

I said, "The tomatoes, when they grow up, they go from green to red. Do you know why they go red?"

Sam shook his head, "No. I have no idea."

"Because they see the cucumbers getting longer!"

Uncle Sam was not impressed at all. He did his lolly, as they say. To punish me for having a filthy mind, he gave me even harder jobs. I was supposed to dig all day. When I would come into the cafe he would say, "I didn't tell you to come in. Stay out there digging."

"Uncle, it is too late. I will do it first thing tomorrow." "I want you to do it now."

"It's sprinkling," I'd complain.

"Don't try to argue with me. When I tell you to do something, you do it straight away. Now do it!" He was that sort of a fellow. When he was in that sort of mood you didn't dare argue with him.

Then I went back to the garden and after a while came back inside. "You finished?" Sam wanted to know. I replied, "No uncle, but I can't see. It's dark."

"You are back in here because you didn't want to do it. You are doing this on purpose. Aren't you? When I tell you to do something you have to learn to do it – dark or otherwise, so you go back there and finish it."

I had no choice. So I went back out and started digging in the dark. While I was working in the dark, I accidentally chopped one of the baby fig trees off because I didn't see it. The next morning Sam went out to have a look at my handiwork in the garden. Then he walked into the cafe fuming and carrying the fig tree. "You did it on purpose," he yelled.

"No Uncle, I'm sorry. I didn't do it on purpose. I couldn't see!"
"You did it on purpose!"

"You little bastard. Others gave you life and yet I brought you up. I'm the one who has to look after you, you miserable bastard." For the first time I raised my voice against him. Things were never the same after that. By the next day, I concluded that I could not work with my uncle any longer.

By then I had just about paid Sam all the money I owed him for the airfares and I had altogether a bit over £100 in the bank. I walked up to see Mr Skinner. He was a gentleman with two sons who sold Holden cars in Trangie. The Holden car first came out in 1948 and so they were very new and much talked about. The Skinners sold cars and did mechanical work on the huge trucks that supplied petrol from Sydney to Cobar, Bourke and Brewarrina.

His sons, who were big boys with huge appetites, were regular customers in the cafe.

Mr Skinner looked a bit like Bob Menzies, the then prime minister, with his big eyebrows and wavy white hair – he was a big man and a very quiet man. I went to him and I said, "Mr Skinner, I want a job. I've had enough of selling milkshakes."

"All right. What are you going to do Nick?"

"I want to learn to be a mechanic," I told him. "To start with I can wash cars."

He thought about this for a second and then asked, "What are you going to do after that?"

"Well," I said, "I want to make money and one day I want to buy a big tanker to carry petrol from Sydney to Cobar and Brewarrina and places like that."

There used to be lot of those trucks going through Trangie and the drivers would eat in our cafe. Sometimes the drivers would show me the interior of their cabins and I admired how they were set up with a bed and things like that. To me, these trucks were huge, and impressive, and I wanted to own one. Mr Skinner asked, "Is that your dream?"

"Yes, it is, Mr Skinner."

He leaned forwards and said, "I tell you what. I don't want to know the details, but obviously you've had a bit of a fight with your uncle. Your uncle has got a reputation. He has got a big mouth. He's a bit hot-headed and tells people off. But don't take any notice of that. It doesn't matter if he has a big mouth. He's got a good heart. God bless him. He means well. Stick with him."

"Really?"

"That's my advice, son. Don't leave him. You stay and work with your uncle, it doesn't matter if you're selling milkshakes. If you can buy the shop – any shop – and you make money and your wallet is full, then if you don't have friends or relatives at least your wallet is full. But I say stick with your uncle. You have no one else. One day you can buy a shop like that for yourself and once your wallet is full you can make changes, but if you don't have family or friends, you'll need your wallet. Nobody wants to know you with an empty wallet."

This wasn't at all what I wanted to hear, but I had a lot of respect for Mr Skinner. Then he gave me more advice. "Whatever, you do, get the idea of buying a big truck out of your mind."

I thought this didn't make any sense at all. "Why?"

"No truck drivers or owners are wealthy people, son. They're always battling and always will. To keep them on the road costs a lot of money – insurance, registration, tyres, mechanical repairs and fuel. The only ones who make a decent pay are the ones who work almost twenty hours a day. They sleep in the trucks, they don't have families. It is a bad, bad, bad line of work." Mr Skinner explained that he and his sons made a good living from servicing and supplying trucks – not from owning or driving them.

Having said all that, he then spoke again about my uncle. "You're just a youngster from another country. You need family and the only family you have got is your uncle. Don't leave him. Stay with him. Even if you have had words, listen to him and in the long run you will be a winner. Go back; no need to apologise; what has happened, has happened; just carry on. Don't leave him until your wallet is full."

I realised that if Mr Skinner gave me a job and something went wrong I would have nowhere to go. If you get sick, where would you go? To strangers? I realised then that if something like that happened I would go to my uncle, or my aunt, or my cousins. Especially in another country, you need your own blood.

"Thank you, Mr Skinner," I said and then left.

Sometimes, I think this was the best advice anyone ever gave me. But I have to admit I am a stubborn person and decided to try working in another industry before going back to my uncle. I thought I'd try to become a shearer. The money was nothing short of amazing. Some of the top shearers earned £100 a week – as much as I had saved in three years. I went to one of the stations in the district where I was given a job as a wool presser – this is where you put the wool in the pressing machine and compress it into a bale ready for shipment. Wool pressers were paid a fixed wage. I can't remember exactly what the pay was, but the big money was for the shearers, so I wanted to try that as well. They used to be paid six times the average wage. Usually, they wasted it gambling and drinking at the pub. Sometimes the shearers got into arguments and fought between themselves.

They would arrive at our cafe with their faces all busted up, and blood everywhere. They'd wash themselves at the back of the shop and then have something to eat. Often the person who they had been fighting would turn up and they'd sit down and have a meal together and joke about what had happened. "Look at you, mate!" one would say.

"Never mind looking at me – look at you!" the other would reply.

"I tell you what, that bloody left hook got me! But if it didn't get me you would have been down on your arse."

That was the way they talked. This was unique in my experience. In Greece if someone has a fistfight, the next minute they will pick up guns and try and shoot each other – or they will never speak to each other again. If a European has a fistfight, it will go to the bitter end. They will pick up a bloody shovel, or pick up a gun, and shoot you. If they are both lucky enough to stay alive, they will not talk to each other for many years.

Eventually, I was given an opportunity to work as a shearer. Some shearers wear a belt which is attached to a spring hooked onto the ceiling. When you bend over this helps hold your back up. And although some shearers didn't use these belts, they recommended that I use it for my first day. I sheared for one day with the belt and was exhausted. After a day I tried it without the belt – after all I felt if they didn't need it, why did I? The next day I was so sore I couldn't get out of my bed. That was the end of my career in shearing.

In the meantime, I had been thinking about Mr Skinner's advice, about filling your wallet up and then you can do what you want to do – but stick to your uncle. It just so happened that around this time my aunt became more insistent about getting out of Trangie and going to live in Dubbo. She used the same arguments which were wearing Sam down: it was a bigger town with more opportunities, their kids could go to a better school there and Maria had a couple of friends there whereas in Trangie she had none. The Trocadero Cafe was put on the market with an asking price of £7,000.

Chapter Nine

There was interest in the Trocadero Cafe from a few buyers. People came and checked the place out and looked at the books. And although there was strong interest in the business, people baulked at the £7,000 Sam wanted. A couple of offers were made, the highest being £5,000, but my uncle refused to budge from his original price. He complained that people wanted him to 'give it away' whereas to him it was a viable and profitable business.

Aunt Maria was not happy that it was taking so long and although she was instrumental in getting Sam to put it on the market, she had no influence on the issue of the price. For Sam, this was men's business, and none of her business, and so he held out for the price he wanted. One day I said to my uncle, "I will buy the shop." He looked at me like I was mad. "You are seventeen years old and know nothing," Sam replied. I could see this was something he would not even consider. There were two things that motivated my actions: my mother saying she wanted me back in eight years, and unmarried; and Mr Skinner saying to me either stick with your uncle or if you can, buy a business and then you can

have a full wallet. One thing was certain – I didn't have £7,000 or anything like it.

Then new buyers appeared. They agreed to take the cafe, but they couldn't raise the money. This time I raised my idea with my aunt. At last I was beginning to learn something about how the world worked. "Why don't I buy the cafe?" I suggested. "You are too young," she said. I started to carefully lay out my arguments: if Sam provided vendor finance I would pay him back each week and in full within two years; he would be in Dubbo which was not that far away and be able to help me when I needed advice or had difficulties; and if I failed they could have the cafe back and put it back on the market. While I was explaining all this, I could see that Maria thought my idea was great. I knew I had convinced her when she said to me abruptly, "Tell your uncle. Tell your uncle."

When I again raised the idea of me buying the cafe with Sam, I said nothing about my conversation with his wife. I trotted out the same arguments I used with her and this time Sam listened. I think that by this time he was fed up with the process of showing these prospective buyers over the place and all the time that took up only to discover it was a complete waste of time. I said to him, "Uncle, when you went away and you were on holidays in Sydney, you came back you said I did a better job than you did. Were you fair dinkum or were you just trying to make me feel good? I will buy it. I am young, if I go broke you can come and take the cafe back and I will carry on somewhere else with my life. Let me have a go. You are only a telephone call away and Dubbo is only a one-hour drive. I will be asking you for advice."

Left: Taking a break with my cousin Bill after he started working for me, 6 June 1959.

He needed time to think about it and to discuss the proposal with Maria. A few days later, Sam came to me and said, "I have thought about it. You can buy the cafe. But you are underage. I will give you my word that it is yours. As from next week, we will open an account at the bank – don't tell the bank manager you are underage." We shook hands. The deal was that I would pay him £100 a week.

Not long after this, the Stock and Station agent came to the cafe. He was a regular and I served him all the time. He was a British fellow named Geoff, and a good friend of my uncle. I could not resist telling him my news. "Geoff, you know what mate? I am the boss. I bought the cafe."

"You are kidding me?"

"No, fair dinkum," I replied. "I bought it. My uncle, we shook hands, done." "Really?"

Above: Cousin Bill; Peter my brother; myself; Dawn, who taught me English through reading comic books; and Hazel, one of the waitresses.

"Yes. My uncle will tell you when he sees you."

Geoff said, "Show me the documents you've got." "No documents. I am underage. We are going to keep it quiet." Geoff shook his head. "No, you still need documents."

"Well, you tell my uncle."

"Ask him to give you a promissory letter, which has the price and says you will pay him £100 a week, and then the account and everything and you leave that with the bank. A solicitor has to draw one up. It is not a dinky-di document, but it is a letter of intent for the selling."

I didn't see the point of this and responded, "I don't understand any of this, Geoff. You tell him." When Geoff approached Sam, he confirmed the sale. Geoff explained to my uncle the importance of having a letter to confirm the arrangements of the sale. If, for example, something happened to Sam and his wife then remarried, that person could kick me out of the shop, and I would be left with nothing. "Nick must have something from you, like a promissory note," Geoff said, "and we will leave this document at the bank." Sam saw the sense in all this. "You're right Geoff. Tell the solicitor to come and see me and I will do one." The solicitor came over and drafted a promissory note which we both signed. This was then taken away to the bank for safe-keeping.

Aunty Maria was very happy with the news. She showed me a lot of love and respect for taking over the shop. Maria always wished me to do well and she said, "I am sure you will do well, but your uncle is only a telephone call away – and so am I – if you need any help call us and we will come up." After I took over the cafe, I did call Sam a few times and he came, as promised. He always came up from Dubbo in a taxi. My uncle never drove. All his life he never drove. Why? I do not know.

One can't see into the future of course, but now when I look back over my life, I can see that buying the Trocadero Cafe was the great turning point of my life. I was seventeen years old. I had an enormous debt to repay. I was now responsible for my own livelihood and the livelihoods of all the cafe's employees. There were to be many trials ahead for me, but I was keen to get started and make a success of the cafe. Here was my chance to return to Greece in four years' time as a man my mother would be proud of.

Chapter Ten

It was like I went to bed a boy and woke up a man. And I was lucky – unbelievably lucky in retrospect – as the times were with me. It was the early 1950s; Robert Menzies was the prime minister and new Australians – Italians, Greeks, Poles, Brits and Balts (those from the Baltic States) – poured into the country hungry for work. The war had finished only a few years before and all over the world people wanted to enjoy their lives and prosper. Meat and wool exports were booming, and my cafe was patronised by farmers, wheat lumpers, fencers, abattoir workers, stockmen and shearers. The shearers used to walk into the cafe and cash their cheques. I was like a bank. I had about ten people working for me. One of the first things I did was to put the wages for the staff up to £10 a week.

The second thing I did was raise our prices in the cafe. I did a tour of some of the cafes in the neighbouring towns and saw what they were charging. What I noticed was that most charged more than we did, and also, they had a bigger range of things on offer. At first when I put up the prices some of the customers kicked up a fuss. "Well, this is the price my uncle told me to charge,"

I explained, as for a long time people did not know I owned the business. However, this excuse did not last long. One of the customers happened to be in Sam's cafe in Dubbo and complained to him about the prices being put up. Unfortunately, Sam denied that he had told me to lift the prices. When this customer came back to me, I had to think up another excuse. "Look, to be honest with you," I explained, "my uncle doesn't want to upset anybody, but he has a new accountant, Mr Ebert in Warren. And Mr Ebert tells me the prices have to go up."

People seemed satisfied with that excuse. Nobody knew much about this new accountant, Mr Ebert – because he didn't exist. I'd just made him up to be the scapegoat for the high prices, and it seemed to work. Slowly, after a few months, the arguments about prices faded and customers became used to the new arrangements.

My strategy worked and for the first time the cafe started to make a profit. Before I took over, my uncle had slaved his guts out virtually working for nothing. I'm not being critical of Sam. This happens in a lot of businesses and is what is known as "churn"; the money comes in and the money goes out, but almost none of it is held onto as genuine profit. And when there is money coming in, sometimes the operator of the business thinks they must be making a profit without really knowing. In our case, money was coming in from the cafe and the fruit shop, and a lot of the success of the cafe was because of my uncle's good name: it was clean, he always served good meals and it was inexpensive.

Slowly, I started to add things to the menu. I introduced a slow-cooked leg of lamb, or shoulder of lamb, just like my mother used to make. It would be in the oven for six hours and just fall off the bone. We started making our own pies with real, dinky-di meat and tasty pastry and people used to come from miles around to buy our pies.

Behind the scenes, one of the greatest influences on my business, and for that matter, all my future life as a businessman, was a man called Les Holden. He was a Jewish man, single and about forty-five years old. Les was the general manager of the Trangie General Store. Being single, he used to eat at our cafe all the time. After I took over the shop from my uncle I said to him, "Les, guess what mate. I'm the boss. I just bought the shop from my uncle."

"Really?"

"Yeah. From now on you go in the kitchen, you cook grilled flounder, fillet steaks, chickens, whatever you want. Cook for us two. You set the table and call me and we will eat. You do the cooking and we will eat and you will never pay a cent from now on, because I am the boss." Les really loved cooking.

"Yeah? What's the catch?" he wanted to know.

"The catch is I don't know how to do the books. My uncle never kept books and you are the general manager of a store. I want you to teach me the books and to help me pay the bills because I don't know anything about it."

Les agreed. "It's easy. We will start on Saturday morning."

I feel that everything I know today about running a business I owe to this man. That is why I have kept his photo. He came in one Saturday as we had arranged. "Get me two wire coat hangers," Les asked. I found them and handed them to him. He opened them up and made them into two big hooks and put these up behind the kitchen door. "Okay," said Les, "from now on we're going to have these two hooks. We're going to write 'In' beside one, and 'Out' beside the other. When the butcher comes in and gives you a bill, you sign the one he takes. Don't pay him from the cash register."

"But," I interrupted, "my uncle paid cash for everything. There were no invoices. When someone gave him a bill, he paid them out of the till."

Les shook his head. "Don't pay anyone from the cash register. When you buy things, when you receive things, like invoices and bills, you put them on either the 'in' or the 'out' wire. Now when the butcher comes in every morning, or the baker, don't pay them on the spot. Tell them you will pay them every Wednesday. And every Wednesday you pay them by cheque."

That raised the issue of my bank account. I had gone with my uncle and opened a bank account in my name, even though I was underage. But no one knew at that stage and no one seemed to care that I was signing cheques. Les also taught me how to prepare the P&L (profit and loss) on a monthly basis. All this was new for me and encouraged me, knowing where I was going and how much better I was doing. I felt confident to carry on. I loved achieving success by working long and hard hours. Les Holden taught me a few other tricks that I've held onto: what to do if you were caught without stock, how to regulate prices and how to find out if your employees were stealing from you. Without him I don't know what I would have done. My guess is I would have done exactly what my uncle had been doing. Thanks to Les, in the next few years I managed to double the sales and profits by adding groceries, more smallgoods, dry goods, guns and watches to our sale items.

During this period, I saw a lot of Les. He used to tell me what happened to his family under the Germans. He didn't have any friends and I think he was lonely. We used to teach him Greek cooking in the kitchen and being Jewish himself, he used to do some Jewish cooking. We used to argue whether Greek or Jewish food was better tasting. Les would come into the kitchen and cook flounder or a mixed grill – one for him and one for me.

Left: Les Holden (left) and me in Trangie, 1951. Les was the manager of the General Store in Trangie. He was my idol and the first person to teach me the fundamentals of business which I still use today.

Although he was only a little fellow, I recall that he used to eat well. I remember another valuable lesson I learnt from Les. We talked about what would happen if we had a visit from the tax man. "He's going to say," Les cautioned, "where did you get your money from? And if you can't explain it, they'll take the shop from you and sell it."

"Oh my God, I don't want that!"

Les said, "Learn to follow the rules and learn to bend the rules. But never break the rules. If the tax man says, 'You are not allowed to do that, you owe us this tax,' you say, 'Thank you very much for bringing it to my attention. Yes, I will pay the tax.'"

It was great advice. Since the day I arrived in Australia, I have never had any problems with the tax man. Les taught me the law and I always listened to him. I didn't have my father here, or someone to teach me these things about business. The only person in the family I could really go to for advice was Uncle Sam, but to me his way of doing business was not sound. He thought it was madness to put up the prices and expand the range of goods we sold.

All these things that Les taught me confirmed my belief that all the years that Sam ran the cafe, he didn't make any real money. He always paid his bills and never owed money to anybody. Sam was always very careful not to owe a cent to anyone. He and his family lived well, but they had no savings and he didn't even want to hear about buying property. At one stage the bank wanted to loan him a quarter of a million pounds. I was standing alongside him when this offer was made: "I have a client who wants to lend quarter of a million pounds on 2½% interest." Sam told them he wasn't interested.

As we were walking away Sam said to me, "See, when you've got a good name, people trust you Nick. Always keep a good name. That banker wants to trust me with quarter of a million."

"But why didn't you take it?" I asked. "To do what?"

"Well, to go to Sydney and buy buildings and get the rent," I suggested.

"No, no," said Sam. "I don't want the headache. Too much money to borrow."

I often think about that conversation. In those days in the early 1950s real estate was not going anywhere. If someone had offered me £250,000 at 2½% interest, I would have snapped it up. Could you imagine what you could have bought and what it would be worth today?

Chapter Eleven

One time I went to pick up the meat from the train, I saw this beautiful girl wearing high heels and dressed up beautifully. She was like a model. I said, "Can I help you? Where are you going?"

"I'm going to the Imperial Hotel. I have a job there."

I offered her a lift and she was very happy about this, even though it was not that far away. As she climbed into the utility, I shoved all the rubbish off the front passenger seat. I dropped her outside the Imperial and said, "By the way, my name is Nick. I own the Trocadero Cafe. It's just across the road here. Come over and see me and I'll shout you a feed." She told me her name was Hazel. She was very nice and very sweet.

I must admit that I was a little surprised when this girl did come down to the cafe one day. Even though Hazel was a barmaid, as they were then called, she seemed a bit fancy for us. But I was as good as my word and shouted her a couple of coffees and a meal or two. I don't think I had seen anyone so beautiful in my life before.

Left: Chris (left) my chef at the Trocadero Cafe, on 10 November 1949 at the Dubbo Public Pool.

She seemed to find it very easy to talk to me and one of the times she was in the cafe she told me she wanted a change of occupation. Without giving it a moment's thought, I said to her, "You come and work for me."

We had a new waitress. Then, Les Holden came into the shop. He took one look at Hazel, and one look at me, and saw all the danger signs. "Oh my God," Les whispered to me, "Where did you get this one?"

"She came from Sydney."

"Oh, she is beautiful," he agreed, "but send her back."

"I tell you what mate, give it a couple of weeks and then I will have a bit of fun with her in my room."

Les would have none of it. "Don't do any such thing!" he warned. "What's the harm in it?"

"Don't put your prick in the till, Nick. You'll close the drawer and you'll lose everything including your dignity and your money!"

I thought he was being a bit harsh. "I just want to have some fun," I explained.

"You want to have fun?" Les asked. "Then sack her first. After that you can have your fun, but not while she's working for you."

I didn't agree with this advice at the time, but I did as he suggested. I distanced myself from her but kept her on. Hazel was good for business – she was bringing business in like there was no tomorrow. According to Les, Hazel had probably been a call girl in Sydney, but as she was now over thirty-five, she was getting towards the end of her working life in that business. He said that girls like Hazel came to the country at that age looking for a rich husband. All the single farmers came in and wanted to be served by her. Once she knew I was not interested, she zeroed in on a couple of young farmers. Since then, over the many years I have been in business, I have never forgotten Les' valuable advice. It was always strictly business with the employees.

Norm, a young farmer, used to come in after hours when the shop was closed to play poker. He played against the Greek boys who worked in the cafe. They talked to each other in Greek and cheated all the time. This fellow was losing hundreds of pounds every time they played. In the end I couldn't stand it. I said to him, "Norm, you can't speak Greek mate, so let me tell you what's going on. The fellow in the kitchen walks around and looks at your cards. He doesn't play, but he tells the others what your hand's like." Norm seemed to appreciate what I was telling him and the next time they were playing he kept an eye out for the kitchen hand who looked at his cards and then told the others in Greek what he had.

But the other players just got smarter. Instead of speaking, the kitchen hand would walk around, then tap out signals to his mates with his foot to tell them what cards poor Norm had. He continued to lose money and I could not bear to watch it. "Mate, you can't win," I told him. "You're throwing your money away, I'm telling you."

Norm didn't seem at all bothered. "Nick, I don't care. I enjoy it. Let me tell you this – all right so what if I lost £1,000 to these cheats? You know while I was sitting here playing cards I reckon I made £5,000 from newborn lambs dropped from their mothers in my paddocks every night."

He was the other card players' Father Christmas, and before long, Hazel's fiancé. I was chatting to a customer one day who told me that he was a salesman who made a living selling watches to people in the bush. He said he had waterproof watches – the first of their kind – and they were very popular. "How much are you selling them for?" I asked.

The salesman said, "Anything from £6 to £8 each." "How many have you got?"

"Eighty."

"Show me."

He opened up these cases and there were all these watches, bands and everything. Immediately I said, "I'll give you £160 for the lot – £2 each."

"What are you going to do with them?"

"I have a showcase here I can put them in." We did have this display case which had fancy items such as pipes and tobacco. The salesman agreed with my offer and I ended up with eighty watches. Because there was not enough room for them in the display showcase, I put some of the watches in the safe.

Not long after that, I saw young Norm looking at my watches with his fiancée, Hazel. She had resigned from her job with us by this time. Norm's father had left him two big properties in Trangie, so I knew he had money to spend. His fiancée was hanging onto him, examining the watches and looking at him with pussycat eyes.

"Nick, do you have anything better than this?" he wanted to know.

"Yes, I have the more expensive ones in the safe – they're £30 each."

"Can we have a look at them?"

I went to the safe and brought out the other watches and showed them to the couple. Of course, they were no different in quality to the ones in the showcase. Then the couple looked closely at one of the watches and nodded their heads. "Ahh, this is what we want. These two. One for me and one for her."

He had his cheque book with him and wrote out a cheque for £60. Those two watches had cost me £4. It was unbelievable in those days. Sometimes I felt like I couldn't stop making money.

It was half luck, and half the will to learn and work hard. When you put that together with a bit of common sense and brains anything can happen.

Someone came in and asked me if I sold guns. It had never happened before and so I said, "I'm expecting some in at the end of this week. Can you come back?" He said he would. There was a gun factory in Lithgow and I bought half a dozen wholesale for £17 each and put them behind the counter and priced them at exactly double – £34 each. This was another profitable sideline until the local copper called in to see me. "For Christ's sake Nick! Bullets here, guns there – have you got a licence?"

"Do I need a licence?" I asked.

"Of course, you have to have a licence to sell guns." He walked out, went back to the station and brought me back a licence. "You should have a licence – and get those bloody bullets out from there. Someone will get shot."

I also obtained my driving licence in much the same way. I never did an exam, or a driving test, or anything like that. I simply went down to the police station and it was typed up and handed to me.

Whenever someone wanted a loan and asked, "Hey Nick, could you lend us £2?" I'd say, "Sure, go out the back and chop three barrels of wood."

"No. I meant can I have the money now because a friend of mine is waiting? I've owed him the money for a long time and he's chasing me."

That never fooled me. "If I give you the money before you chop the wood," I replied, "you will go straight to the pub and get drunk."

One time a fellow came into the cafe with four live chooks. "Nick, how much will you give me for these chooks? A mate of mine asked me to sell them." I gave him £2 from the till. He said, "Thanks, where do you want them?"

"Take them out the back and put them in that little shed."

He did that and came back and asked, "Do you want any more?" "Do you have more?"

"Yeah, yeah. I think there's quite a few, but I will check. Do you want me to bring another four chooks?"

"Yes. All right," I agreed.

He walked off and I should have been suspicious because he was back in no time with another four chooks. Again, I paid him, and again he took them out the back, and again said he might have more. When he brought me the third lot of chooks that was more than enough for me. I told him I didn't need any more. He went on his way very happy with his £6 payment. After he left, I began to think about what had just happened. So I went out the back to check and discovered I had only four chooks. The rascal had sold me the same chooks three times over!

My uncle came to see me. We talked about things and then he asked, "Can you afford to pay me back a bit earlier than we agreed – like maybe half?" He said that he wanted to go back to Greece with his family – something they had never done. Up until then I paid Sam £100 a week. I thought about it for a moment, and then said to him, "I'm in the position where I can to pay you the lot, right now." This look passed over his face which I will never forget. He stared at me in disbelief – then he looked thrilled at the prospect of getting all his money – then he looked at me suspiciously – what had I been doing to be able to do this – and back came the look of amazement. He must have asked himself why it was that he didn't have this sort of money. I paid him the whole balance I owed him after eighteen months owning the cafe. Afterwards, Sam was telling everybody that what I made in those eighteen months he didn't make in all the years he was running the cafe.

Chapter Twelve

I continued with the cafe roster that let us watch a movie once a month at our local cinema – they were almost always cowboy movies. Most Sunday afternoons, a couple of us from the roster would go and watch the football. Those were our outings. In a country town, there was nowhere else to go and not much else to do. I bought an old 1928 Oldsmobile utility for £28. It had wooden spike wheels and on Sundays I used to take the staff from the cafe out shooting. Out in the bush we'd shoot mainly feral pigs and kangaroos and occasionally emus.

Sometimes, we'd go to my orchard at Bundemar and shoot rabbits. While we were there, I'd take out the axe and saw and cut wood for the stove. At the time I was into building muscles and weight-lifting and enjoyed filling the utility up with firewood and bringing it back to the cafe. In time I imported a Hudson from the United States, and also bought a Studebaker. That was one of my eccentricities – I loved owning beautiful cars and still do.

I drove my 1928 Oldsmobile all over the place. I went to places like Warren, Gilgandra, Condobolin – even down to Forbes and Parkes. In a lot of these towns there were restaurants run by

Greeks. I'd check out the menu, what they charged and what their meals were like. I'd ask myself, "Is their cafe better than mine? If so, why? Or, are they offering better value for money?" And I didn't do this in secret. I would introduce myself and ask all these questions. I think because I was so young the other cafe owners were quite open with me and told me a lot about their businesses.

Also, I used the car to give my friends a lift to the local dances. Not many young men had a car and a lot of the kids in country towns didn't have money. I had both. And I was always generous. I never hesitated to shout my friends drinks and because of this I was a popular boy. Although I was only about eighteen, I had money coming in left, right and centre.

I can't say I was smart. There was a lot of luck in it, such as buying what was already a very successful business from my uncle. There were plenty of attractive young ladies in Trangie. I loved giving these girls a lift and taking them to dances, but that was it. These ladies behaved differently to the Greek girls that I had known and grown up with. They were more outspoken and more independent. And dowries were almost unheard of. In Greece the parents of a young woman had to give *prika* to the groom. If you don't pay *prika*, you don't get married – it's as simple as that. Normally, a good *prika* was a unit in Athens or a house in a country town. At least the boy will marry and work and make a living, but he doesn't have to pay a mortgage because he received a decent *prika*. These days it is very different in Greece because the girls are all educated – some of them are even better educated than the boys. I learnt that if you married an Australian girl, there was no *prika*. And I remembered my solemn promise to my mother to return to Greece a single man.

We had a chef named Chris, who was a Cypriot and a great wrestler. He was a good chef, but he wouldn't do anything else.

When you work in a small business, you have to lend a hand with all the work. For example, it annoyed me that Chris would never sweep the floor – it was always dirty. I said to him, "Sweep the floor sometimes. Or ask somebody else, like the fellow you have peeling the potatoes. Get him to sweep the floor." He made funny faces, but after a while I noticed that the floor was cleaned a few times, so that pleased me. Then one day I opened the kitchen door, wanting to put something behind it, and when I pushed the door to close it, nothing happened. Chris had swept up all the rubbish and just left it behind the door. He was too lazy to even pick it up and put it in a bin.

I walked back into the cafe and picked up a salt shaker from a table. "Chris, here mate. Come here," I called. Other staff looked at me wondering what was going on. Chris walked over. "Do you know what this is?" I asked, holding up the salt shaker. "Yeah," he replied warily. "So, what do you want?"

"Come here." With a bit of a flourish I opened the kitchen door and revealed the pile of rubbish behind it. "Put some salt on top of the rubbish, because it is going to go bad pretty soon." Chris was furious.

At first, I thought he was going to punch me in the nose, and because he was strong man, a wrestler, I moved back. He took his apron off, threw it in my face and he walked out. He picked up his things, went up to the railway and caught a train to Sydney. I was in tears. I'd lost my only chef. I never saw him again.

Chapter Thirteen

A couple of years into living at Trangie I started playing rugby league. Originally, it was because I used to see the butchers working across the road and my God, were they fit! They'd cut heavy meat and lift enormous boxes and trays and were going about it like there was no problem. Then there was me on the other side of the street, carrying around cups of tea or coffee – like a woman! I wanted to be manlier! At the beginning, the team trainer said I wasn't fit enough for the game. Even though I was working seven days a week, it wasn't physically draining enough. After he told me that, when we closed the restaurant at night I used to get one of the staff from the kitchen to ride a pushbike and I would run alongside them about three kilometres out and three kilometres back in, every second night. Also, I didn't have proper shoes to run in – they were made of leather which made it hard running on the bitumen. Usually, my German Shepherd dog Leon ran with me. They are such intelligent dogs. A friend of mine, Johnny, used to breed dogs. He had them trained. I used to get them when they were six months old. I bought Leon from a lady, a local customer of mine in Trangie. They had some puppies and she more or less gave him to me. Leon always made good company for a run.

After doing some solid training I was soon quite big and strong. We had an Italian trainer for our rugby league team and Trangie was in the Western District competition. We played against Cobar, Brewarrina, Bourke, Gilgandra, Nyngan and Warren. For our away games, the club used to hire a small train with about half a dozen carriages, and the whole town used to go with us to the football on Sundays. If there were thieves around there in those days, they would have been able to break into the supporter's houses and take everything. But I don't think too many houses in Trangie had valuables.

To start with, they put me in the front row – when I was in the juniors – before I played first grade. Then, they put me in at five-eighth and I also played a couple of games at inside centre. I had to watch myself so that I didn't get injured, so I wasn't putting everything that I could into my football. However, I must have been a reasonable player as they never kicked me out of the team and I played with them for two years.

Our half-back was a fellow by the name of Digger Clark. He had fought in Korea and he used to wear his army clothes all the time. I guess that's why they called him Digger. He was only a small fellow, but he liked to go around and stir up trouble, which usually ended in a fistfight. Typically, he'd go up to someone and say, "Dave, what do you think about Johnno?"

"He is a friend of mine, a good bloke," Dave would reply.

Then Digger would frown and say, "That's all right. I'm not going to say anything more."

"Why, what happened?"

"He has a big mouth, you know. He says you are a bloody no-hoper and any day he's going to smash your face up."

Dave would be all fired up and then Digger would then go and see Johnno and repeat all of this, just switching who supposedly said what to whom. He was a real troublemaker.

Another player in our team was Pat, whose nickname was 'Itchy'. I have no idea how he got that nickname. Itchy was a strong boy with a reputation for being a good fighter. No one would pick on him. We played football together and were good mates, or so I thought. One day I was reading some comic books on the counter at the cafe. Itchy came in and said, "G'day mate!" and sort of touched me on the face. But this was a little bit harder than a touch. I replied, "G'day." I could see his face was becoming serious. "Have you got a bone to pick with me?" he wanted to know.

"No," I said, but it made no difference. "Well, let's sort it out now, mate!"

I refused to budge. "What is it Itchy?"

"You're going round telling everybody that you're going to bash me up because I've got a big mouth."

"No, I didn't say that. Come on now."

"If that's what you think, Nick, let's get it over with. Let's go out to the footpath."

I tried to say no, but then I knew it would be all over town if I chickened out of it when he challenged me. So I said, "If that's what you want, let's go." We went out to the footpath and sized each other up. We each threw a few punches and while this was happening, the cause of all this trouble, Digger Clark, was running into every one of the three pubs in town and calling out, "There's a big fight on. Come out quick."

All the people came out – it wasn't far from the pubs to the cafe. Everyone was standing around watching. Itchy and I sparred with each other – he hit me a few times and I landed a few on him. After a while we both had had enough of this. There was blood coming out of his nose and I had a few cuts here and there. We sat on the footpath and put our arms around each other. I looked at him and said, "Ha. Jesus Christ look at you!"

"Have a look at your bloody face!" Itchy said.

We laughed and went out the back to the bathroom and washed up. Then I said to him, "What was this all about Itchy?"

He said, "Well you shouldn't be saying things about me."

"What did I say about you?" I asked.

Then he told me all the dreadful things I was supposed to have said. None of it was true. "Who told you this?"

"Digger Clark," he replied. "That bastard."

We went out the back and washed up and walked back into the cafe. All the crowd were still there waiting for some action. Then, I saw Digger Clark and said to Itchy, "There he is, let's get him." Digger bolted! We ran after him down Dandaloo

Above: The Trocadero Cafe in 1953 with floodwaters lapping the floorboards.

Street. Everybody was laughing because they knew who had caused the problem by spreading the false rumour. That is the only time in my life I boxed in a brawl on the footpath, the Australian way, with bare fists. That was what life was like in Trangie.

One time our rugby league team played Cobar, which had a population of around 5,000 people, in the grand final. It was a much bigger town than Trangie and they thought we were easy meat. From the sidelines, opposition spectators called out, "Kill the Froggie! Kill the Froggie!" It took a while before I realised they were referring to me. I had no idea why this was. When I asked someone why they called me 'Froggie', back came the answer, "Because they think you're a Frenchman."

At that time, I had no idea that English people called Frenchmen 'Frogs' or referred to them as 'the Frogs'. My hair was brown, it wasn't dark like most Greeks and although I had olive-coloured skin, I didn't have a dark complexion. "Kill the Froggie! Kill the Froggie!" continued from the sidelines.

For some reason, spectators mistaking me for a Frenchman and howling for blood fired me up. It is strange what motivates a human being. During the game I took out three Cobar players and stopped them scoring. One of our players, Brian, had at one stage played for Australia. He was a formidable player who weighed about fifteen stone. People were surprised when I pointed out that I was heavier than Brian. He had a thicker neck, and bigger shoulders, but his legs were slim. With me, my thighs were just about as thick as my waist and so I was far more powerful than I looked. Anyway, this turned out to be the best game of rugby league I ever played and afterwards there were comments made that they didn't realise what a ferocious player they had in their team! For the first time ever, Trangie won the competition.

Before we caught the train back, I rang Ernie Andrews and said, "Have you heard the good news? Trangie won the grand final." I told him we were coming back on the train and that we were going to have a party in the cafe. I asked Ernie to go to the pub and buy a lot of beer, and to go to the butcher and get some meat because everything was going to be free tonight. And so there were a lot of happy faces on the train back when I told them the news – free food and drink at the cafe tonight on me for all of the residents in Trangie.

By the time we arrived, the word had spread and the cafe was packed. People were spilling out onto the street and we celebrated our win well into the early hours of the morning. It made me very happy to do this. I wanted to show my thanks to this wonderful town. I could not have made a success of the cafe without their support.

Chapter Fourteen

Having been raised in the countryside of Greece, I always had a dream of becoming a farmer. My business was going well, and I bought an orchard which had about 1,000 orange trees on it at a place near Bundemar, some twenty kilometres west of Trangie. There was a little house on the property and I found this Chinese fellow who agreed to look after the orange trees in return for living there rent-free. Before I purchased this place, I specifically remember asking the agents if the river ever flooded. I had lived in the district long enough to know that although there always seemed to be a shortage of water, sometimes floods appeared and ruined the crops. " Well, yes, it is flood-prone," the agent admitted, " but they only get floods here about once every one hundred years or so. The last flood was about fifty years ago." I liked those odds and took the risk. My Chinese friend turned out to be a real find. The oranges did well and then he started growing mandarins, tomatoes and watermelons. I used to take them to the shop and sell them there.

This Chinese fellow was a strange sort. He lived on his own, and as well as looking after my crops he also had his own garden. He seemed perfectly happy with this arrangement.

My Bundemar farm was good for about five years. Then in 1953, the once-in-a-century flood arrived, about fifty years early. All the trees were under water and everything was lost – including the Chinese gardener – he was nowhere to be seen. I went to the police and reported him missing. They conducted searches, but sadly, he was never found and presumed drowned.

There was also an experimental farm nearby which was owned by one of the private schools in Sydney. Students from the school would spend a year on the farm after they sat for their leaving certificate. On this farm, there were well over three hundred people. It was like a big school and they lived like soldiers. The teachers used to take them out and teach them about sheep and cattle, about feral animals and pests, about which chemicals to spray, about wheat and barley – basically anything that grows on the land.

It amazed me what these young men were taught – like how many breeds of grasshoppers there were, which flies do good things and which flies you should kill with spray. These students were only allowed to go and see their parents at Easter and Christmas. For the rest of the time they were at the farm.

I knew a few of the boys, as they would come into the cafe on the weekends. I learned a lot from them and felt I was very lucky. One bloke I remember was called Jack – we used to call him Jackaroo. He was tall – over six foot – and very slim and very funny. In later years when I used to watch the comedian Jerry Lewis, I was reminded of Jack. He was both funny and clever. I learnt a lot from talking to Jack about what he was studying on the experimental farm and about various things. When I think about it, Jack was the closest friend I ever had when I lived in Trangie. We had a lot in common – we loved football, and boxing and flying. Both of us became interested in flying and took lessons at the flying school in Narromine. Also, I used to give Jack a lift to the local dances.

There were very few cars around and the majority of young men didn't own a car. Whenever there was a dance in Nevertire, Narromine or Dubbo, people would ask me for a lift. I used to give a couple of the local girls a lift to the dances and paid for their tickets into the dances and the drinks and things like that. I remember at one dance in Nevertire, Jack slipped outside with a girl. The only place they could find a bit of privacy was this chicken pen. Apparently, Jack was a real gentleman and laid his jacket on the floor of the chicken pen for the girl. We know this because when he came back into the dance hall we could smell him from a mile off. When he walked into the hall everybody was saying, "Oh Jack, get out, you stink mate! What the hell!" He realised then that he had chicken poop all over his jacket, but Jack was always good for a joke. "I have just been in the fowl yard with Beryl!" he announced. "Kissing chicks in the chicken pen!"

One Sunday morning at about 7.30 am, Jack came into the cafe and asked me if he could cash a small cheque, like £10 or something like that. He had recently flown solo and was now qualified to take a passenger. I'd only done twenty hours flying. Jack was going to Narromine and asked me to go with him. As he had his full licence, I would be his first passenger. I was very enthusiastic about flying and agreed to this. But as it was Sunday and I had given some of the staff the day off, I told him I would meet him at the aerodrome in a couple of hours' time at about 11.00 am. "See you then mate?" Jack said and off he went.

Not long after that I received a phone call from a bus driver from the town of Wellington. He said, "I'm running late, and we've had a few problems. I have thirty-three passengers and had arranged for lunch in Nyngan, but we'll be too late for lunch there, so we are going to stop at your cafe." He apologised for the late notice. Then I explained to him that I didn't have the staff on to cater for thirty-three people.

"Just give them a ham salad," the bus driver suggested. "Whatever you have got will be enough. And some toast. And olives if you have them. Something light."

"Okay," I agreed.

After I put the phone down, I called together what staff we had and we set to work. We prepared everything so that when the bus passengers arrived all we had to do was hand out the food. While I was working in the kitchen, I completely forgot that I was supposed to go flying with Jack. I had the radio on. Then the music stopped, and the announcer said, "We have some bad news. There's been an accident. A light plane has crashed in the middle of the town of Narromine."

When I heard that I froze. I just knew it was Jack. I quickly jumped into the car and drove to Narromine. All the roads were closed off around the town and the police didn't know who the pilot was. I drove out to the airport and told the police I knew the pilot. It was my friend Jack. If that bus driver hadn't rung me and asked me to feed his passengers, I would not have been delayed and would have been on that plane with Jack. His death was a very big loss for us all. My best friend was dead.

About a year later, this man came into the cafe and introduced himself as Jack's father. "I believe you knew my son."

"Yes, he was my friend." I remember how he had the same look in his eyes as Peter, the local shopkeeper whose son had drowned.

"He used to talk about you a lot when he came to Sydney," his father said. I made him a cup of coffee and told him that Jack and I had been close friends and how we had fun at some of the local dances and things like that. Then, I told him how Jack had come into the cafe on that last day and cashed a cheque to get the money for his flying lesson.

"In fact," I added, "I still have the cheque. I couldn't bring myself to bank it."

"Could I see it?" he asked. I walked out the back and came back with Jack's cheque. We both stood there looking at this cheque and his son's handwriting for £10. "I know it's your money," his father said, "but I wondered if I could have this cheque." He told me he didn't want anything of his son's to be left behind and pulled out his wallet and took out a £10 note. "Don't worry about the money," I insisted. We shook hands and his father walked out of the cafe.

Chapter Fifteen

Over the time I was in Trangie I kept in touch with Ernie Andrews, who had been our chef. A couple of times we went to Sydney together to see a fight, or to go to the wrestling. At one stage, he became very rich and had two shops in Warren, but he lost the lot to gambling. Not long after that, he got married and asked me for a job. He said he was doing it tough. I put him back in the kitchen, but he wanted to keep the kitchen door shut so people would not see him working in the cafe. I agreed to this, but I knew it wouldn't be long before people found out – in a country town almost nothing can be kept secret. And of course, when customers learnt that Ernie was back, they were delighted because he was such an entertaining man.

Then one day he came to me with a proposition. "If I was an SP bookie I would make a lot of money. Give me some money to start an SP book." I should explain that an SP bookmaker is a 'starting price' bookmaker. In the 1950s, 1960s and even into the 1970s, most forms of gambling were illegal. The only legal way to bet on a horserace was to be at the racetrack where you could put on a bet with a legal bookmaker. Most people couldn't do this, and so the easiest way to have a bet was to ring an SP bookie and lodge your bet over the phone. They paid the odds listed by race officials at the start of the race – hence the name 'starting price' bookie. If, for example, you put £1 on the horse you backed, and it was listed at 10 to 1, and won, you would collect £10 in winnings. The police knew who the SP bookies were but turned a blind eye to it.

I can never say that I went into this with my eyes closed. I knew Ernie very well; I knew he had gone broke and lost all his money. But I also knew this was due to his gambling – not because he was dishonest or anything like that. I thought about his idea and decided to put down £500. "But," I said to him, "I will handle the money. You tell me who wins, and I will pay them out." Also, as part of our deal, I told him that I wanted the option of being able to cut it anytime I wanted to. He agreed to this, and now I found myself in the SP bookmaking business.

Out the back behind the kitchen were our bedrooms. It just so happened that one of the bedrooms had a window which faced onto the back of the pub. Ernie set himself up in this bedroom and before long we had punters from the pub turning up at this bedroom window with their bets. Naturally, the police soon found out about this. It wasn't long before they rang with the news that they would be around to do an 'inspection'.

The police would come in, have a bit of a look around, and then they'd go back to the station. At first, I didn't understand at that time what was going on. I was quite naive. Once, after the police had called in I asked him, "What the hell is going on?" Ernie nodded towards the police leaving and said, "Don't worry about it. We're mates."

"Do they know what we're doing?"

"It's all good Nick. The coppers and me are sweet."

After a couple of weeks with Ernie running this business, I discovered we had £16,000 in the bank. It was a lot of money – at the time you could have bought forty or fifty homes in Sydney with that kind of money. This put a very big smile on my face I have to say and whenever I walked past Ernie I had to resist the urge to give him a huge hug.

One day this fellow came in. His name was Ron. He was a half-caste and had one leg shorter than the other. Ron was a footballer, and a surprisingly good one. He played inside centre. The thing I remember about him was that having one leg shorter than the other made him a very difficult player to tackle. His slight disability gave him an unpredictable side-step – you never knew which way he was going to go. Ron was a shearer earning big money. He pointed to the name of a horse and said, "£1,000 on that horse." I went out the back and told Ernie.

He almost had a fit. "Oh Christ!" he moaned, "That's the favourite. It's at three to one." "Will I take the bet or not?"

Ernie thought about it and said, "I suppose I can offset half of it to another bookie. Play it safe."

"Do what you think is best," I replied. Unfortunately, Ernie didn't offset the bet. Ron's horse won and he picked up £3,000 in winnings.

The following weekend Ron was back. I almost had a heart attack the moment I saw him. "I'd like to place a bet on two horses," he announced, and then pointed to his selections. "£500 on this one and £500 on that one. If you need me, I'll be in the pub." I took the money and ran out the back to discuss it with Ernie. "He can't win two weeks in a row. Let's take his money and we'll claw back some of what we lost last week," was Ernie's sound advice. That afternoon both of Ron's selections came in. He arrived, half-drunk, to collect his winnings. By this time, he had a couple of 'girlfriends' hanging off him.

Imagine how I felt when Ron came back the next Saturday. Again, he was betting big, £1,000, and again Ernie explained to me that this kind of winning streak could not continue. This was how the game was played. Eventually, he would lose and lose again, and we'd get all our money back from him and more. However, again Ron's horse came first, and he was fast sending us broke. Something was going on – either Ron had inside information or he was scamming us somehow and we were too dumb to see it. Ernie couldn't work it out.

When Ron walked in the next Saturday, I figured it was time to tackle him head on. "What's going on Ron?" I wanted to know.

"What do ya mean?"

"How come you can always pick winners?"

He smiled. "Sure, I'll tell ya." He paused and then said, "I see the winners in a dream." "A dream?"

"Yeah. I dream in the night-time the name of the winning horse." "And what, you write it down?"

"No," he said, "I have to wake myself up to remember the name."

He explained that he had to remember the name of the horse because he couldn't write it down. He didn't know how to read or write. Ron had never been to school in his life. When he signed anything, it was with a cross. Before I took his bet, I went out to see Ernie. "Ron is back." Ernie sighed.

I said, "We have got to stop taking bets from him."

"No," said Ernie. "We have to get back what we lost. He can't continue a run like this. We have to get back what we lost to him."

"Ron says he sees the names of the horses in a dream," I explained. Ernie rolled his eyes. "Sure, he does," he said dismissively.

The same thing happened that day. Ron's selections came home and again we were seriously in the red. I remember going to the bank and withdrawing the last £500 we had. A smarter man than me would have started copying Ron's bets and putting them with other bookmakers. But Ernie and I were under so much pressure because of this one punter that in hindsight we just couldn't think straight. Sure enough, Ron was back the next Saturday, and when he again won I had to take money out of the cafe's takings to pay him. I told Ernie that I was no longer in the SP business. He was very disappointed, but what else could I do?

By this time Ron was probably the richest man in Trangie. He started living the high life. He'd hire Ray Aston, the local taxi driver, to take him to Sydney, which was a seven-hour drive. Ron would live it up in a hotel, and of course put Ray up in a room; then they'd spend the day at the races and drive back to Trangie. But Ron's run of good luck was over. Either the Sydney bookies were smarter than us, or the dreams had disappeared. He lost all his money gambling in Sydney. Then tragedy struck. On the way back on one of these trips, they had a puncture in Dubbo. They jacked up the taxi and Ron helped Ray to change the tyre. He was pulling the tyre off when he slipped and fell backwards into the path of an on-coming car. He was killed instantly. Poor Ron was only thirty-five.

Chapter Sixteen

Buck collected all the rubbish from the kitchen as well as the fruit shop. He had a horse and cart and would take all the offcuts of veggies and the half-rotten fruit which we threw out. Buck had a place just out of town with about forty pigs and he used to feed them our scraps. Originally, our deal was that he had to take the lot – all the scraps as well as all the rubbish. Then I started noticing that he took all the scraps yet left behind things like empty bottles, cartons, boxes and tins. Soon, they were cluttering up my yard. After a few arguments I lost my temper and went crook on him. "Take the lot, or none," I yelled.

Buck shook his head. "Well, I won't take any of it then." And off he walked.

It was a huge setback. What was I going to do with all this rubbish? In the end I decided to do it myself. I bought an old truck and then loaded it up with all the rubbish and then took it out somewhere to dump it. I know this sounds terrible, but that was how people got rid of rubbish in those days – they just drove out into the bush and dumped it. I had to get up at five in the morning because that was the only time I could do it. And the truck was very old and would not go faster than about ten kilometres an hour. It wasn't long before I was sick and tired of dumping rubbish. One day I was talking to a customer called Dennis in the cafe. I explained my run-in with Buck and asked, "Do you know anyone who can take my rubbish?"

"Mate, my mother has got two sows and they are a good breed." I wondered what this had to do with my rubbish but kept listening. "These sows give birth three times a year and every time they give you around about twelve or thirteen piglets."

"Really?" I said. "Thirty pigs a year?"

"Yep. There are two of them and they are expecting to have the little ones soon – next month in fact. My mum is too old to look after them. Why don't you buy 'em – £20 each? Chuck 'em in the back yard here. I'll show you where you put the concrete on one side, put a bit of cardboard for the little ones, a bit of straw and feed them yourself with the veggies and all the things from the kitchen that pigs can eat."

"This is fantastic," I said. "Go and get your mother's pigs and bring them in."

Dennis put a hand up. "Hang on a sec. Before we bring them in, let's get the concrete laid. I know a bloke who'll do it." We did everything in a week and then Dennis brought the pigs over. The little ones, they were like little kittens, you could hold them, and they wouldn't try to get away. They would just look at you. They were beautiful pigs. And they were all given names. After I bought them customers would go out the back to use the toilet, and then when they came back in they'd say, "Oh Nick, those are beautiful pigs!" Before long people were bringing them into the shop to play with them.

Next minute I had an angry Sergeant Wedlock knocking on my door. "Jesus bloody Christ! What the hell are you doing Nick?"

"What do you mean?"

"Someone told me you've got pigs …"

Before he could finish I said, "Ah, they're beautiful mate. Come and have a look. When they're bigger, we'll cook them…"

"Get them out of here! Get them out!" "Sergeant Wedlock what's wrong?"

He said, "Look, you're not allowed to have pigs inside the town limits. They're supposed to be at least five miles from the edge of the town."

"I didn't know that."

"Obviously not. They're not allowed. They bring disease. If the health inspector comes around here, you'll lose your licence to run a restaurant."

"Are you serious?"

"Yes!" Sergeant Wedlock replied. "Get them out before I get into trouble. They have to be gone in a couple of days. If they're not gone by then I'll have to ring the health inspector, otherwise I'm in trouble."

What the hell was I going to do with these pigs? Someone suggested I speak to Buck's son. He was getting married and just in the process of building a house. He was a nice boy – not like his father – his father was a drunk and a no-hoper. I explained to Buck's son about my pigs and suggested he put them in his father's piggery. I offered him 50%. "When you sell them," I explained, take out what you're owed for expenses, "and give me half of what's left. The other half you put in your pocket."

To him this was an unbelievable bargain. He came and picked my pigs up and put them in his father's piggery. The pigs kept on multiplying and in the end, we struck a deal where I bought all his father's pigs – about forty or so – and the son and I had the same arrangement – he got half of all the profits. What I hadn't counted on was just how hardworking and enterprising the son was. So, I ended up owning a pig farm with over 2,000 pigs and we made a lot of money. We called the company Linsa Pigs – it was a good name. This young fellow would bring me a cheque from the auction sales and we'd deduct his expenses and split the profits. And all that happened because of an argument I had with Buck, his drunken father, over our kitchen waste.

Sometimes, I wondered if I should go into the meat business. But we already had a butcher in town. His name was Bill Scott. He had over the years run all his competitors out of business and wasn't someone you would want to take on.

Chapter Seventeen

In those early years in the cafe, I did wonder what lay ahead for me. Today people would be amazed if you sent a boy of thirteen halfway round the world and expected him, more or less on his own, to survive and thrive. There were lots of tears. I missed my family and always the question kept coming back to me, "What is to become of me? Where is my future?" Sometimes, all I could see in the years ahead was more of the same – more loneliness – more work – and a sense that I had failed.

I did experiment with various things: like shearing, wheat lumping, owning an orchard and being part-owner of a piggery. I was always looking, searching for my future. In the back of my mind I thought I would probably sell the cafe to one of my relations when I turned twenty-one and return to Greece. But what then?

One day at the sheep sales in Trangie, I met a Greek fellow who was very wealthy. He had several sheep stations and would buy thousands of sheep at the auction. He was my idol. Unfortunately, I don't remember his name anymore. He was an old chap who had spent his whole life in farming. This fellow was quiet and reserved and never much of a talker. And because he was such a big buyer, he was usually surrounded by agents or people from the auction. I do remember him saying to me once, "You are doing a good job. Keep at it." At that time, I wanted to be like him, to be a rich and successful farmer. I couldn't see how that was ever going to happen by just continuing to work hard in the cafe.

Also, because I was the oldest, I knew that my entire family were depending on me to make a success of the business. I was put into this leadership role by circumstances, and it was a role I enjoyed. And just as my uncle had helped get me to Australia and set me up, I did the same for my family. My brother Peter arrived from Greece in 1952. He worked in the Dubbo cafe with Uncle Sam for a few months and then came to work with me at the Trocadero in Trangie.

All these things were going through my mind, but no matter how much I thought about it, there seemed to be nothing on the horizon which would help me move to another level in business. I made good money out of the cafe, and dabbled in this and that and was doing okay. But life is strange and rarely predictable, and the thing which was to change everything for me came out of nowhere when big Jack Vangi, a larger-than-life bookmaker, arrived on my doorstep one Saturday morning wanting a feed of steak and eggs and chips.

BOOK FOUR

The Australian and British Empire Butchery

Chapter One

Bill Scott was the only butcher in town. It concerned me that the meat he was selling to us was not good quality. Customers had complained. I spoke to Bill about this several times, but all he did was try and make fun of me. He said he couldn't supply me with prime cuts like rump, fillet or T-bone because there were no steers or cattle that grew only rumps and T-bones. According to Bill it was my problem – I had to learn how to cook low-quality meat like topside, round and brisket – if I did this properly the customer would never notice the difference. And yet they did. Too many times I had customers leave half their meal on the plate and say to me, "You should change your butcher."

My customers wanted rump or T-bone, and they knew the difference between that and round steak. When I told Bill that customers were telling me to find another butcher, he said, "You can go wherever you like."

"Well, you're the only butcher in town," I replied.

He was very arrogant. "You're not going to tell me what to do. You take whatever meat I give you." When I told my staff and customers about this, they couldn't believe it.

Although it made me feel better when people told me Bill Scott was in the wrong, it didn't solve my problem. I was also very conscious of the fact that I was a Greek, and Bill was a local. I was always careful not to give a bad impression in such a small town. There was always prejudice about us 'wogs', that we were dirty, or slippery, or dishonest. I was once told that Greeks could only fight with sticks and knives. That was one of the things which prompted me to go and learn to be a boxer at the Police Boys Club.

In the end, Bill Scott pushed me away from his shop by continuing to supply low-quality meats. I drove into Dubbo and made arrangements to be supplied with meat by a company in Dubbo called Canary Smallgoods.

An order of meat would arrive on the train at about ten o'clock every morning. Bill Scott must have realised I was buying elsewhere, but said nothing. The customers noticed the difference immediately and suddenly people were commenting on the beautiful steaks we were now serving. I thought all my problems had been solved until one morning when a living legend arrived on the doorstep of my cafe.

As per usual, very early one Saturday morning I was out the front of the cafe hosing down the footpath. It was just before seven, and out of a car stepped Jack Vangi and a mate. Jack was a big man, six foot two, tall, strong and lean. For twenty-five years he was the mayor of Nyngan. He was nicknamed 'Ned Kelly' because he looked like an outlaw and when it came to business, he certainly acted like one. I first met Jack when I was playing rugby league in Nyngan. After the match this man came over and put out his hand. "I heard there was a young Greek boy playing, and so I came to watch him," he explained. "And you didn't disappoint, son. Jack Vangi's the name."

Jack was also a Greek-born emigrant. He told me this was the first time he had ever watched a game of rugby league. He and his father owned most of the shops in Nyngan and they were very shrewd businessmen. From the moment I met him, I liked Jack and felt I could learn a lot from him. He was a very knowledgeable person.

And so there he was at my cafe bright and early one Saturday morning. The two men came in and took a seat. "Nick," said Jack, "give us a rump steak, four eggs, onions, chips and six slices of toast." He pointed to his mate and said, "He'll have the same." Then he added, "And make it quick because we have to be back in Narromine for the races." It turned out the man with him was a bookmaker.

There was a silence and Jack looked at me. "I'm sorry, Mr Vangi, but I don't have any steak." His mouth dropped. I could see they were both really hungry.

"What?"

"I'm waiting for the train to get in and then I'll pick it up."

"Train? What train? Jesus Nick, there's a butcher across the road." Jack listened stony faced as I told him about my dispute with Bill Scott and the poor quality of the meat he supplied. "Do you owe this man any money?" Jack wanted to know.

"No. But he won't sell me anything because he now knows that I'm getting my meat from Dubbo."

Jack sat in his chair and pointed his finger in the direction of the butcher shop. "That man," he said, "has a licence to sell meat to members of the public. Go over there and tell him that. You're a member of the public and he must serve you. If he doesn't give it to you… well… just go and ask."

I left the cafe and walked across to the butcher shop. Bill Scott greeted me with, "What the hell do you want, you wog." I ignored this and told him I had two hungry customers – Jack Vangi and his bookmaker friend. "They want a steak before they head to the races," I explained. Bill couldn't have cared less. While we were in the butcher shop arguing, the door burst open and in walked Jack Vangi. "What's this bullshit I hear," he thundered, "about you not supplying him with steak. My mate and I are sitting over there twiddling our thumbs waiting for our breakfast! Who's the owner of this joint?"

Bill Scott was not a man to be intimidated. He might not have been very tall, but not only was he wiry and strong, he was at the time holding a meat chopper. "I'm the owner," he said. "And if you think Ned Kelly can throw his weight around here, you've got another thing coming."

While this was happening, the employees of the butcher shop had moved in from the back to the front to see what was going on. Bill turned to them and with a laugh said, "Boys, this is Ned Kelly from Nyngan. He's come here to swing his tail."

Jack asked Bill the same question he had asked me: "Does this man owe you any money?" Bill admitted I didn't. "It's not about money," he claimed.

"If your brain was half as a big as your nose," Jack countered, "You wouldn't say that. You've got a licence to serve the general public. If you refuse, that licence can be taken away."

"Too bad," said Bill. "I'm not selling him so much as a sausage."

Then Jack Vangi looked around. "You have quite a few boys working here. If you keep this up, I'll see you're stripped of your licence and you'll all be out of a job."

"I'm the boss. I give the orders here, Ned," Bill replied.

"For God's sake, cut the meat he wants, he'll pay, and we can have our breakfast and be done with it."

Bill Scott stood his ground. Jack turned to me. "Nick, we're wasting time arguing with this idiot. Get yourself into the coolroom, cut us two steaks and give the man a couple of quid."

To get to the coolroom I had to walk past Bill who was standing there with his meat chopper. "Surely he won't hit me with his chopper," I hoped. Somehow, I plucked up the courage and started walking. Then Bill grabbed my shirt and warned, "No you don't. No wogs in my shop." Suddenly, Jack Vangi had his hands around Bill's throat, lifted him into the air, like he was a toy soldier, and slammed him into the back wall. "I've had enough of this bullshit," Jack announced.

Poor Bill was a short man and so Jack held him up against the wall by his neck and his boots were off the floor with his legs swinging in the air. He was swearing and screaming, it was f-this and f-that. I went into the coolroom and one of the butchers followed me. It was common knowledge in the town that all the butchers hated Bill, so I knew this bloke would help me. Quick as a flash he cut me two nice, big, juicy steaks. Meanwhile, the commotion was continuing out the front. I could hear Bill swearing his head off and Jack saying, "You call me what you like. You have a big nose, but your brain is smaller than your nose. Look, you've even got knives, I've got nothing. Stab me. Go on. See – you've got no guts you little bastard. You've got no guts, but by the Jesus you've got a big mouth. Idiots like you shouldn't be in business."

I walked to the counter where Vivian Coffey was standing. We played rugby league together and I could see that it was an effort for Vivian to stop himself from laughing. When I pulled out some notes Vivian said to me on the quiet, "Don't worry about paying. It was a pleasure to meet Jack Vangi. That man has got guts."

Jack Vangi turned and gave me a look which asked, "Did you get the steaks?" Then he saw them wrapped up and under my arm.

As I walked out the doors he lifted Bill even higher and threw him against the wall. "Fool," said Jack with a look of disgust at Bill, and followed me out of the butcher shop.

One of the best things about growing old is that you can look back on your life and see what mattered and what didn't.

I was but a boy when this incident happened in Bill Scott's butcher shop, and yet I now know that this was one of, possibly the greatest, defining moment of my life. Almost everything that happened to me in the next ten, twenty, thirty, forty and fifty years came out of the consequences of this moment with Jack Vangi on the warpath on a quiet Saturday morning in Trangie.

Back at the Trocadero I threw the steaks on the stove and moments later Jack and his bookmaker mate were tucking into their breakfasts. While he was eating Jack said some very complimentary things about me. "You were very young, seventeen I believe, when you bought this cafe from your uncle. All you wanted was to serve good meat to your customers and that butcher wouldn't give it to you. So you went elsewhere. Not many young people would think, in a small town, to take that action. I reckon you are going to get on in life." The two of them then congratulated me on the meal and headed for the door. I knew they would have to drive flat out to make it to the races in time. We shook hands and Jack said, almost as an afterthought, "You know, if somebody opened up a butcher shop in opposition to this idiot, they'd send him broke." Then he added, "See ya mate."

I must admit that as Jack Vangi drove off a terrible feeling came over me. Obviously, there was going to be trouble over what had happened to Bill Scott. Everyone in Trangie would know about this before the day was out. And as I have said before in this book, it was not an even playing field. Bill was an Aussie and I was a Greek, and together with another wog, we had humiliated him in front of his employees. I knew that many of the locals would say to each other, "These bloody wogs are taking over the place. Who do they think they are?"

The most sensible thing I could do was to go back to Bill Scott and apologise for what had happened. I waited a couple of hours, hoping that in the meantime Bill might have calmed down a bit. Eventually, I forced myself out the door and walked back over to his butcher shop. There were no customers in the shop – only Vivian, the butcher I played football with. I told him I wanted to speak to Bill. He went out into the coolroom and a few moments later Bill walked in. Before I could say anything, he said viciously, "Get out!"

"Mr Scott, I'm sorry for what happened …"

"Out of my shop you wog bastard!"

"I want to apologise for what happened. I couldn't control him …"

Bill wasn't having any of it. "Get the hell out of here you bloody Greek bastard. You wog bastard. Vivian, if he owes me any money you go to his stinking cafe and get it. But don't let this bastard into this shop ever again."

He tried to push me out the door, but I wasn't that easy to move. I was very fit and strong from playing football and was also doing boxing. I put up my hands with open fists towards him – as if to say, 'hands off'. He backed off a little and I walked to the door. But I could not resist the urge to say something. I turned and said to Bill, "Mate, Jack made you look like a frightened little rabbit. He told you to stab him and you didn't have the guts to do anything. And now you talk like this – why didn't you talk like this in front of him?"

Then Bill sent a punch in my direction. I knew how to protect myself from my training at the boxing club. I lifted my left arm in defence, but a second punch hit me on the neck. I knew it was better not to retaliate. He pushed me and by this time we were in the doorway, and then outside on the footpath. "Bill," I said, "I came here to apologise." I knew that if I behaved like a cheeky little bastard, I wouldn't get the town's sympathy. Once the town goes against you, as my uncle taught me, you are gone. I was then very popular in the town, and I always showed respect to everybody. That is why, even though Bill was behaving outrageously, I tried to show him respect.

Then I heard myself repeating the words of Jack Vangi. "You know Bill, if somebody opened up in opposition, they'd send you broke." Bill scoffed, but I continued. "I am a customer of yours and you don't treat the customers like that."

"No one's got the guts to take me on," Bill sneered. "Two opened up and I sent both of them broke."

"I'm not scared of you," I said.

Then he went too far and said something which I can still hear in my ears decades later. "You wogs are only good enough for fish and chips and hamburgers," Bill said loud enough for everyone to hear. He could see that the insult had stung me, and so he repeated it. "You wogs are only good enough for fish and chips and hamburgers." That was a remark which motivated me for the next sixty years.

I had tried to apologise, but he wouldn't accept it. He had manhandled me, but I had not retaliated. I went back to the Trocadero and had a coffee. I sat there thinking and brooding. Then, I decided it was worth going back to him. So I walked over to the butcher shop and the abuse continued. When he'd finished I said, "Listen mate. Yes, I am a Greek and I'm proud of what I am. Now, I'm proud to be Australian."

"You're not an Aussie," he called out.

I ignored him. "But I can promise you I am not a bastard. I have a mother and father." "Wog bastard," was his reply.

"And what are you?" I asked. "I'm an Australian."

"Really?" I said, "I thought the real Australians were Aboriginals. You don't look like an Aboriginal to me. So you must come from somewhere too, mate, from England or somewhere."

That stirred him up. He came over, shoved me and then punched me in the jaw. This was a big mistake. By this stage we were out on the footpath. At 14½ stone I was a bit heavier than him, and a bit taller, but the difference was, I was a boxer. Before he knew what had happened I hit him four times – boom, boom, boom, boom – and down he went. Vivian and the other butchers were all there watching. It was all over. There was blood everywhere. I turned to Vivian and said, "Take your boss inside before the cats and dogs start licking him up, and tell him to have better manners next time." One thing for sure – Trangie was never going to be the same after this.

Chapter Two

This terrible and public brawl gave me the idea to start a business and for the wrong reason – revenge. I'm sure there are plenty of textbooks out there on 'How to Succeed in Business' which will stress the point that you should never ever decide anything in the heat of the moment, and secondly, never ever go into business for revenge. But that's exactly what I did. Being called a wog, or a dago, didn't bother me much, but I kept thinking about Bill Scott's throwaway line, "You wogs are only good enough for fish and chips and hamburgers." Also, I remembered what Jack Vangi had said about how someone should set up a butcher shop in opposition to Bill Scott, and decided I would do this.

It was still early Saturday morning. I had a shower, changed my clothes and then told the cafe staff that I was going to Dubbo. I drove to Canary Smallgoods – the people who supplied us with meat – and there spoke to the boss – Dick – I can't remember his surname. I said nothing about what had happened, and just told him that I was thinking about opening a butcher shop. Straight away he said, "What, in opposition to Bill Scott? Gee, I don't think that would be smart, Nick." Although this was really a spur-of-the moment decision, I told Dick I had given it a lot of thought, and figured it was worth the risk. "Well, if you're serious about this," Dick said, "then you'll need to go to Sydney and see Harry Lesne. He's on the Pyrmont Bridge Road. Lesne's the man to help you with this." So I rang the cafe, told them I was going to Sydney and would be gone a few days.

I caught a plane from Dubbo, flew to Sydney and went to see Harry Lesne. I explained to Harry that I needed to know what was involved in setting up a butcher shop from scratch. I said I wanted my butcher shop to look as good as the smartest butcher shop in Sydney. Lesne was a real professional. He and his team drew up the plans and before long started building my shop on their factory floor. Whereas Bill Scott had timber benches, an old timber saw and sawdust on the floor, this was going to be electric saws, stainless steel counters and very large glass display cabinets. Naturally, it cost me a lot of money.

We filled up two railway carriages and shipped it to Trangie. Then Harry Lesne's team arrived and installed the fixtures and equipment in what had been our fruit shop. As we had plenty of land area, there were no problems with space. Within a couple of weeks, the job was finished and I was now the proud owner of one of the best butcher shops in the state. It had everything – well, almost everything. In my haste to make this come true I had neglected two very fundamental factors in the butchery business: first, we had no meat; and even worse, we had no butcher.

As the shop was being built I did have a word on the sly with Vivian Coffey at football. He had told me many times before that he hated working for Bill Scott. So when I decided to open this butcher shop I approached him about coming to work for me. He agreed to be my manager, but later changed his mind. I couldn't blame Vivian for doing this. Bill Scott made it very clear to his butchers that if they came and worked for me, there would be no job to come back to after I went broke. Bill was very confident about this – he had twice before sent rivals packing – and they were at least qualified butchers. How the hell was someone like me, who did not know the first thing about meat, going to be a competitor for a butcher as experienced as Bill Scott? And he knew that Vivian and I were mates. He had pulled Vivian aside and said to him, "When the wog closes up, don't ask for your old job back because it won't be there anymore." Vivian was getting married soon and in the process of building a house. "I don't get paid for my football," he explained. "Where am I going to make my money to live on if I have no job?" The poor bloke was in tears. I said, "Vivian, stay with him. I don't think Bill will send me broke, but I don't want you to feel anxious – in case I am wrong, stay with him." His face lit up and he seemed to be happy. Vivian hugged me – and then he kissed me!

As I had to buy meat, and didn't know anything about it, I rang up Mr Bodey, from Bodeymar Station. He was a farmer who owed me a favour. When the floods had struck I picked him and his wife up in my car and took him to a safe area. Because I was always shooting out in the bush, I knew the area. And when they were in danger from the floods I was able to find a way to their place and get them out. He came into the cafe and said, "Thank you Nick. I would like to give you something for what you did for me and my family." He then handed me a cheque for £30, which was a fair amount of money in those days.

Without even thinking about it, I handed the cheque back. "No, I was just helping out. I didn't do this to be paid. I thought you were in trouble at your house and knew the area because I used to go shooting around there. I had a good car and knew where the high water levels were." Anyway, Mr Bodey was very grateful and I considered him to be a friend of mine.

After I spoke to him on the phone and told him about needing meat for my butcher shop, he put me on to his station manager. I arranged to meet up with the manager and together we went around the property and he selected the best cattle for my meat. They would then be slaughtered in Dubbo, and the meat sent to my butcher shop.

While I was waiting for the meat to be delivered, I started to have this gut feeling that something was not right. Then I happened to pass Bill Scott in the street, and he did something which confirmed my suspicions – he smiled at me. When the meat came in, I noticed that it was a very distinctive dark colour. So I rang up Mr Bodey and told him this. "Oh, don't worry about that," he said. "Leave it in the coolroom for two or three days and it'll become a light colour." Every day I kept checking the meat and it became darker and darker in colour. I thought I was going mad.

As luck would have it, another farmer, Mr McKay, came into the cafe to have a meal with his wife. He was a very wealthy man and owned several cattle and sheep stations. He used to come to the sheep sales in Trangie and he would buy thousands of sheep. He was an older chap who had spent his whole life in farming. He never talked to me much at all; he was always with a group of buyers or people from the auction and he would sit down and eat, but he never made it his business to stand and talk to me. Once, he said to me, "You are doing a good job. Keep at it." And another reason why I admired Mr McKay was because he drove a Rolls Royce.

Every Sunday he would come by the cafe from church. He would pull up out the front and give a honk of the horn. That was the signal for me to bring out two bricks of ice cream wrapped up in dry ice and newspaper – we didn't have plastic then. I would open the car door and his wife would be sitting there. I'd then say, "Mr McKay, I will put the ice cream down on the floor in the back seat." Then as a special favour to me I'd ask, "Could I stay here and smell the Rolls Royce for one minute?" Mr McKay would laugh as I breathed in and got a good whiff of the leather.

"Remember one thing, son, all that a man wants to achieve in life, he will achieve it, as long as he believes in it. If you want a Rolls Royce, you will get a Rolls Royce."

It was my turn to laugh. "Me? Own a Rolls Royce? Selling milkshakes and fish and chips?"

And so while Mr McKay and his wife were eating he turned and said to me, "Hey Nick, I heard you'd opened a butcher shop." When I nodded he added, "What do you know about being a butcher?"

"Not much," I admitted, "but I'm willing to learn."

"Fair enough," he said. And I remembered that Mr McKay didn't like Bill Scott and the pair of them had fallen out over something. I told Mr McKay that I was still looking for a butcher, but was confident I'd find one in a few days.

"And what about meat?" he asked. "Yeah, I've got meat."

"Would you mind if I had a look?"

"Yeah," I agreed.

There was a door going directly from the cafe into the new butcher shop. I showed Mr McKay into my brand-new butcher shop, hoping he would be impressed, but he said nothing. He walked into the coolroom and then cried out, "Jesus Christ! Jesus Christ!" "What's the matter?" I wanted to know.

"Who sold you this meat?"

"Mr Bodey. From Bodeymar Station."

"The bastards!" He was furious. "I'm sorry Nick, but this is meat from a bloody bull. You couldn't drive a nail through that meat. This meat is only good for smallgoods. If you sell that to the public, they'll never come back again. It's inedible."

I had also bought some lamb from a farmer and Mr McKay took one look at this meat and again hit the roof. "This isn't lamb! It's hogget." I had to admit to him that I didn't know the difference between lamb and hogget, which is meat from old lambs. "This is disgraceful," Mr McKay said and then asked, "Where's your phone?" We walked back into the cafe. I pointed to the phone. He picked it up and asked to be put through to Bodeymar Station. Mr McKay asked to speak to Mr Bodey and then tore into him.

"How the hell could you do that?" he yelled. He accused Mr Bodey of taking advantage of me and of sabotaging my new business.

As I was listening I felt like I grew another ten inches taller. I thought, "There are people like that trying to kill me before I start." And it really shocked me that I saved Mr Bodey from the floods and he repaid me with a knife in the back. I had mistakenly assumed that everyone would be happy with me putting my money down to open up in opposition to Bill Scott. I thought people would congratulate me because everyone was complaining about him being a robber. Many times he used to serve the meat and in those days they didn't have plastic bags; it was wrapped in newspaper and greaseproof paper and flies could get in. I remember once there was a woman in front of me who took her meat back and complained, "It's full of maggots, Bill."

He threw the meat at her and said, "Get out! Those maggots were created after you left my shop, in your car; not from here." This woman started crying and then walked out.

After Mr McKay got off the phone he started giving me instructions. "All that meat you have in the coolroom – tomorrow send it to the smallgoods factory and tell them to use it for smallgoods. Just give it to them. Don't leave it here because you will be the laughing stock of the town if you open the shop and try and sell that meat. Send it to the smallgoods factory and take whatever they give you for it. Take it and cut your losses."

I did as he said. I went into the coolroom, loaded the bull meat on my shoulders, put it in the back of the ute and drove to Dubbo. They paid me a fraction of the price I paid for the meat when I bought it from Mr Bodey. I have to say I learnt a lot about life that day. It is a dog-eat-dog world.

Chapter Three

Sometimes, fortune favours the brave. While I was wondering how I could get myself out of this mess with the butcher shop, a telegram arrived from Dr McGirr. He was my landlord. His father had been the premier of New South Wales for twenty-seven years, back before the war. Dr McGirr owned a lot of properties in country towns and owned the Trocadero Cafe and the fruit shop. This was bound to be bad news – someone must have told him that I had converted the fruit shop into a butcher shop – I was in breach of the lease. The telegram said: "I want to see you 5.00 pm tomorrow at the Royal Hotel, Summer Street, Orange. Bring your boxing gear." That was the message. Nothing at all about the lease. As I had great respect for Dr McGirr, I went straight out the back where I had boxing gloves and bags hanging up. I collected my boxing boots and shorts – threw everything into the boot of the car and took off.

Left: This photo was taken at the back of the Trocadero Cafe in 1951 when I was eighteen years old.

When I arrived at the Royal Hotel in Orange, I met Dr McGirr and he introduced me to George Barnes, who was then the Welterweight Champion of the world. Dr McGirr pointed to George and said, "You can have three rounds with him." He then explained that Pat Ford was going to fight him to raise money for the Orange Base Hospital, but had rolled his car and sprained his arm. "We looked around for someone with an Italian name as a draw card," Dr McGirr said, "and because your Greek name is Androutsos, it sounds like a foreign name and it draws attention." In those days the Italian boxers – like Muchano and Louis Calrotzi – had reputations for being fierce fighters. At that time Pat Ford was the British Empire Lightweight Champion – I was handy with my fists – but not in the class of people like Pat Ford. "What do you say, Nick? Three rounds with George?" I pulled Dr McGirr aside, "No bloody fear. He'll kill me."

Dr McGirr put his arm around me and said, "You have nothing to worry about, Nick. It won't be a fair dinkum serious bout – it's just for show – people just want to say they saw George Barnes in action. We'll fit you up with some headgear and you'll be as right as rain." And to clinch the deal he added, "It's all for a good cause, mate."

What the good doctor said was true. George Barnes and I sparred for a few rounds and he just played to the crowd. At one point he took hold of the referee and started dancing with him. The crowd were laughing and having a great time. By the end of the night we collected almost £7,000 for the hospital.

It was time for a celebratory drink. As you can imagine, I had a lot on my mind with my problems with the butcher shop and must have looked a bit down in the dumps. "You're not looking too happy, Nick," Dr McGirr noted. "You did so well, mate!" Later, I realised that I had not had a chance to talk to anyone about what was going on, so when Dr McGirr looked at me like a true friend, I opened up. "Doc, I have done something silly. Your property, the fruit shop I've converted it into a butcher shop and I didn't get your permission. I didn't know you had to get permission. In fact, it was a fellow from the council who told me because I had put in a butcher shop I needed to apply for a 'change of use' permit."

"What's to worry about?" Dr McGirr asked. "Do I have to pay anything?"

"No. It's all paid."

"Good. That's all right then. You have my permission. Now, come on, cheer up."

Then I explained to him about my plan for the butcher shop and about my failure to find a butcher to run the place.

Dr McGirr smiled. "Well," he said, "I can find you a butcher. In fact, there's one right here." With that he turned and called to Pat Ford, the injured boxer who I had stood in for. "Hey Pat! Come here." It was the first time I had met Pat. Although his arm was in a sling, he looked as lean and fit as they come. Dr McGirr introduced us and said, "Pat's a butcher by trade. And his old man manages Springfield Butchers. They've got about twenty butcher shops, and their biggest one is right opposite this hotel."

He then told Pat the story about my new butcher shop and suggested that I go and meet his father. Pat then rang his parents and invited me over for dinner. We made our way over to their house and Pat introduced me to his mother and father. Bill Ford was a tall, imposing, heavily built man. He had a reputation for not taking any nonsense. In Orange he was famous due to an incident involving another butcher, Mr Kelly. They had butcher shops on opposite sides of Summer Street and were in the middle of a price war – one would put his prices down, then so would the other. At some point they met in the middle of Summer Street and started abusing each other.

They ended up having a fistfight in the middle of the street – cars screeched to a halt, a crowd gathered and the police were called. It was a different world then – the police weren't there to stop the fight, this was the accepted way for men to sort out their differences – and so the police were there to make sure it was a fair fight. Bill Ford soon had the better of his rival, the fight was over and the meat price war came to an end.

Obviously I was a bit nervous meeting a man like Bill Ford, but he was a real gentleman. After dinner he listened very carefully to what I had to say about my butcher shop, and asked lots of questions like, "So is the shop ready to trade? Have you got meat? Where are you going to buy your meat?" In the course of this conversation I mentioned what had happened on the day Jack Vangi and his bookmaker friend wanted a steak for breakfast and how Bill Scott had abused me and so forth. Bill turned around to his son. "Pat, we will teach this fellow Scott a lesson." Then, Bill looked at me and said, "I have to say you've got guts, son. I admire that. We're going to help you out. Pat, as you know, is a butcher. He'll be in Trangie on Monday morning and he's going to run the shop for you."

I couldn't believe what I was hearing. We talked about money. I offered to pay Pat £17 a week and I'd put him up at the local pub. They were very happy with that. Bill also had some ideas about where we could buy meat and the name Charlie Rush came up. Charlie had a butcher shop in Narromine and he ended up supplying us with meat. He was now buying for two shops and this gave him more buying power. It turned out that there was no love lost between him and Bill Scott. The arrangement with Charlie Rush was he'd buy two calves for me, two for himself; then he'd give me my share of the bill direct from the stock and station agent. Not once did I ever have to check an invoice from Charlie. I had good meat, and better meat than Bill Scott. As it turned out, people hated Bill Scott not just in Trangie, but all over the place. Slowly, the game was turning in my favour.

That night at the Ford's home in Orange, I stood on the front steps as I was about to leave and shook hands with them on the deal. Mr Ford pointed at me and said to his son, "Pat, don't let him down. You hear that?" Then he said to me, "He'll be there on Monday." I walked back to the hotel in the brisk night air wondering what the hell had just happened.

This changed everything for me. To me the Fords were men of honour. They didn't give a damn that I was a Greek, or a kid running a cafe in the middle of nowhere. They were real men, men who would be as good as their word.

Chapter Four

It seems to me that in the course of my lifetime the sport of boxing has become a lot less popular and a lot less distinguished. When I was a young man, boxing was regarded as a noble pursuit and boxing champions were household names. Boxing matches were attended by big audiences in an era when the only entertainment was movies, the theatre and radio. Pat Ford was the British Empire Lightweight Champion and at that time a rising star in the world of boxing. He may not have been a household name, but he was very well known, and verging on being famous. To have someone with his fame and prestige managing my butcher shop in Trangie was incredible. It was like having someone like the footballer Laurie Daley working for you.

On our first Monday there was a crowd of over a hundred people lined up outside the shop as word had got around that Pat Ford was here. He had arrived on Sunday night and worked

Left: Pat Ford, the lightweight champion of the British and Australian Empire, in his prime, 1953.

through the night preparing the meat for our opening day. I said, "Pat, come outside and say good day to the crowd."

Pat shook his head. "No. But tell them I do apologise. I'm busy. They can come in to see me when I serve them over the counter." He was fantastic. I could not have asked for more – Pat was a hard worker, he was very popular with the customers – and he and I became good friends.

We put him up at the Imperial Hotel and supplied all his meals from the cafe. He could have whatever he wanted to eat, but Pat was not a big eater – he was always in training. We put all his gym gear out the back on the verandah of the cafe. The verandah was then closed in and Pat was able to train there.

Unfortunately, I knew nothing about meat and couldn't really help Pat. My contribution was to drum up business and make deliveries. I used to door knock at people's houses to tell them about the new butcher shop. I'd say that Pat Ford and I were partners – I never said that he was an employee. I'd joke that we were Pat the Lightweight and Nick the Heavyweight and called our shop the Australian and British Empire Butchery.

I'd give people a price list and housewives would ring up and I'd take their order. They'd say, "Two pounds of rump, three pounds of T-bone," and so on. I'd pass the order to Pat and between customers he would cut the orders and wrap them up. We didn't have plastic. We would wrap them up in greaseproof paper and newspaper. I tried to deliver the meat as quickly as I could. This was something new then – home deliveries – and certainly not something that Bill Scott offered.

But there was a downside to home deliveries. We lost money on some customers who delayed paying us, or 'forgot' altogether. They would sometimes say to me, "My husband's not in yet. I'll pay you next week," or, "Oh, we're a bit short at the moment. Can

I fix you up next time?" What could I do? You couldn't refuse to serve people and some of the families who did this had little kids and were doing it tough.

Pat was reliable and conscientious. Many a time he walked into my room at the back of the cafe at four in the morning to get me out of bed. He'd pull the blankets off and say, "Get up! I need you next door!"

I'd mumble, "Okay, okay." He'd walk out and then I'd grab the blankets, put them over me and go back to sleep. Then Pat would be back and drag me out of bed. When he was busy he needed me to help him prepare meat and do sausages. I'd get up, go to the bathroom, have a wash and make us both some breakfast – scrambled eggs on toast. After that we'd go next door and set to work.

Pat's girlfriend would come and visit and he'd bring her to the cafe. They would sit down and he'd say to her, "What would you like to drink?"

"Pat, it's a bit late and I'm hungry."

"No, you're not hungry," he would usually say. "You only think you're hungry. Keep saying to yourself 'I am not hungry' and you won't be hungry." Pat was obsessed about eating the bare minimum and keeping the weight down and this applied to his girlfriend. We used to make jokes and laugh about this, but Pat was always adamant that people also thought they were hungry when they weren't. The best way to keep everyone happy was to get one of the waitresses to ask his girlfriend what she would like and then bring this out to her "on the house". Pat didn't seem to mind as long as he was not paying. He might have been careful with his pennies, but Pat was an honest person and a fantastic butcher. Without him I would have been lost.

Chapter Five

When I have told this story to people over the years, they often find it strange or odd that a champion athlete would work as a butcher in a small country town. But this was in the days before professional sport developed into the industry it is today. No matter what your status was, for example, if you played for the Australian Rugby League team, the Kangaroos, you still had to have a job to provide you with an income. The money you earned from playing only supplemented your everyday income. A champion boxer like Pat Ford won prize money – but it was never big money. And sponsors didn't hand out loads of cash – they tended to give you things like a pair of gloves, or training equipment.

Having such a famous boxer around could cause problems. Some of the local lads would have a few too many drinks at the pub and then come down looking for a fight with Pat. One such fellow was Jack Lamb, a big half-caste boy with a reputation as the town's best street fighter. He used to fight two or three people at a time in the pubs and had a name for himself. Young Jack was always very good with me. If drunks were having a go at me at the cafe, Jack would volunteer to toss them out.

One day Jack went out the back to the toilet and he saw Pat Ford training. He watched Pat sparring with a trainer and then came back inside. Jack was one of the few people who did not know who Pat was. He pulled me aside. "Hey Nick, that little fellow out there, that little skinny bloke, he is bloody good. He can fight. I wouldn't mind putting the gloves on with him. Can you ask him?"

I went out to the verandah and told Pat that Jack wanted to have a spar with him. He said, "Fair enough." We put some gloves on Jack, they then touched gloves and started. Jack had a reputation for having a big right swing. If he threw it and it connected, you would be out for the count no matter what. That's how he knocked them out in his pub brawls. However, Jack was throwing big punches but Pat Ford seemed to be everywhere. Every time Jack swung at Pat, he connected with nothing. He'd try again and still only hit air. Again and again and again this happened. Pat seemed like he was nowhere and everywhere.

The next minute there were two lightning jabs and Jack Lamb had a bruise on one eye and a bit of blood tricking out of a cut on the forehead. "Stuff this," he said, and threw his gloves down. Jack walked out to the front of the cafe in a daze. "What's the matter mate?" I asked.

He shook his head from side to side. "I can't believe it. What happened there? I can't believe it. I couldn't lay a glove on him."

"Do you know who that is?"

"No."

"That's Pat Ford," I explained. "The British and Australian lightweight champion." Poor Jack was shocked. "That's him? Pat Ford?"

"That's him all right." I then pointed to a newspaper article I had cut out of the paper and hung up in the cafe. "Last week in Melbourne he fought the French champion, Yves Germain, in front of 15,000 people."

Jack went and stared at the photo of Pat in the article. "That's him, for sure." Then he added, "Nick! You have made my day. I would have been a very sad man if somebody else had belted me around like that. At least I was beaten by the best." Back to the verandah he went and thanked Pat for having a spar with him. After that, Jack became a regular visitor and watched Pat training and became an occasional sparring partner.

I had driven to Dubbo airport to pick Pat up after his fight with the French World Champion. When he walked down the steps of the plane, I noticed that both his eyes were black, closed and swollen. There was the tiniest slit open on one eye which enabled him to see. His jaw was swollen, possibly broken, and one hand was wrapped in a towel. "Jesus Christ mate!" I said, "What have they done to you?"

Pat laughed. "Ha, ha. You wanna see the other fellah! I beat him in the last round!" That was Pat – no matter what happened to him in the ring, he was never an angry man. After that he'd be sore and sorry for a while and then get back into it. We had someone replace him when he was away and when he was too sore to work.

Chapter Six

Butchers like Bill Scott took advantage of the ignorance of their customers. He would take a cheaper cut of meat, such as blade, and cut it in a way to make to make it look like scotch fillet. Some customers, particularly old ladies, or old men, who didn't have a farming background, or a meat background, would see the 'scotch fillet' and order it not realising they were buying an inferior cut and paying a premium for it. Most customers didn't know the difference. To be fair to Bill Scott, he was not alone – a lot of butchers did this. If customers did complain, Bill would dismiss them with the comment, "If you don't like it, go to Dubbo." Naturally, this all changed when I opened up in opposition to Bill across the street.

When we first opened, we were flooded with customers and no one set foot in Bill Scott's shop for days. The only way Bill could retaliate was to lower his prices. In those days there were price controls set by the government which had been in place since World War II. The price of essentials like bread, butter, milk, sugar, potatoes and meat was set by the authorities. It was illegal to sell higher, and very hefty fines if you were caught doing this. But you could sell lower.

Also, prices had to be displayed on the windows of the shop. Bill put up a sign to announce he had dropped his prices by 20%.

"Look what the bastard has done!" Pat fumed.

This was something I had anticipated. "Pat, drop our prices 20%." "No, we're going to lose money."

"Too bad, Pat. This is a war."

"Righto Nick," he said. "20% it is."

We heard from customers that Bill was telling them that it would not be long before he sent us broke. He claimed he could always sell cheaper than us because he had his own cattle. This was an exaggeration – he had a few cattle somewhere – but nothing more than that. What Bill did not take into account was that we offered a better service and had a very different approach to him. We had better quality meat, better service, we did deliveries and advertised on radio 2UE in Dubbo. In those ads we used to say it was the Australian and British Empire Butchery in Trangie, operated by Nick the Heavyweight and Pat Ford the Lightweight of Australian and British Empire title.

Then Bill dropped his prices lower again and we followed him. One thing which we never did was threaten our customers. However, this was very much Bill's nature. He started telling the customers that he was going to close me down and that they had better stick with him, because once I was put out of business he would refuse to serve anyone who had bought meat from Nick the Greek.

It is a golden rule of business that two income streams are better than one, and this is where I had a tremendous advantage over Bill Scott. His survival depended on his income from the butcher shop. That was it. Whereas I had the continuous cash flow of the cafe coming in, plus I also had money coming in from the piggery and other business ventures.

We went tit for tat, as they say. Word reached us that Bill had hired a couple of young kids from the school to make deliveries for him on their pushbikes. So we did the same thing. Bill then put the price up to the maximum allowed by the government. We did the same. A few days later he dropped his prices 50%. We matched that.

After almost a year of this 'warfare', one day I received a phone call at the cafe. When I put the hand-piece to my ear and a male voice said, "You rascal." My English was getting better, but calling me a 'rascal' was pointless as I didn't have any idea what the word rascal meant. However, I recognised the voice which was unmistakable. Before I said anything, the male voice then added, "Bill Scott here."

"Oh yeah Bill. How are you mate?"

No exchange of pleasantries – straight to the point: "What time do you close tonight at the cafe?"

"Eleven o'clock."

"I'll see you then."

"What's this about, Bill?"

He said, "I just want to talk to you mate." And added ominously, "Make sure you're on your own. I don't want anyone else there." Then he hung up.

My concern was that there was going to be a punch-up, or at least trouble of some sort. Bill and I had been in a brawl a couple of times, and one time he put the cattle dog on me. He had this vicious cattle dog and I had jumped the gate and was bitten by the bloody dog. He wasn't a person I could trust, but what could I do? As a precaution I pulled aside Jack, who worked in the kitchen. He fought as a Greek soldier with the United Nations in Korea in 1951. If there was a fight, Jack loved it. Another time a couple of blokes tried to attack me in the shop and Jack came in like a mad man with his gun and scared them all off. I explained to him that I was expecting someone around eleven and that there may be trouble. "Listen mate," I said. "Don't go to sleep. Have your cup of tea out the back on the verandah and if I need help I'll call you twice – Jack, Jack! Then you come in, and run on up because I might be getting belted."

"All right, don't worry about it." He was as pleased as punch that there might be a fight.

On the dot of eleven Bill Scott came into the cafe. Everyone had gone and it was just me and him. He didn't say hello or anything, just, "Have a look across the road Nick." "Yeah?" I glanced out the window.

"What do you see?" "The CBC Bank."

"What's in the front of it?"

"Your truck." It was a huge livestock semitrailer for carrying lambs. On the side of the prime mover was the sign 'Scott's Meats'. It was built for carrying two or three floors of stock. I noticed the trailer was empty.

"It's not mine anymore," Bill said. He paused for a moment, like he had to control himself. "The bank took it off me. I just delivered it to them now. And my house is gone. The bank took it too." I could see he was in shock. He then told me that he'd had to pull two of his boys out of Scot's College in Sydney and bring them home. "Everything I owned – the little farm I had – it's all gone. I have lost everything by selling under the price."

Bill Scott was an enemy of mine, but at that moment I felt so sorry for him. He was as tough as old boots and as ruthless as they come. I said, "I'm sorry to hear that."

"That's all right," Bill replied, "I can only blame myself. But the reason I have come to see you Nick is this. I want to know how the hell a young boy like you, who comes from Greece, and can't even speak English, with no experience in the meat game, how you open a butcher shop and …" His words trailed off. Then, he paused and continued. "Here was I, a very experienced butcher, and I did close down two other butchers who opened up in opposition which is why I was the only one in town. Everyone was scared to open in opposition to me and you turn around and open a butcher's shop and you send me broke."

I didn't know what to say. Bill said, "I can't leave this town until I hear from you, and from you personally, how you did this. All I want from you is the truth. It doesn't matter if it hurts or how painful it is. I just want to know the truth. Because one day I am going to have to explain to my grandchildren what happened here."

"Bill," I replied, "number one: I would never have dreamt in my life that I would have put you out of business. I can't believe it. I was going to be your opposition, nothing more than that. I always believed it was possible for us both to make a living here. When I opened the butcher shop I was lucky to have a person like Pat Ford work for me and Charlie Rush supplying us with good meat. I was told many times that my meat was better than yours, and that gave me more confidence."

As I was telling him all this, Bill nodded his head in agreement. I admitted to him that I knew nothing about meat, and explained that when he called me a wog and said I would only ever be good enough for hamburgers and fish and chips, I took that as a challenge. I told Bill that his attitude fired me up and I made a commitment to open a butcher shop in opposition to him to prove I could be more than just be a wog who made fish and chips. Also, I pointed out to Bill that the tricks he played like having his friend supply me with inedible meat from bulls only toughened me up and motivated me more. "Many times I did wonder what I had done," I went on, "and it went through my mind that I might lose everything and end up on the street. But I also told myself that if I did go broke and lose everything, I was still young."

As we talked, I did give credit to the fact that my lack of experience didn't matter thanks to the assistance I had from Pat Ford and his father. If it wasn't for them, the butcher shop would not have been a success. "But even if that happened, Bill, I would still have the cafe." I pointed out to Bill that it was always going to be a battle for him to beat me. He had a house, a farm and a large family to support. He worked five days a week and his only real income was his butcher shop. On the other hand, I was a young, single man with no dependants, and very few expenses. I worked seven days a week. My cafe had nine employees and turned over a lot of money.

He wanted the truth and so I gave it to him. He was old, didn't work as hard as me and had all these expenses. I was young, and inexperienced, but ready to learn. "Nobody could beat me," I said, "because of my youth. And to be honest with you Bill, when I came to Australia, I didn't come to look at the kangaroos, I came here to make money. I was hungry for money, and the people who work for me, they work long hours and they're hungry for money. They'll work twenty-four hours if there's money to be made. You know the award wage is £10 a week, but do you know what I pay them? I pay them £15 a week and they can't even speak English."

I went on to say that my employees, most of whom were cousins of mine, came from families who had lost everything in the war. These workers wanted to make money so they could buy a home for their parents in Greece or be able to contribute to a dowry so their sisters could marry. "What it all boils down to Bill, is this: in Greece we have this saying: 'You were the maestro, but I played the music.' When you signal with your baton 'down', I go down. And when you say 'up', I go 'up'. You were the master. Whatever you were doing I was copying you, mate – you go up, I go up – you go down, I go down. But the difference is that I am less than half your age and I'd guess my expenses were about 20% of yours, but my profits were 300% to yours."

It gave me no joy to think that I had 'won' my battle with Bill Scott. Before me was a broken man. This was not something I ever wanted. All through my business career I have always had the attitude that there are more than enough opportunities for everyone. I never was a 'win at all costs' type of person. Bill stood up, grabbed his hat and said, "Thank you Nick. Thank you."

"What will you do now?" I wanted to know.

He looked down at his shoes. "I have found a job in Dubbo. In a butcher shop."

I opened the front door for him, and he walked out. Whereas I had sometimes dreamed of beating Bill Scott in our butcher shop war, now I felt terrible, as if someone had just died.

Chapter Seven

What I told Bill Scott was the truth. If I didn't have the cafe to support me, I would have been on the street before him. From that experience, I learnt that in business and in life you have to have a backup plan. In Greek we call it *'karta atou'* – the trump card. You don't play all your cards; you always try and hold in your hand a trump card. My *karta atou* was simple – if the butcher shop didn't succeed, I'd close it up and concentrate on the cafe. The worst that could happen would be that I would be paying the wages and I would be breaking even and not making much money at all. That was the worst that could happen. But the butcher shop was a great success and together with the cafe, it was very profitable.

Also, I had a good name. All through life I have never tried to cheat or swindle anyone – I never said one thing and then went behind somebody's back and did the opposite. I often remind people that life is so full of wonderful opportunities – you don't need to be dishonest to take advantage of them. My father always told me to 'keep to your word', whatever you do in life, 'keep to your word'. If you make a deal with someone, and you've made a mistake, you have to live with it, but learn from that mistake.

My life as a businessman began in a small country town where the attitude to emigrants was not welcoming. At best, I was tolerated and this made it even more important that when locals had dealings with me they found me to be as good as my word. Slowly, but surely, I went from being tolerated, to being respected – which was a massive leap. After respect, there comes admiration, and then, acceptance. It's different today – by and large people don't care where you come from. Also, in case you may get the wrong idea, I didn't decide to use honesty as a business strategy – honesty was in my nature, it was how I was raised.

Pat Ford worked for me for three years by which time the butcher shop in Trangie was well established. And in that time, I learnt about the meat business. Pat moved back to Orange and continued to pursue his boxing career and I would often fly to places where he was fighting. One day, I was talking to Pat on the phone and he mentioned he was in the process of buying a butcher shop in Orange and waiting for that to go through. He was also between bouts and so had time on his hands.

One of the things I wanted to do before I eventually returned to Greece was to see more of Australia. Apart from Trangie, the surrounding towns and Sydney, I had seen nothing else. So after talking to Pat we had this idea of going on a bit of a holiday and exploring Australia.

We went in my car and headed north. It was a fantastic experience because nothing was planned and we stopped where we liked, when we liked. All up, we were gone for about four weeks and reached as far as Mackay in North Queensland. We stayed in the best hotels and I paid the bill. But we always booked the rooms under the name Pat Ford, and when the receptionists saw that name they'd either give us a 50% discount or give us the rooms for free. Pat was famous, and whenever we had a meal together, other diners would come over and want to shake his hand and ask for autographs. I found the friendliness of ordinary Australians amazing. We also met a lot of Greeks when we ate in their cafes. Some knew me by name and some knew my uncle. There was always something to talk about. The main thing was that in those early days, all the new Australians were like me, young and ambitious. They'd ask me: "What sort of business have you got? How much are you making? What sort of car are you driving? And what are you going to do when you go back to Greece?"

A highlight for me was the time we spent in Surfers Paradise. I realised that Australia was not just Trangie and Dubbo – at that time I didn't know much about Sydney. When I drove around with Pat what I saw and experienced was so beautiful I began to think for the first time, "Do I really want to go back to Greece? This country is fantastic!" Then I would remember the promise I had made to my mother.

Not long after that holiday, Pat decided to get married. He bought a house in Orange and gave up boxing. Many years later, I took my sons to meet him in his butcher's shop in Summer Street, behind the Royal Hotel in Orange. Had it not been for the friendship and help of Pat and his father, my life may have gone in a completely different direction. In the space of a few short years, I had become quite knowledgeable about the meat industry in general and butcher shops in particular.

Chapter Eight

Three years after he helped me out with the butcher shop, it was announced that Mr McKay, the prominent grazier, had died. A couple of months later, I had a phone call from his widow. She gave me the news that Mr McKay had put in his will that she was to sell the Rolls Royce to me for £2,000. This was about a third of the price of a good second-hand Rolls. I was stunned and almost dropped the phone. "Mrs McKay I can't have it."

"Nick, this was Ray's wish. There will be no going back on it." She told me that Mr McKay wanted me to have the Rolls Royce. He said I was one of the few people who really appreciated the beauty of that motor car. He had instructed his wife that she was to sell it to me for £2,000, and that it didn't matter whether it took me ten, or even twenty years to pay it off. She quoted Mr McKay as saying, "Give him the registration and it is his Rolls Royce. Tell him to pick it up."

About a week later I went out to the McKay's property with the chef from the kitchen and the cleaner. I promised Mrs McKay I would pay it off quickly. She handed me the keys and I drove it back to the shop. I locked it up in the back of the garage where no one could see it. At first, I felt it was so precious I didn't want to drive it anywhere. Then, after a while, on Sundays, when it was quiet, I would reverse the Rolls out and drive to Narromine or Dubbo with my friends. Then we'd come back to Trangie and I'd put it back in the garage and lock it up. Sometimes, I'd have to remind myself that this was not a dream and that I did own this amazing motor vehicle.

One day Norman McInerney and his fiancée, Hazel, were having lunch in the cafe. She looked so happy, and I noticed she was still wearing the watch I had sold them. I sat down at their table and said, "Listen Norman, you're a rich man, hey?" He nodded his head in agreement. In truth, he was filthy rich. "So," I asked, "why are you driving a Holden?"

"Why not. It's a good car. What do you drive?"

"A Rolls Royce." When I said this he burst out laughing, then realised I was not joking. "A Rolls Royce? What Rolls Royce? There's a three-year waiting list."

I explained about how I had been friends with Mr McKay and how after he died he instructed his widow to sell it to me at a generous discount. Norman said that he had wanted a Rolls, but found the idea of waiting years for one too much trouble. They then followed me out the back to the garage where I showed them the car. "Look at that," I said proudly.

"Oh my God, I can't believe my eyes," Norman replied.

"You want to buy it?" I asked.

"Can I?"

"Yes. £2000."

I didn't want to make a profit because it was a gift from a special friend. To make it simpler I said, "Just give me a cheque for £2,000 so I can take it to Mrs McKay and give it to her." She will understand. Much as I love this car, I can't drive it around, because it doesn't seem right for someone running a small business to be driving a Rolls Royce. If I left a Rolls Royce out the front of the cafe, I soon wouldn't have any customers. We shook hands. He wrote me a cheque made out to Mrs McKay and the Rolls was his.

When I went to see Mrs McKay, I was very apologetic and explained my reasons for 'giving' the car to Norman McInerney. She was very understanding. "Nick, after you drove off from here the other day, the car was yours. Now it is your decision. You have done what you have done." I handed her Mr McInerney's cheque.

"Your husband once told me, I would one day own a Rolls Royce," I said. "But maybe that day will be when I am ready and old enough." I was still under the age of twenty one. Plenty of years ahead to make that dream come true.

Chapter Nine

Perhaps my proudest achievement during this time was to be able to be in a position to build a dream home for my parents. This was in about 1951. Because I was making good money, I was able to fund this project. Les Holden, who was really my financial adviser, used to say to me, "Don't ever interfere with the business paying its bills. Pay your bills in the business first, otherwise you will have no business." Les was my idol! Anything that was left over could go to other things. And so what I had left over went towards the cost of building a house for my parents.

After looking at various options, I purchased a large block of land, about 2,500 square metres, in Akrata. It was in the exact spot that my father had pointed to during my last days in Greece. I had kept my promise and I knew that made him happy. It was located alongside the creek so there was a lot of water available for the vegetable garden and it also had an orchard. We built a large stone, two-storey house with four bedrooms upstairs, three bedrooms downstairs and two shops at the front on the ground floor to lease. From start to finish it took about three years and became the home of my parents, my grandmother and my three brothers.

Above: The house I promised my father I would build for the family, under construction in Akrata, 1950.

Above: The second house in Greece I built for my family. The first was resumed and demolished for new roads. My mother, father and brothers and neighbour on the balcony, 1961.

I must admit that one of the reasons I wanted to build a large stone house was because I wanted to show off. I was proud of the fact that I had made it in Australia and that because of my success, I was not a peasant anymore. And even though I admit to being a bit of a show off with this house, I was also making a statement that my mother and father were the ones who made me what I was. I can still hear my father saying to me, "Logic and common sense mate. If you tell somebody green is red, they might believe you, but he'll go away and think and next time won't swallow your bullshit." Building that house meant so much to me – it was a way of honouring my family.

During this time, members of the family continued to come to Australia seeking a better way of life. Uncle Sam brought out my cousins Jimmy, Leo, Peter and Andrew Kostis. They all worked for my uncle in Dubbo for about a year and I had my brother

Above: The day my younger brother, Peter, and my cousins, Leo and Jim, arrived from Greece in 1951.

Peter working with me at the Trocadero. I think my uncle Sam was proud of me in a way.

I was the leader with my cousins and all the others. I was leading and the others were following. I always tried to bring the others with me, not only in sport and in my work, but with all my ideas. I was always an open book, there were no secrets. Even financially I used to help, especially when I had been told by my parents: "You are the oldest, look after your brothers."

All my life with whatever they needed, I was there. As a human, you know after all that and you reach eighty-three years of age, you look back on what made you really pull through. Someone close to me once said, "Without you Nick, I would be nothing, but don't expect me to walk around the streets saying that whatever I have got I owe it to you. I have a wife and kids and I want to show them that I did it myself. But the reality is that without you I would be nothing." I have heard that a few times from relatives and friends. That is human nature and I accept it. You think to yourself, "What would I have done if I was in their position?"

BOOK FIVE

My Early Years in Sydney

Chapter One

On 16 August 1954, I left Trangie and drove to Sydney in my very smart Hudson sedan, which I had imported from America for £4,000. In those days, you could buy a brand-new Holden for £800. I loved motor cars, and in Trangie they had nicknamed me 'the king of the cars'. The exact date of this journey is easy to remember and why that was will soon make sense to you. In eight years my life had been transformed. I was pleased to be able to return to Greece as a success – in truth I had succeeded beyond my wildest dreams, through hard work, perseverance and a bit of luck, I had a lot of money in the bank. I had built a beautiful home for my parents and a wonderful future awaited me in Greece. My mother would be happy that I was still single and it was fair to presume that when I landed in Athens she would soon be suggesting prospective brides for her well-to-do son.

Before leaving Trangie, I sold my interest in the Trocadero Cafe to my brother Peter and my cousin, Peter Poulos, for £10,000. They were there for a couple of years, but they couldn't get on with each other and the cafe came back to me. As I just didn't have the time to manage a store back in Trangie, I sold it to another cousin of mine, Andrew Kostis. He and his wife were looking for a business. I took them up there and they bought it for the same money, and did well. As none of my relatives were interested in the butcher shop, I sold it to an Australian chap from Narromine.

As I drove from Trangie to Dubbo and from there on to Sydney, I thought about my experiences of the past eight years. I had grown to love the people and the town of Trangie – it had been very good to me – and had a special place in my heart. If it were not for the promise I had made to my mother, I could easily have stayed there, and who knows, could have lived there to this day. In the pocket of my trousers was a Qantas ticket for my flight from Sydney to Athens. The plan was to spend my last night in Australia at the Ritz Hotel, the same hotel I had stayed in on my first night in this country.

Not many people know this, but the biggest hill between the Blue Mountains and the centre of Sydney is a place called Taverner's Hill. It is so built up today it's hard to notice what a high hill it is. Taverner's Hill is on Parramatta Road in the suburb of Petersham. And it was while driving up Taverner's Hill that my journey had an unexpected interruption. I heard the wail of police sirens, and having lived in the bush for eight years, it was a frightening sound. Obviously, some terrible crime was being committed somewhere and the police were racing to the scene. However, it soon became apparent to me that the sirens were coming from two police motorbikes and they were signalling to me to pull over.

On the side of the road in front of me was a police car and standing there was the sergeant indicating me to pull over behind him. I had no idea what was going on. I pulled up, opened the door and jumped out. "Hello Sergeant," I said.

"Jesus Christ!" the sergeant greeted me. "Do you hold a driver's licence?"

BAR
Sundaes
TROCADERO SPECIAL
AMERICAN BEAUTY
PEACH MELBA
FRUIT SALAD & ICE CREAM
Drinks

CAFE
P.K.

"Yes," I replied, getting out my wallet.

"Then how is it that you're still alive?"

"What do you mean?" I asked.

The sergeant was beside himself. "You ran a red light. Twice – not once – twice. Then you were crossing double lines to pass cars. Not once did you put your hand out when you turned left, or right, or stopped. Even now when we pulled you over you didn't give a hand signal to stop. For the last three miles you broke every rule in the book – God only knows what you did before that."

I stood there feeling very foolish. Everything he had said I did was true. By this time he had my licence and was looking at it.

"Ah, Trangie," he said, reading from the licence. "Who gave you this licence?" "Senior Constable Richards," I answered.

"All right," said the sergeant, "I know who he is."

"I've been driving for a few years in Trangie, but this is my first time driving in Sydney."

"Really?" he said sarcastically, "Who would ever have guessed it? What the hell am I going to do with you? You wouldn't know what the rule book was even if I threw it at you!" Suddenly, the sergeant saw something on my licence and looked at me with a mixture of amazement and suspicion. "This is your licence?" he asked. I nodded. Then he said, "You do know what day this is, don't you!" Through my mind I tried to think what might be important about this day – it wasn't Australia Day, or Anzac Day, or anything like that. While I was thinking, the sergeant repeated his question: "Don't tell me you don't know what day this is!"

"Monday?" I heard myself say meekly.

Previous page: A return visit to the Trocadero Cafe circa 1956. Left to right: Uncle Sam, myself, my cousin Andrew; Peter, my younger brother; cousin Leo; and Jimmy; all were working in the Trocadero Cafe.

"You idiot! What does this day mean to you?"

I thought for a second and said, "I am very happy because I am in Sydney."

He dismissed this as nonsense and then said, "According to this licence of yours, if it is your licence, that is, it's your birthday!"

"Oh, that," I replied, relieved.

"Date of birth: 16 August 1933." He paused and looked at me. "That is your date of birth?"

"Yes, yes."

"So today is your twenty-first birthday!" the sergeant said with some amazement. I couldn't see what the fuss was about. "Yes, that's right."

The sergeant looked confused. "I don't get it. Today is your twenty-first birthday and you couldn't care less." I realised I had some explaining to do – it was a cultural thing. "Sergeant," I said, "I am a Greek, and in Greece we celebrate birthdays up until the age of twelve. After that, we are men. Celebrating birthdays is something for boys, not men."

As I explained this I could see the sergeant was beginning to understand. "We Greeks celebrate name days. My name day is 6 December. St Nicholas – my name is Nicholas. We go to each other's houses and have drinks and a party. All the Nicks celebrate together. But on name days, not birthdays. That is why I forgot it was my birthday. You don't have to make an appointment to go in for a drink. Everyone walks in to each person's house and if there is enough room they sit around and have a drink or a coffee or something – a scotch or sweets – whatever they are offering in the household. They offer you something and you wish them happy name day and you have a drink to good health. You don't stay too long because there are others coming in and you go to the next Nick and the next Nick after that and there might be ten or fifteen places to go to wish them a happy name day." I could see the sergeant was beginning to regret that his motorcycle officers had pulled me up.

"Enough, thank you," he said, putting his hand up like a stop signal. "What the hell am I going to do with you?"

Then I thought of something to say. "My father was a policeman. In Greece." The sergeant could see that I was telling the truth. "This was in the war. He's retired now." "I see."

"Yes, and when I go back to Greece I might join the police force." When I said this the sergeant pointed to the pouch on his hip which had his gun in it. "That is my gun. I have been carrying it for thirty-five years. The moment I retire I will throw it as far as I can. Don't do it. It's a hard job, a thankless job."

Above: My imported Hudson car during my early days in Sydney, parked opposite my butcher shop in Annandale.

"Perhaps you are right," I replied.

"I'll tell you what I am going to do, son. And I have never done this in my life. Because you have an honest face I am not going to book you. But you must do something for me – and for yourself – otherwise you won't be alive too long in Sydney."

"Whatever you say sergeant, I will do it."

"I am going to drive down to the police station and you're going to follow me. When we get there, you are going to book yourself into a learn-to-drive school – no ifs or buts – all right?"

And that's what we did. I drove very carefully behind the sergeant all the way to Newtown Police Station. I booked myself into the learn-to-drive school he recommended. We shook hands and off I went. I had neglected to tell the sergeant that I was flying to Greece the next day – that would have complicated things too much – better to book in to the school as he has insisted – and when the lesson was due to start I would be far away in sunny Athens.

That night I stayed at the People's Palace which was in Castlereagh Street in the city. In those days people coming to the city from the bush always seemed to stay at the People's Palace. They had a reputation for providing affordable accommodation and I think they were run by the Salvation Army. There were no meals provided – it was just a room and a bed. When I went to sleep I wondered if I should open a butcher shop in Athens – that would be a clever thing to do.

Chapter Two

A phone call to my uncle Milton in Athens the next day changed the course of my life. It still amazes me that it was a call I didn't have to make. It was what Australians call 'a courtesy call', where it is polite to let someone know something. Everyone in my family, except as it turned out, Uncle Milton, knew of my plans to come home.

What was not known was the exact time of my arrival. So when I went to the trouble and expense of making an international phone call to Uncle Milton's office in Athens, I was stunned when he said to me, "Don't come." I couldn't believe what I was hearing. "What?" I asked.

"Don't come home. The army will seize you at the airport." Milton went on to explain that because I had turned twenty-one I was required to make myself available for three years' national service. Being a citizen of Greece, I understood my obligations as a citizen. If everyone was required to do this, then so must I. However, by now I was also a businessman, and I heard myself ask Uncle Milton, "What's the pay like in the Greek army?"

"Perhaps enough to keep you in cigarettes, but nothing more." Then he explained that under the current legislation if I waited in Australia for twelve months, I could then pay a fine of £700 to the Greek Government and would then be legitimately exempt from military service.

I knew immediately what the right decision was and agreed with Uncle Milton that I would cancel my travel plans and remain in Australia for one more year. I knew this would be an enormous disappointment to my mother and father, but I also knew that they would be in complete support. I asked Uncle Milton to break the news to my mother.

This threw all my plans into confusion. What was I going to do? I wasn't the sort of person who could have a holiday, or simply do nothing for a whole year. I would have to do something, but what? There were a couple of options – one was to find a job, or find a cafe for sale, or perhaps look for a butcher shop to run.

By this time, because of my last few years working in the meat business, I did have contacts who could help me. I was put in touch with a man called Cec Phillips, who was a butcher shop broker. Cec made a living by buying and selling butcher shops for vendors and for would-be purchasers like me. When I met with him, I explained my unusual personal circumstances; that I was looking to buy a butcher shop somewhere in Sydney, but only wanted to own it for twelve months. He understood all this – that it would have to be a business that I could sell without too much trouble in a year's time. According to Cec, he had just the business which fitted the bill – it was a butcher's shop on Parramatta Road, in the suburb of Annandale. By coincidence, it was only a couple of hundred yards from where the police had pulled me over on Taverner's Hill.

Cec and I went out to the Annandale shop and checked it out. I really liked what I saw and it was as good as Cec had claimed.

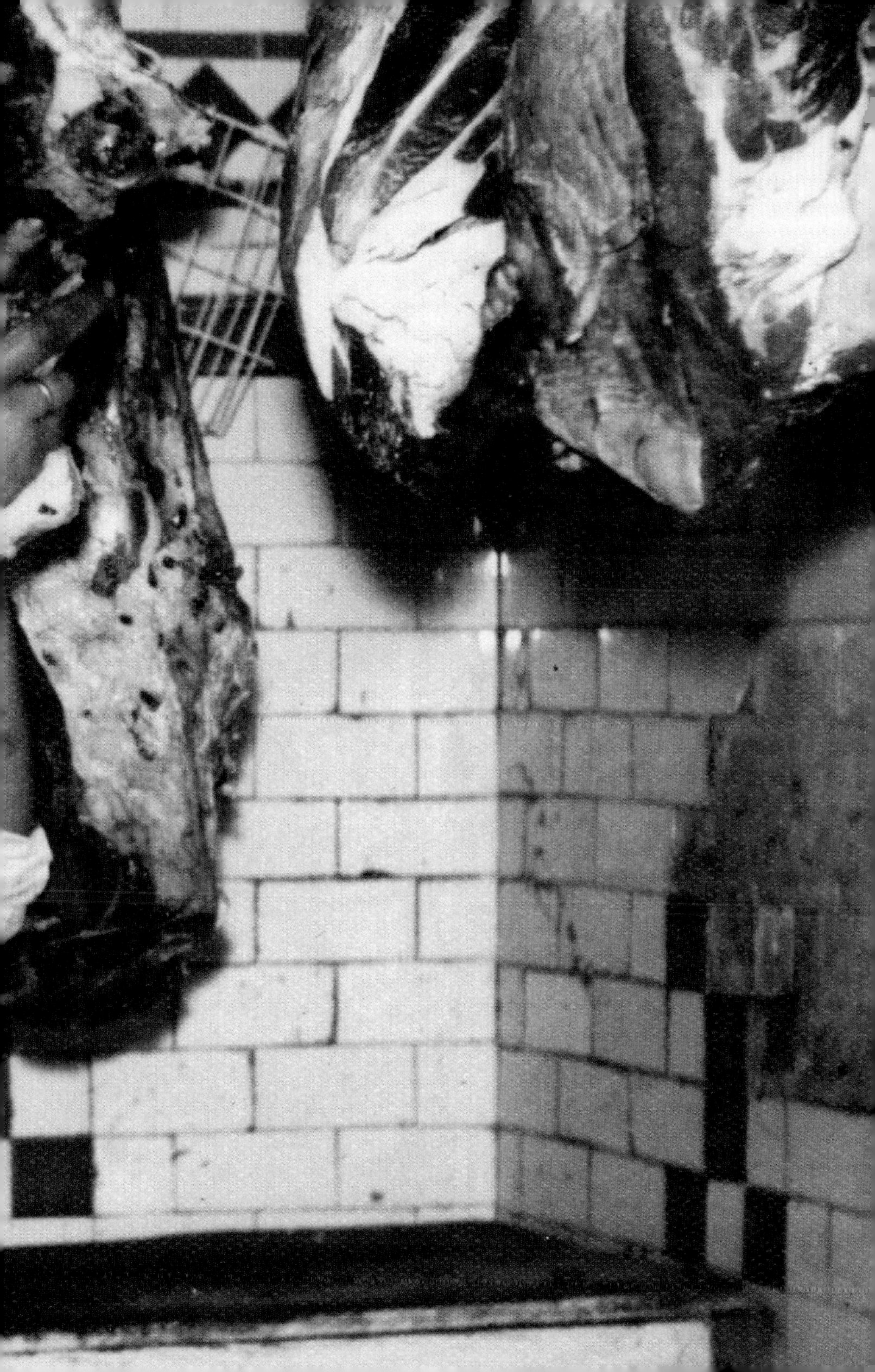

It was a well-run business with lots of customers and I could just imagine me working there and running the place. Cec advised me that I could buy this business for £5,000 – this was only for the business, not the property itself. Again, he reassured me that when I wanted to sell it in twelve months' time, he would be able to find a buyer for me at that price. It sounded like a fair deal. "But," I said, "before I commit to buying it, I would like to work there for a month, for nothing, just to see if it is as good as it looks."

They accepted this condition. I worked there and it was soon pretty obvious to me that this was a very good business. Cec organised all the paperwork and I was now the proud owner of the butcher shop at 247 Parramatta Road, Annandale.

Previous page: In the cool room of my butcher shop in Annandale, 1955.

Chapter Three

As you would expect, owning a butcher shop in the heart of Sydney, which then had a population of just under two million people, was very different from being a butcher in Trangie. Everything was bigger, faster and more expensive. The vendor, Mr McNamara, was a real gentleman of the old school. When I asked him why he was retiring he said to me, "I have a few greyhounds and I like to take them for a walk and go to the races once a week. I don't want to work hard all my life Nick. I think I have enough, which is why I wanted to sell it." He offered to come in once a week, even once a day if need be, to help me get used to the business.

There were six butchers on staff, and a girl behind the till, who also did the books. They had their own accounting system and I modified it only a little bit from what I had learnt from Les Holden in Trangie. Mr McNamara introduced me to everyone including the manager, Reg. I remember at one point saying to Reg, "What will I do?" and he replied, "I don't want you to do anything. Just sit there and watch." It soon became apparent to me that I had purchased a very well-run butcher shop – the staff worked very well – and for a while I did wonder what I could do to make myself useful. Some people buy a business for the purpose of sitting back and doing nothing more than counting the money as it came in. That was never my style, never my intention.

I thought I knew quite a bit about butchering, but watching this store in action made me realise that I knew virtually nothing. Every Saturday the shop was packed and I noticed that many of the customers were Greeks and Italians because there was a huge migrant population in Annandale and nearby Leichhardt. Customers soon learnt that a Greek fellow now owned the butcher shop and came in to see for themselves. At that time there was only one other Greek butcher in Sydney – he owned a shop in Oxford Street in Paddington.

In order to occupy myself, I decided to answer the phone, but even that seemed a bit pointless at times. I'd pick up the phone and say, "Hello, Nick Androutsos." The caller would then say, "Can I speak to Reg?"

"Can I help you?" I'd suggest. "He's just serving a customer at the moment." "I'll wait," they'd say. "I want to give him my order."

"Actually, I'm the new owner. I can take your order and give it to Reg."

"Thank you. That is nice. Yes, I was in the shop and I saw you last time, but I would rather talk to Reg if you don't mind."

At the end of trading every Saturday Mr McNamara would come into the store and together we'd count the takings and work out the profit for the week to see if I was making money. The transition from one owner to another had gone smoothly enough and the figures showed that I was doing just as good as Mr McNamara, or slightly better. Because of this, I changed nothing.

My plan to keep busy for one year before returning to Greece was working better than I had imagined. I had managed to buy a good business at a fair price, but now I continued to rack my brain to find something meaningful to do.

As I was a single fellow, I used to go out quite a lot and noticed that many of the cafes in Sydney were owned and operated by Greeks. When I chatted to these cafe owners, they were impressed that I owned a butcher shop. One day, a cafe owner said to me, "You have a butcher shop, okay? Then why don't you supply meat to my cafe?" This was like throwing a life buoy to a drowning man – here was an idea I could explore.

Our retail prices were much higher than what the cafe owners were paying, and also they were buying a different type of meat to what we stocked in the Annandale store. I went to the wholesalers who were based in Homebush and looked into the whole set up – what cuts they supplied to cafes and what prices they charged. Then, I went back to the shop in Annandale and spoke to my manager, Reg. "This part of the coolroom," I explained, "I want to keep separate – for myself. I'm going to bring in meat from Homebush – T-bones, sirloin and fillet steak – and I will sell it to the cafes."

Reg was fine with this, just so long as we kept the meats separate – he didn't want our shop customers being sold the wrong meat. I was very pleased with this as I had the use of a coolroom for this new area of business without any cost. The next thing I needed was a little panel van so I could make my deliveries to the cafes.

That is how I started in the wholesale meat business – and all because a Greek cafe owner had suggested I supply him with meat. The people who had previously supplied the Greek cafes could not compete with me. I spoke the same language as the cafe owners and made the deliveries myself. Almost all of these cafe owners were a lot older than me and they were very proud of the fact that a young Greek man like me was doing well.

I never understood why the only other Greek butcher in Sydney didn't move into the wholesale market. George, who was then about sixty years old, had the shop in Oxford Street, Paddington. One day he actually came to my shop in Annandale and introduced himself. We soon became friends. He took me out to lunch and then invited me to his home for a meal. George seemed to like me, and he was so friendly I found myself asking, "Why does he like me so much?" Then it all started to make sense when I went to his home and was introduced to his daughter. She was very pretty and he wanted us to marry. And so he was disappointed, but very understanding when I told him of the solemn promise I had made to my mother to return to Greece a single man.

Chapter Four

It has occurred to me as my story is coming out, that the reader may gain the impression that I was so hardworking that there was no fun in my life. This was not so – I was only young and a single man, financially well off – and living in a very exciting city.

In one of those strange twists of fate, the place I used to go to the most on a weekend was the Trocadero. The locals called it the 'Troc', and on Friday and Saturday nights it was 'dance central'. It was located in George Street, and south of Bathurst Street. The Trocadero had been going since before the war and there was always something happening there – debutante balls, dances, charity functions and parties.

My mates and I spent a lot of time hanging around the Troc. I used to park the car outside – in those days you could park anywhere in the city. What I usually did was watch the girls dancing and when I saw one that I liked, I would wait for the end of the dance and then see where she was sitting. Then, just before the band started playing again, I would go up and ask her for a dance. I would say to my mate, "That is the one I am going to go for." When I think about it now, the girls said 'yes' about 70%

of the time. This was 1954, and some girls didn't like foreigners, preferring Aussie fellows, but most of the girls liked the fact that I was foreign and different.

There were also dances at the Petersham Town Hall and I used to go to those with my friends. There were a lot of nurses at Kogarah Hospital and they used to go to the Petersham Town Hall in droves. I liked the nurses – they were good sports. In Petersham I was a bit cheeky and use to park my car illegally right out the front. I knew the police from Petersham Police Station because they used to come into the butcher shop to buy meat. Whenever the police were a customer, I gave them meat free of charge – and they all soon knew who I was and what car I drove. We'd be at the dance and one of the cops would come to the door and say, "Can you tell Nick that his Hudson's parked illegally?" It was all good fun, but parking did get me into trouble on another occasion.

I made the mistake of parking illegally in one of the zones reserved for the post office. This was in Castlereagh Street. The postman saw me walking to my car and abused me. He was very cheeky and called me a dago. This was a mistake. During this time I also continued to train and was very fit. On Saturdays I used to carry a lamb weighing twenty-five kilos up three floors, on my shoulders. I'd run up and down the steps fifteen times. After the postman called me names, I confronted him and we had a punch-up. Because of my fitness and my boxing background, I made very short work of him and actually knocked him out. Not knowing what to do with him, I picked him up and threw him into the back of his van.

When I arrived back at the shop in Annandale, I told the boys what had happened. "For Christ sake ring up the police," they suggested. "He might die, or suffocate in the back of the van." This seemed unlikely to me – I had slammed the doors, but he wouldn't suffocate. Anyway, the boys urged me to do it and so I rang up the police and said, "There is a postman locked in his van in Castlereagh Street." I didn't give my name and never saw that postman again. Hopefully, he would think twice before calling someone a dago.

As I was still an eligible bachelor, a lot of Greek families would ask me to their homes for lunch. Most of these families had daughters who they wanted me to marry, but I had to tell them that I couldn't marry in Australia because I promised my mother I would go back to Greece and marry. I always wanted to be upfront in my dealings with people. That was my father's advice when I left Greece – be honest, don't tell lies, be respectful, be respected, and above all, respect yourself first. If you respect yourself first, you can only improve as time goes on. In some cases, when I told my Greek hosts that I had promised not to get married in Australia they didn't invite me back. Others continued to invite me to their homes – perhaps they thought I would change my mind. The thing about keeping a solemn promise to your mother is that it is something you must fulfil, but often in life the unexpected happens and throws all your carefully made plans out the window.

Chapter Five

There is a Greek expression which goes: "The liar and the thief are happy in the first year only." It takes many years to get ahead. My butcher shop in Annandale was going well and in 1956 I bought another shop at 10 Oxford Street, Paddington. The suburb of Paddington in 1956 would be unrecognisable to anyone living there today. It was a working-class area where rents were cheap and property values were low. A lot of Greeks lived in the area and I thought the butcher shop would be a good investment. I paid the owner of the Paddington shop £3,500 – that was for the goodwill. I could have bought the property outright for half as much, but only paid for the goodwill and rented it. The rent was only £15 a week. My uncle used to say, "Why would you buy the property if you are only getting £15 return a week?" For about double the same money you could buy the business and make £200-300 a week." However, there was not a lot of interest in real estate at that time and in today's terminology you would describe

Left: At the iconic Bondi Beach, 1956.

the property market as 'sluggish'. Later in my story, I will tell you about how I steadily moved into buying properties – and not big places, but small ones – thanks to the advice of an American friend.

I organised for one of the butchers who was working for me at Annandale to manage the new business at Paddington. He was a Greek fellow, Harry Pappas, and I offered him 30% of the net profits while I looked after the cost of running the shop. He thought this was a great opportunity for him and worked very hard. A few years later I was the best man at his wedding. Paddington was a tough place to do business – customers used to walk down the street and check out the prices of our beef mince and tell us if it was two or three pennies higher per pound that the opposition.

Sometimes, when you buy a business, you haven't done your homework properly, and something nasty lands on your plate. And sometimes, you buy a business, and you discover it has buried treasure and no one else seemed to notice it. The Paddington shop was quite small, but one of its customers was P&O Cruise Lines. The shop supplied meat to P&O's ships when they berthed in Sydney Harbour. In those days we supplied no more than a handful of ships per year. Today, this is a major part of my business and we now supply hundreds of ships every year.

Another customer of the Paddington shop was the shipping company A.W. Miller. They had a fleet of seven cargo ships transporting cargo from Newcastle to Sydney. Occasionally, Mr Miller would come into the butcher shop in Annandale and ask for some eye fillet. In fact, I used to save the best eye fillet for him and put it aside. However, sometimes we wouldn't have it and I would say to him, "Don't worry Mr Miller. I will bring it to your home tonight." After work I would drive over to Point Piper. He was one of those fellows who was always up for a chat and we'd sit and talk while his cargo ships would go past on the harbour. The ships would signal him with their ship's horns: "Beep, beep, beep." Mr Miller explained, "If they have no problems, they pull it three times. When they pull it twice it means there have been problems. So I then contact the ship."

Around this time, I met a Greek fellow who had been working on ships but was having trouble finding work. He came to me and asked if I would be able to get him a job as a chef on a ship. I thought I would ask Mr Miller of A.W. Miller himself, because of my friendship with him. He lived in Point Piper and never ever drove. To get home he always got a lift from one of his workers. They wore dark blue uniforms which were always filthy black from the coal they shipped and handled. I spoke to Mr Miller about my friend who was looking for work and he was soon working for them. Although Mr Miller was a wealthy man, I found him to be very down-to-earth and very approachable. It was from talking to people like him that I slowly built up my knowledge of business.

Chapter Six

As a rule I never mixed business with pleasure, but sometimes my leisure time was interrupted by the demands of business. The company A.W. Miller had seven ships bringing coal from Newcastle to Pyrmont. Each of those ships had a crew of about ten sailors, and we used to supply them with meat. Today, my company supplies meat to cruise ships carrying over 5,000 passengers, but this was where it all started.

The arrangement was that we were on call twenty-four hours a day. If one of their ships docked at Pyrmont, we would be contacted and be expected to drop off the meat they had ordered. Because of the way shipping charges were levied, these ships often came in at night and left before dawn the next morning. Their orders were stored in coolrooms at Sydney Cold Stores, Harris Street, Pyrmont.

I was at a dance one night enjoying myself when one of their ships came in and they wanted to have their order delivered at 1.00 am. I was a single man and so this was not a problem for me at all. I leaned over to my dance partner, Jenny, and told her I had to leave. "Why?" she wanted to know. It was only about 12.30 am.

"I have to get going, but I will come back, soon."

"Where are you going?"

"A ship has come in." I then explained to her that I was on call and had to drop off a delivery of meat to this ship.

"I'll come with you," she suggested.

Perhaps she thought I was making excuses or something. I tried to explain that what I had to do wasn't very pleasant at all. "You don't want to come with me," I warned. "I have to go down to the butcher shop, go inside the coolroom, pick up some boxes of meat and deliver them down to the ship."

"No, I insist," she replied, taking no notice of what I was saying. "I'm coming with you." There didn't seem to be any point arguing with her, so I said, "All right then, let's go."

I knew what would happen – once she saw me carrying these boxes of meat – some of which might be dripping blood – she would change her mind and just sit in the car and wait for me to make the delivery. When I was picking up the first box in the coolroom, I turned around and there she was. "Shall I take this one?" she asked. I nodded, more in shock than anything, and she lifted up a box and carried it out to the van. Young women wore mini-skirts in those days, and she was a thin, wispy girl and obviously stronger than she looked.

After that, I drove down to the wharf and when we arrived I turned to her and said, "Stay here. I won't be long."

"Why?" she wanted to know.

"Well, because the only way on to the ship is by walking along this plank of timber and it's not very safe."

"Don't worry about me," she responded. "You look after yourself."

"Okay," I said.

I took the first box and made my way up the plank. I dropped it in the ship's kitchen and noticed that Jenny had not followed me.

Clearly she had taken one look at that gangway and changed her mind – it was after all a pitch-black night. When I arrived back at the van I was surprised that she was not there. I picked up the second box and as I made my way up the plank I heard this very faint cry, "Nick!" I looked around, but could not see her.

"Where are you?" I wanted to know.

"Down here."

She was in the water! Mind you, I was really impressed with this young woman because she had fallen into the water, and there was not the slightest sound of panic in her voice. It was such a sight to see her treading water in the dark. I quickly went out to the fellow on the gate. He was a student studying medicine at university and

Above: Interior view of Ampco and Andrews Meat factory we owned at 40 Harris Street, Pyrmont.

working at night as a security guard. "Mate, we have a girl in the water. Have you got a torch?"

He said, "We'll need a rope."

This fellow had a look around and being on the waterfront we had no trouble finding a decent length of rope. We went back to where Jenny had fallen in. Then the security guard lowered the rope down and instructed her to wrap it around her arms and waist.

After she did that, he and I pulled her up on the rope – just like she was a fish we were hauling in. Apart from being a bit cold and wringing wet, she was fine and uninjured. I thought it would be a good idea not to ask what had happened to the box of meat she was carrying. I said, "What am I going to do with you now?"

"Take me home."

She lived in Annandale. When we pulled up I was just about to say goodnight to her when she said, "Wait here." When she saw the confused look on my face she added, "I'll change my clothes and then we can go back to the dance." Jenny was a very determined young woman. And very attractive. But I had made a promise to my mother.

Chapter Seven

Some of the workers from the shop used to go to night school, which was free, to learn English. This was a course for teaching new Australians how to speak English and was held in some classrooms in Johnston Street, which was a few blocks from the butcher shop.

The day after their first lesson, I overheard these butchers talking about one of the girls in their class. They thought she was unbelievably good-looking. When I heard this I thought to myself, "How typical of Greeks – they went to learn English and instead spent the whole evening gawking at women." A few weeks later, they were still talking about her – and it was always the same – she was about seventeen years old and beautiful. Then, one of the butchers suggested I come to the classes and ask this girl out. "Why don't you take her out?" I wanted to know. Apparently, they had tried and come up short. The girl wouldn't go out with anyone, and it was difficult to get her alone. The family lived only a short

Left: Three years after meeting Maria, and prior to our marriage.

distance away in Booth Street, Annandale, and either her brother, or mother, or father walked her to and from the night school classes.

I asked what I thought was a fairly obvious question, "Why do you think she'd go out with me?"

One of the butchers said, "You have the talent, the experience, you're a business man, but most of all you own a beautiful car."

"What about my looks, mate?" I joked. "What about my personality?" He replied, "Well, let her tell you that!"

One of the other butchers said, "Seriously Nick, with your car, your personality; you could win her."

"One of these days," I remarked.

I was intrigued about this girl, but did nothing. Because I was now very busy with work, I didn't have time for night school. Also, I'd been learning English since the day I arrived and didn't see the point. And yet the butchers who went to the night school classes

Above: Christmas lunch with the gentlemen who worked in my butcher shops. Left to right: John, Peter, Harry, myself, Bill, Peter and Jim in a Greek restaurant in Pitt Street, 1955.

continued to talk about this girl – I learned that her name was Maria – but apart from that nothing changed.

One day, I was standing inside the front window of the shop arranging the meat display when I saw this young woman walk past. It was like being struck by lightning! I had never seen anyone so beautiful in all my life. She was with her little brother, holding onto his hand, and I remember she was wearing a knee-length dark blue skirt. She had a green blouse with the collar up and her long black hair was tied at the back with a bow. Then, she was gone.

I climbed down from the window with my mind in a spin. Harry, one of the butchers, had seen what happened. He came up to me and said, "That's her! That's her! The girl I've been telling you about. The one from the night school."

"She is incredible!" I said, still thinking about the vision of that young woman. "I know! That's what we've been telling you!"

Into my head came the plan to attend the very next night school in Johnston Street. But then Harry said to me, "She'll be back."

"What?"

"I've seen her do this before. She walks down the street with her little brother to the paper shop, and then walks back."

"Listen," I said to Harry. "You know her, don't you?"

"Yeah, yeah."

"Well, get the chamois and go outside and start cleaning the windows. When she walks back say hello to her and say something to her."

"Okay," Harry agreed. "And then what?"

"Let me look after that. Quickly now." Harry went and found a chamois and set himself up outside on the footpath wiping the windows down.

As predicted, Maria soon appeared walking along the footpath with her little brother. Through the glass I saw Harry turn and speak to her. My timing was perfect. I then walked out and announced, "Harry, you're wanted on the phone."

"Oh, okay," he said. Then he added, "Oh by the way, this is my boss, Nick. Nick this is Maria." She smiled at me. I swear to you she was like a Greek goddess. Harry rushed back into the store to answer the imaginary phone call.

Meanwhile, I was too eager, but couldn't help myself and fired off a barrage of questions: "Where are you from? Where are your parents from? Are you local? Where do you live? What are you doing? Where are you working?" The poor girl didn't have a chance to answer one question when I'd hit her with another. Eventually, I shut up and listened. Her name was Maria Andoniadies. She was working as a seamstress at a clothing factory in Surry Hills and lived with her parents just around the corner in Annandale.

Then an idea hit me. "Do you work on the weekends?" I asked. That day was just full of luck for me. That same morning the young lady who was my cashier every Saturday told me she wanted to leave. "Don't leave me! Don't leave me!" I had cried. She was married with a couple of kids and had been working there for about fifteen years. She said she would help me find someone and wouldn't leave until her replacement was settled in. This prompted me to ask Maria, "My cashier is leaving. Would you like to do our Saturdays for us?"

"I don't know anything about being a cashier," she answered honestly. I explained what it involved and of course made it sound very simple. Maria listened and then said, "My English is not the best. I don't think I could do it."

"I will teach you," I replied, then quickly corrected myself. "We will teach you." She nodded and smiled and said, "I think I will come back with my mother." That was it. She took her brother's hand and walked off.

I felt like she had seen through me and guessed that I was interested in her for romantic reasons. One week went by and no Maria. Then two weeks went by. One Saturday morning I was closing the shop up just after twelve o'clock when Maria arrived with her mother. With the two of them standing there listening, I explained about the job and showed her the books. She was still a bit hesitant and undecided. Finally, her mother said, "I will leave it to her." Nothing was decided and the three of us left the shop and I locked the doors. That day I had parked my car out the front. It was a brand-new car, a Chrysler Ariel. Like a true gentleman, I offered the ladies a lift, and they accepted.

"Now, where would you like me to drop you?" I asked. "We're going home," Maria's mother explained. "Where do you live?"

She said, "Booth Street, Annandale."

We drove off in my smart new car and arrived outside their house within minutes. As we pulled up Maria's mother asked, "Would you like to come inside for a coffee?" "No thank you," I replied. "I have to get to another appointment." The truth was that I had nothing else on, but thought I needed to sound less keen. I was trying to be the big businessman. They then gave me a wave and were gone.

The following Saturday Maria was back. "I would like to try and be a cashier but no guarantee," she explained.

"Of course, of course."

"If you could hold on to the other girl for another week to show me what to do," she suggested. I arranged with my girl to stay for a couple of weeks to show Maria the ropes. As I had suspected, Maria picked it up really quickly and became the store's cashier. I learnt that she had been to high school in Greece. From conversation I found her to be very knowledgeable, and very clever. I soon realised that she was not the kind of girl who was impressed with a big, flash car.

Chapter Eight

Maria's mother, Androniki, continued to come to the store around closing time to walk her daughter home. And I continued to give them a lift home. After a couple of times her mother asked me if I wanted to come in for a cup of coffee, and this time I accepted. I met her two brothers – Nick, who was about my age, and Con, who was much younger – and her father, Anthony.

Her father had come from Asia Minor. Greeks had been living there since the Trojan Wars, but during the First World War the Ottoman Turks attacked the Greeks living in Asia Minor – there were massacres, forced deportations, death marches and arbitrary executions. Altogether about two million people died. At the time of this, Maria's father was eleven years old. His family escaped to Thessalonica in northern Greece, and after a few years there, went to America.

He worked in restaurants as a waiter and then had his own little business, a paper shop. Then, in the early 1930s America went through the Great Depression. All businesses were under financial stress and the government started chasing all the businesses to see if they were paying tax. A lot of these people, such as Maria's father, came from different countries all over the world and they were paying cash for everything. They avoided paying tax and were sending money back to their own country. So Maria's father was sending money to his mother and buying blocks of land in Thessalonica.

Soon after, Maria's father Anthony left America and went back to Greece. He worried that if he stayed he would be caught and have to pay a massive tax bill. He went back to Greece where he had a couple of blocks of land and started building units. In one spot he built three blocks of units, totalling sixty-five units. Then, the Greek Government resumed the site to make a railway station. The compensation they offered him was far less than they were worth. All the units were pulled down and in its place they built a railway station to serve the Balkan countries like Yugoslavia and Bulgaria. That station is still there and in use today. This all happened around 1938 and he tried to get more appropriate compensation.

The Greek Government offered to pay him for the value of the land without the units. He took them to the High Court and then World War II started. When that happened – everything was frozen.

Maria's father told me there was this thing they call the statute of limitations – if nothing happens in seven years, you can't continue your legal action. I mentioned that my uncle Milton was a lawyer in Athens and suggested he look into his case. Maria's father was happy for that to happen. The court files were in a basement in Athens and Milton was given a dust coat and a mask because of all the dust on the files. My uncle tried to do something about it, but nothing could be done legally and we had to forget about it.

Although he was a man of few words, I learnt a lot from Maria's father. He told me other stories about his life. He had returned to Greece a rich man, despite the Great Depression, but after his units were bulldozed and then the Italians and Germans occupied the country, he was a poor man. At the time he was building his units he employed about thirty people. Under German occupation he was starving and he didn't have enough food to feed his family. He used to take a wheelbarrow to the markets, buy fresh vegetables and then sell them to the German officers. He became friends with a couple of German soldiers and officers. Then, when the Germans lost the war, the British came in and their soldiers occupied the same barracks where the Germans had been. He became friendly with the British soldiers and also met some Australian troops. Anthony spoke English well, because of his time in America, whereas not many Greeks spoke English. So those were better days for him.

During this time, he became friends with a fellow from Newcastle, and he offered to sponsor Anthony to come to Australia. "Why did you prefer to go to Australia, rather than to America?" I asked him.

"Between you and me," he admitted, "I did owe the American Government lots of back taxes. I thought if I went back to America they might grab me and make me pay back money which I didn't have. I was broke. Therefore, I thought the best thing would be to try and make a fresh start in Australia."

When this soldier from Newcastle returned to Australia, he kept his word. All the paperwork was done and everything was arranged. And so in about 1949, Maria's father and his oldest son, Nick, arrived by ship in Sydney.

However, the soldier from Newcastle who had invited him and brought him to Australia wasn't there. For some reason their sponsor didn't turn up. They had no contact number for him. Anthony and his son waited for a couple of hours, but he never showed up. They hailed a taxi and asked the driver to take them to a Greek club. The taxi driver took them to the Greek Club at the corner of Elizabeth and Castlereagh Streets.

Some members of the club helped him, and temporary accommodation was found for them in Glebe. A lot of the men in this place were in the same situation – they had come here without their families – and were looking for work. One of the fellows at the boarding house took him down to Hudson's Timber Mill at Blackwattle Bay where he was hired as a labourer operating a power-saw cutting timber at the mill.

He was an interesting man and I learnt a lot from him. He used to call me *tavromaho*, which is bullfighter in Greek *tavro* meaning 'bull' and *maho* meaning 'fighter'. One piece of advice he gave me I never forgot – he said to never put any money in Greece. He was very negative about Greece's future. He said that from way back Greece was a holiday place where the locals didn't believe in hard work. They see all the holiday-makers sitting in the sun and having a good time and they think, "Why should I work?" Because of this attitude, they don't work hard. But people like my father, who had a farm, had to work hard to produce crops like wheat and barley.

Anthony stayed at Hudson's Timber and after a few years they bought a small home in Booth Street, Annandale. At heart, he was still a businessman. He paid off the house, then mortgaged it and used the money to buy five units in Johnston Street, Annandale. Today, those units are worth about $3.5 million.

While it is true that I enjoyed talking to Maria's father, he wasn't the reason I was at the Booth Street house. She was their only daughter and the family rule was that she was not allowed anywhere without her mother, her father or a brother with her. Once I joked with her, "Have you still got a policeman looking after you wherever you go out?"

She laughed at this, "Yes, I even have a policewoman – my mother!" And so I only ever saw Maria at their family home or at work.

At the butcher shop she worked as the cashier and did things like answer the phone. She was a happy person, and everyone liked her. If it was someone's birthday in the shop Maria would organise a cake and things like that. Also, I noticed that she always left everything spotless. The other girl in the shop would leave leftover cups of tea in the sink, or rubbish around the place for the cleaner to clean up. Not Maria – she kept the shop spick and span.

My visits to Maria's home continued. I soon noticed that they didn't have a television. One day I went out and bought a television and took it down to their house. This was after I had been seeing her for a while. Television was such an unusual thing then – once you sat down in front of it – you stayed sitting there for hours. Together, we watched television and slowly got to know each other and fell in love.

Chapter Nine

It was an unfortunate fact of life that I was given by my father an unpronounceable surname: Androutsopoulos. Even for a Greek speaker, it is a name that causes tongues to trip. Whenever I had to reveal this name to someone – like when getting a licence or opening a bank account – the person I was talking to would look at me dumbfounded and say, "Sorry, what was that?" I'd repeat the name slowly and they'd say, "I didn't quite catch that." When I moved to Trangie, 'Androutsopoulos' became 'Androutsos'.

By this stage in my life, I knew that I would not be returning to Greece. I had been in Australia over ten years. I loved this country and I knew without any doubt that my future was here. I decided to become a naturalised citizen. It was at this time that I formally changed my name from Androutsos to 'Andrews'. My brothers later did the same, as did many of my other relatives. Recently, when I counted the numbers, there were something like thirty-six relatives using the surname 'Andrews'.

The television I bought for Maria's family was a great success and although we spent a lot of our time together watching it, we were not allowed to be on our own. Slowly, but surely, her

family relaxed, as they began to know me. Nothing was said, but at a certain point in our relationship, the two of us were able to go for a walk on our own, and gradually that became going for a drive, and then going to the pictures and then to a dance. I could see the basics were good and I thought if my mother and father met her they would be happy with her. Whilst I had not forgotten my promise to my mother, everything changed when I met Maria. Sometimes, I used to think, "Am I missing something? Is there any more to it?" She always showed respect to her parents, she always talked to my relatives with respect and she was respectful even to strangers.

And she was also fun. Between us we used to play jokes that were a bit naughty and would laugh a lot. We were very much in love and I knew she was the one for me. The time had come for me to speak to Maria's father, Anthony.

Greek families always want a son, rather than a daughter. This was a fact of life. And because of the hardship of the war years, this was even more the case. When parents had a daughter, they had to pay a dowry to get her married. It is not like that today, but in those days, if you had one girl, or even more, the father would be very upset because having to pay a dowry could ruin the family's finances.

I turned up at the Booth Street house and everyone knew that something was up. Maria, her mother and the two boys had gone somewhere and there was only her father at home. I had a bit of a speech prepared in my head and told Anthony that I was in love with Maria and wanted to marry her. "I ask for her hand in marriage and your blessing," I said. Maria's father replied, "If she

Left: Engagement night with the beautiful Maria Andoniadis, 1958.

wants you and you want her, fair enough. It is okay with me. But one thing I will tell you now, Maria has no dowry."

"I'm not asking for a dowry. I don't want anything. I just want to marry her."

"Well you have my approval. It's up to you and her from now on."

I was a happy man indeed. "That's all I need." We then shook hands, and hugged.

The next thing I had to do was tell my parents. It was never going to be easy, but they could see that my life had changed enormously since I had arrived in Australia and that the business ventures I was involved in were very successful. My parents were

Above: Our wedding day, 18 October 1959.

delighted with the news. Plans for our wedding now took over our lives.

We were married on 18 October 1959 at Agia Triada (Greek Orthodox Church of the Holy Trinity) and had the reception with family and friends in our home.

While I had reached the stage where I knew an awful lot about the meat business, I knew nothing about homes, or their values. Around this time I was buying a lot of meat from a fellow called Elliott who was based in Darling Harbour. He told me he had been looking for a house for his daughter and son-in-law. They saw one in Wahroonga, but at £10,500 it was too dear for them. I thought I'd go and see what kind of a house you could get for that money.

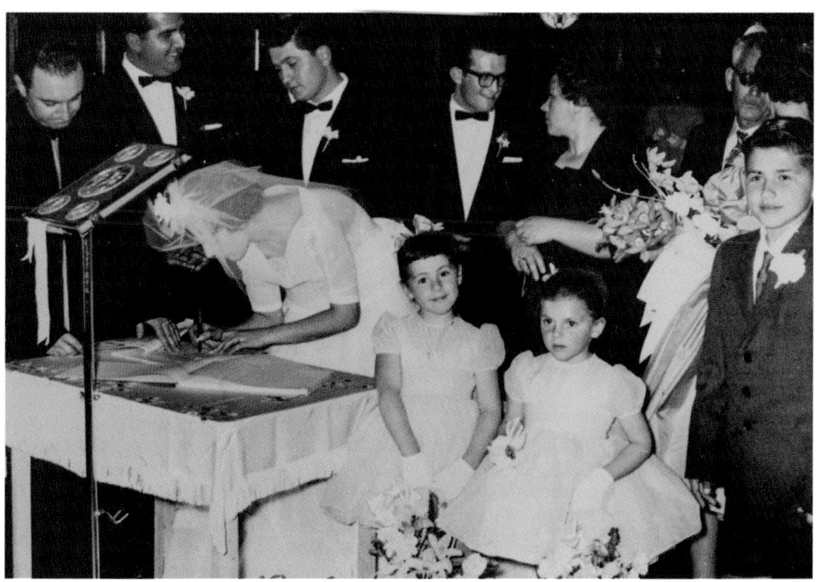

The moment I saw No. 1 Eastbourne Road, Wahroonga, I loved it. It was peaceful – there were very few cars – and the birds and the trees reminded me a lot of the village in the mountains where I came from. It was a large double block of land on the North Shore with about a hundred rose bushes in the garden. I had never seen such big roses – as big as your head.

When I went to see the house, it was spring time and the roses were in bloom and it smelt beautiful. I simply couldn't resist it. I fell in love with the house and decided that I would buy it and give it to my bride as a surprise wedding present. Before the wedding, I went to Grace Bros and paid for the house to be furnished with all the latest things. Then I arranged for it to be painted.

This was going to be a total surprise to my young bride. At night I dreamt about what her reaction would be – a new home in the leafy and prestigious suburb of Wahroonga, and a home fully furnished – once she walked in the door she wouldn't have to do a single thing. I was a very happy man.

Chapter Ten

When I tell people about the surprise wedding gift of a Wahroonga home, I only ever get two reactions: men think this is as good as it gets when it comes to gifts, and women always react with horror. I guess the Wahroonga home purchase tells you a lot about me, as I then was, the twenty-six-year-old businessman. Whilst I was formidable when it came to working long hours, or stitching together a deal, I was but a babe in the woods when it came to that difficult subject called 'what women want'.

I had arranged things so that during the wedding ceremony, a couple of my cousins and my brother, told people at the church where the reception was being held: No. 1 Eastbourne Road, Wahroonga. No one knew who lived there, or where it was. When everyone arrived at the house I turned to Maria and said, "This is your home."

"What?" she said in her native Greek.

"We are going to live here. This is all yours."

My mistake, which was a big one, was not to involve my future wife in this very important matter. I was blinded by love – love for Maria and love for this wonderful house. I didn't have my parents,

Above: Maria and Marietta at our Kirribilli Avenue unit, 1962.

Left and above: The property I bought Maria as a wedding present – 1 Eastbourne Road, Wahroonga.

or my grandmother, or some other grown-up telling me that what I was doing was not something any woman would like. My wedding surprise was a disaster. Maria was horrified – she still talks about this even today. Thankfully, I was blessed with a darling wife, and I am still blessed for her to be with me today.

About five years later we went looking for somewhere more to Maria's taste and found a beautiful apartment in Kirribilli Avenue, Kirribilli. It had views over Sydney Harbour and was also very handy for my work. After our marriage, I looked after the business and Maria didn't interfere. She has been in charge of looking after the family and the house, and I don't interfere. And she has done a tremendous job. In the blink of an eye we had marriage, house, dogs, cats, cars to wash, lawns to cut, barbecues on weekends, and then children. As Nikos Kazantzakis says in his book 'Zorba the Greek', we had "the full catastrophe!" Marietta was born 15 February 1961, Anthony was born 7 September 1966 and Harry 6 December 1969.

And I'm the first to admit that I was hardly a perfect human being, but my heart was always in the right place. Fifty-eight years later we are still in love, with three wonderful children and eight grandchildren.

Above: Out on the town with Maria, 1962.

Above: A family photo outside our unit in Kirribilli.

Chapter Eleven

In 1963 I returned to Greece for the first time since my flight from the country seventeen years before. The plan to go back in 1954 had to be abandoned because of compulsory military service. Now, my circumstances could not have been more different – I was now a married man with a two-year-old daughter.

We planned to stay overseas for six months. Because of the time we would be there, I decided it made more economic sense to take a car over rather than rent one, or buy one there. Also, it has to be remembered that it was hard to get a car in those days because of the impact of the Civil War. I bought a brand-new Falcon car and had it shipped over on a Greek cruise liner, called *Patris*, which is a Greek word that means 'my country'. At that time Greeks were migrating to Australia all the time and there were a couple of ships bringing them over.

We flew to Athens where we were met by my parents. The car was ready to be picked up when we arrived and over the next few months we travelled around Greece because I wanted to know every corner of it. There is a lot to learn about Greece, especially its history. I didn't go to school and I didn't know a great deal about my country, only what I had been told from other people. That was a big experience. We travelled around, mainly with my mother; my father wanted to stay in his club, but my mother wanted to be with us all the time. We enjoyed it very much and it was a great holiday.

In later years I travelled the world exporting Australian meat. That gave me the opportunity to hear and to learn; especially when you go to different countries and try and sell them meat. You talk to people over lunch, or over breakfast in the office, formal or informal, you see factories, you see workers, you ask how much people get paid, how much money they are making, and to me, that is the school where you learn from the street. You don't have to go to university to learn these things. It depends on the people. For example, some people don't like to ask questions, they think the other person will be offended. I always like to ask questions, and if they don't want to answer, I say, "Well, don't answer mate. Don't worry about it. Let's go to the next thing." If you ask, you might get something; but if you don't ask at all, you'll always get nothing.

At that time, I noticed the Greeks didn't pay any taxes in Australia. They would put money in biscuit tins and they had cash everywhere, instead of putting the money in the bank and paying the tax or buying the properties in the city. They would have made millions, but they did it the other way around and everybody was always seeing what the next person was doing and they were copying each other. I had my own ideas but I wasn't ignoring what I heard, and I was learning from the older people, what they were thinking, how they were doing it. Even today, at my age, I still listen to people – perhaps not too many older people than me, but even a ten-year-old kid, I will listen to them. I will sit down and listen to what they think, even if they are only ten years old.

Between trips, we stayed in Akrata most of the time. We would go off on our travels and come back and stay for a week, and then be off again. My house, the one I started building in Greece during my early days working in Trangie, that I promised to build for my mum and dad, was now ready. We were just finishing up the two bathrooms, everything else was beautiful.

Akrata has an unbelievably beautiful beach. It is very well known all over the world and we often spent time there. The beach would be four kilometres long. I know that because I used to walk down its length and then have to ring my nephew to drive over and pick me up because it was too hot to walk all the way back!

One day while I was down at the beach I saw an older gentleman reading the New York Times. I can't really explain it, but there was something about this fellow that intrigued me. I noticed that he went to the beach every day, and he always had with him the New York Times. After a couple of days I went up to him and said, "By seeing what you are reading, you must be American. Are you American?"

"No," he replied. "I am Greek, but I lived in America most of my life."

I introduced myself and so did he – his name was Pablo. "Sit down and have a coffee with me," he suggested.

I said, "I'll take Maria and the little one home and I will come back."

When I returned, he was still there. He was casually dressed. We started chatting again and ended up having lunch. At the beach the council allows restaurants to have tables on the sand because the tide never comes up too high. Each restaurant has a different coloured table cloth to show they pay rent for the space to the council. While we were sitting there, I explained to Pablo how I had left Greece after the Second World War and had gone to Australia where I now lived and worked. Pablo told me he was a builder, then a developer, had struck it lucky and made a lot of money in America. He said he was very successful developing these high-rise buildings, which, from the way he described them, must have been over forty floors high. He asked what I did and I replied that I had five butcher shops. Pablo asked, "Have you got any properties?"

"A couple," I replied, "but I mainly rent."

"The properties you don't own," he suggested, "buy as soon as you can. If you have say three or four shops and own no properties, then sell one or two butcher shops and buy the properties."

Instinctively, I felt like this man knew what he was talking about. He asked why I hadn't bought the properties and I repeated to him my uncle Sam's theory about property. I could see from his reaction that Pablo was horrified to hear this. "Wrong, wrong, wrong," he said. "The business is only as good as you are looking after it. One day if you are not around, and the business goes down, the property still stays. Eventually, the property value will go up. If you manage it, or you don't manage it, it will still go up. One thing I can tell you Nick, do not take the gamble. Do not lay your eggs on somebody else's nest."

It was advice I have never forgotten to this day. I can still see in my mind's eye, Pablo and I sitting at the table on the beach at Akrata and listening to this. "When the lease for your shop is finished, if they don't want to renew it, then you have no business. This is because someone else is going to throw your eggs out." The other incredible thing he said to me was that when it came to buying properties, buy small. He said that too often people stretch themselves to be able to afford a place instead of buying relatively inexpensive, smaller places which are more easily developed, or on-sold.

I listened to this man and we met a couple of more times over the next few days. He had an interesting story to tell. He told me how he had lost it all.

He invested in high-rise buildings because they had big corporate tenants, but when the Great Depression started, the tenants closed down and walked out leaving him with no income. The banks sold the properties for 25% of their value. They took the lot. He remained in the United States until the Second World War finished and then lived in Greece on a United States pension, which at the time was four times more than the Greek one.

Pablo was a naturalised American. He said, "I sent a few bucks to my mother to help some relatives who had land on the beach," and pointed to the boats nearby and two blocks of units. "Those units are built on my land and because I owned the land the developer gave me 40% of the building. That's how it works – you give them the land, they spend the money building – and give you 30%, or 40%, or 50% of the units."

Another thing to consider he said, is this: "If you have bought a big property, you'll have to hand over the title to the bank to secure the mortgage. If instead you have, for example, six much smaller properties, they can give you many more options. You might own one or two of them outright, which means you have the title, which can be very important when you have to negotiate with the banks. If you have a few properties unencumbered and then go to a new bank they will look more favourably at doing business with you. The bank will know you have the power and the guts to do it. I have never been knocked back by a bank in my life because I don't ask silly questions. If you tell the banks, 'Oh, I have a grandmother and she has ten gold teeth.'

'Yeah? Bring her in to sign the guarantee!'"

The formula, or the strategy for success, is never to borrow up to the valuation of your house. Pablo's advice was this: "Stick to the little properties; with the little ones, if you get a vacancy in one it is not a big deal, the others can carry it, providing your borrowings are not exceeding more than 40% of the market value."

There and then I promised myself that when I came back to Australia I would focus on buying properties, and focus on picking up smaller places. A lawyer I knew noticed I wasn't investing in large properties and said to me, "Nick, what's going on? Why are you getting all these smaller places?" I had to explain to him about what I had heard from Pablo in Greece. It made sense to me.

BOOK SIX

Building the Business

Chapter One

My butcher shops seemed to be going well, and as the business grew I depended more on managers. I liked to motivate people and give them real rewards for their efforts – not just praise and a box of chocolates – but something more substantial – money. Usually, I gave them 30% of the profit, and nine times out of ten, that did the trick. However, sometimes things didn't go according to plan, as in the case of a Frenchman called Mervyn. For a while there he managed the shop at Annandale for me and seemed to be going okay. Then one day he just disappeared. This happened to coincide with the fact that I had lent him some money, which he had promised to repay, but never did. When people do this I am always disappointed, but I never get angry – life is too short to get all fired up over a debt. This happens in life – people make promises and most of the time they're as good as their word – but occasionally, one lets you down. It's like separating the sheep from the goats – you soon become good at looking at people and making a decision about whether they're honest or not.

Mervyn was gone and so was my money. Then, one day when I was at the Annandale property, a commercial traveller dropped in who was supplying the butcher shops with equipment. He said to me quite casually, "I saw Mervyn the other day." I knew from the way he said this that he had no idea Mervyn had 'disappeared' on me.

"Yeah?" I replied. "What's he up to these days?"

"He's in a very nice set up – managing a butcher shop in Chippendale."

After the commercial traveller had left, I jumped in the car and drove to this butcher shop in Chippendale. It was only a small shop and as I walked in I could see Mervyn was there on his own. Bold as brass I marched in the front door, went straight behind the counter, rang the till and started taking all the money out. Mervyn stood there in shock – shocked to see me – and shocked to see me taking money out of the till. "You didn't do the right thing," I said. "Who the hell are you working for, because I will tell them about you and you'll get the sack."

He was very apologetic. "My boss died a couple of months ago," he explained. "And the widow has two shops, one here and one in Forest Lodge." Mervyn was managing both shops for the widow. Then he said something which pricked my ears. "But she is selling the shops – both of them."

From the till I took a substantial amount of cash and said to him, "Good luck explaining how short you are to your boss."

"She can take it off my wages."

"Okay, let's do something sensible," I replied. "You said she's selling?" He nodded in agreement. "Well, I got nowhere near the money you owe me, so I suggest you make a deal with the lady so I can buy both shops and both properties for the right money. Okay?" He then asked, "I don't suppose you'd have me as a manager, would you?" You had to give Mervyn credit for having a thick skin.

"It depends how good the deal is. I will think about it."

Mervyn spoke to the widow and we reached an agreement that I would buy both businesses and properties for £20,000. It was a very good deal. But Mervyn was dishonest, and there was no way I could employ someone I didn't trust. I gave him his marching orders and put in a fellow by the name of George. George was a Yugoslavian fellow who worked as a butcher in the Annandale shop. I offered him the same arrangements I had with the manager of the Paddington shop – 30% of the profits.

George was a wonderful fellow who did very well for himself. A few years later he told me he wanted to own his own shop and was looking to buy. So he went out and bought his own shop, but I also had him manage two of mine for years to come.

I purchased the Chippendale and Glebe properties and businesses in 1958, and in 1960 bought another shop at Kiora Road, Miranda. As the Miranda butcher shop was brand-new, I paid around £7,000 for the goodwill. As I had done with the other shops, I put in a manager and gave him a share of the profits as I had done with my other shops and properties using the same formula.

Chapter Two

All this time I was still busy learning about the meat business. I was eager to learn and there were lots of people to teach me. I was introduced to many people in the game, but one who made a big impact on my life and became my idol was Steve Varvaresos. He was very successful in the meat business. His nickname was 'Mr Stainless Steel', because all his butcher shops had stainless steel everywhere. Using stainless steel for benches and counters was a new idea and very expensive, but the customers loved it. Steve Varvaresos also had a smallgoods company called Sutton's Forest.

Steve loved telling stories and I learnt a lot from him. He had a tremendous reputation and was very respected. No matter who you spoke to in the meat industry, whenever his name came up people would say, "Steve Varvaresos is a gentleman and a half. His word is a contract – when he gives you his word, it's done. You don't have to sign a contract with Steve." That made a huge impression on me, and it was the kind of reputation I sought for myself. He was very successful and bought this mansion in Vaucluse which had been owned by Anthony Hordern – the department store people. The house looked like a castle and the land went right down to the harbour. At a time when houses were being sold in Sydney for £12,000 to £25,000, Steve paid £475,000 for his Vaucluse home. He and his wife had two sons. When they were young men, Steve bought them each a cattle station – one was 3,500 acres and the other about 5,000 acres. The boys competed against each other to see who was going to produce the best cattle.

It was always an experience having lunch with Steve. He was obsessed with quality and obsessed with service. If he saw a waiter doing something wrong, he would politely pull the man aside and suggest he do something different. He was always preaching to people and wouldn't hesitate to walk into the kitchen of a cafe and have words to the chef. Although he was demanding, he was never rude. To me it was a real eye-opener to be able to meet and talk with such successful people. I tried to copy what he did.

I noticed that Steve helped his extended family and always tried to give, rather than take. When you do well financially, families can be difficult to deal with. Steve would say, "You may not believe it, but giving people money is never a good idea." Loaning relatives money is always a risk, yet I believe it is important for someone like me to do good for society, to do good for the community and to help people where I can.

Getting ahead of my story, I had a strong friendship with Steve for many years. In the 1960s there was a terrible credit squeeze – the banks stopped loaning money because of some global situation. Everyone in business was feeling it, including me, and I wondered whether I should ask Steve for a loan. He was a very intuitive person and during our lunch he brought the subject up by telling one of his stories. "I heard from a friend of mine the other day," Steve said, "and he came and asked me for money. I told him, 'I can't lend you money mate, I'm sorry. I have this contract with the bank.' My friend then asked, 'What contract with the bank?'

So I told him. 'The deal is that I don't sell money and they don't sell meat.'" I had the answer from Steve even before I had asked the question – that was the kind of man he was.

Many years after that I was having dinner with Steve when he said, "Nick, I don't know if you know, but the doctor has told me I have six months." He had been diagnosed with cancer.

"I'm sorry to hear that Mr Varvaresos."

"That's all right mate. We all have to die sooner or later. Sometimes it's good not to know, but when your time is up, it's up."

"The doctors can be wrong."

Steve shook his head. "Yeah, they can be wrong, but I give them 80% that they are right and 20% they're wrong. I have to prepare my businesses and sell them." Then he looked at me and asked, "How old are you Nick?"

"I'm thirty-four." "Oh, you are a baby!"

I said, "Christ – I'm not a baby – I'm thirty-four! I'm about to hit the top and roll down the other side of the hill – down."

Steve repeated, "You are a baby." I have never forgotten that conversation. You worry that you are getting old, but as the decades slip by you reach an age when you don't give a damn about your age. You just don't worry about it and that makes you feel good. Now that I'm in my eighties, I look back at what I was like at sixty, at fifty, at forty and at thirty, and I say to myself, "Oh, I was just a baby then!"

Chapter Three

In 1962, I sold the Paddington butcher shop to my brothers, Peter and John. Soon after that, I purchased a large butcher shop at 306–316 Willoughby Road, Naremburn, as well as the property next door. The shop was a wholesale and retail butchery and I bought it from the official receiver for £350. It was unbelievably cheap, but there were no other buyers. It was three times bigger than the Paddington shop.

When I bought the Willoughby Road business, it was not running. I met with the property owner, a lady, and offered to increase the rental on the shop from £15 to £25 a week. She thought she was hearing things – but then I told her I wanted an option to purchase the property within two years for £7,000. The property was RTA-affected – meaning it was reserved for future road usage – and she may have thought I didn't know that. She signed on the dotted line. While I did get the business very cheaply, I spent a small fortune on smoke houses, coolrooms and other equipment.

One weekend I was there helping with the painting. Maria came in – she had brought lunch for the painters. Then a fellow walked in and introduced himself as Les – he owned a butcher's shop close by. He pulled me aside and said, "What are you doing mate?"

"What do you mean?"

"The three butchers here in Naremburn including this one went broke. So why are you opening a butcher shop?"

"Because from now on I will start to bring people here. I'm going to make money and you're going to make money." He didn't believe a word I said and walked out.

Above: My double-sized butcher shop in Naremburn which I extended further downstairs to handle semitrailer deliveries from interstate and for smoking 1,000 hams at a time.

My meat was purchased from an abattoir in Blayney – we'd buy a semitrailer-load full, 250 or 300 lambs at a time. When it arrived and was being unloaded, the truck took up half the street. This did create some problems with the neighbours, but eventually we'd get bigger coolrooms, and this would happen less often. One day, I saw Les, the neighbouring butcher, and we started talking. At some point we moved on to the subject of what he was paying for his lambs, which he bought from Homebush.

He was hesitant to tell me. I said, "Listen, Les. Play straight with me, like I am with you. I will make you money, right? But cooperate for Christ's sake – for your own sake. You have to tell me how much you are paying." He told me the price he was paying which was about 30% higher than what I was paying for my meat from Blayney. When I told him what I paid he didn't believe me, so I showed him the delivery docket. Then I pointed to all the stock we had and said to him, "Take your pick from all this. Weigh it up, take it to your shop and pay me exactly what I paid." Poor Les, he couldn't believe I would offer to do this.

After that, he used to come to our coolroom very early in the morning and get the meat he needed. Les would cover it up with a sheet, then double-check no one was looking when he walked back across the road. He didn't want his customers to know that he was buying from me. But it suited me to have Les still operate his shop, plus the other butcher there. They specialised on cuts that I didn't handle, such as yearling steaks, veal, special sausages etc. which the customers in the area still wanted. My focus was to move in the direction of wholesale orders.

There was only Les and his wife working in their shop. I told him that before long he would need to employ a couple of butchers. "How will that happen?" he wanted to know. "Because," I explained, "I advertise and I bring a lot of people here. I am also supplying the restaurants, but people will come here and there will be plenty of business for everyone." Les ended up employing two butchers, which made his wife happy because she didn't have to work in the shop anymore. One day his wife came over and said, "Thank God you came here Nick. I don't have to work anymore in the bloody butcher shop."

The Naremburn shop was a goldmine. We used to serve a lot of people on the upper North Shore. Most of these people were professional people. The wives would ring in with their orders and their husbands would pick it up on their way back from the office. We would stay in the shop till about six o'clock, or later, so these customers could drop in and pick up their orders on their way home. People like the newsreader Brian Henderson and his wife Margaret were regular customers. Before long, we had about twenty employees in the shop and I had established eight panel vans doing deliveries to the five-star hotels and restaurants in the city.

The business became so successful that the local residents and even some shops complained that we were taking all the parking on Willoughby Road, and they didn't have enough parking for themselves or their customers.

While I was operating Andrews' Meats, I came up with the slogan "Beef eaters make better lovers!" This slogan was printed on the sides of our panel vans. I think it got our name out there because of its shock value. I also had some funny moments because of it. One woman rang up with a complaint. "That is false advertising," she said very seriously.

"Why?" I wanted to know.

"Because, Mr Andrews, "I gave my husband a lot of beef lately and all he did was fall asleep."

"And you bought the meat from my shop?" "Yes."

"And he just fell asleep?" "Yes."

"That's no good," I said. "But tell me, what did he have with the beef?" "Oh yes," she replied, "he did have a couple of glasses of wine."

"Beef eaters make better lovers!" I said, "But this is no good if he has wine." "Really?"

"Yes," I explained. "The beef will make him a better lover, but it's the wine which is putting him to sleep. Give him more beef, and no wine." Then I hung up.

Another woman rang and abused me for making money out of killing poor, defenceless animals. She was a vegetarian. "I didn't start people eating meat," I explained as politely as I could. "It started many, many years ago when beef became so popular in the first place. You should blame the people from before Christ, and even before the Romans. Give the ancient Egyptians a ring and complain to them after we're done here, because I wasn't around then."

Fair to say that she was not amused. When I pointed out that if we didn't eat lambs, chickens and beef the world would starve, she said "Now you're making fun of me." I told her I didn't have time for arguments.

Chapter Four

In 1966 at my butcher shop in Naremburn, I was personally cooking and smoking about 2,000 leg hams every Christmas for my customers. I worked very hard with my staff after hours for about two months of the year to get these 2,000 hams done. I was experimenting for two or three years to find an easier and a more profitable way to do the hams and for better quality. What I decided to do was build under the shop a walk-in oven to cook hams. It was very well set up and we cooked five hundred hams at a time. What usually happened was that butchers doing hams would pump them with 10% brine, then leave them in a vat to soak. After that they'd bring them out and boil them in the boiler, then hang them up and smoke them. That was the traditional method, so I did that for a while, then started to think that there had to be a better, more efficient way to do this. The question in my head was, "Why can't we do it all at once, rather than having all these steps?"

After thinking about it and experimenting with a few ideas, I came up with a new system which in hindsight I should have had patented. What I did was pump the hams with 15% brine and hang them in a special room where the heat from the gas circulated and slow-cooked them for six hours. While this was happening, smoke from burning sawdust outside came in and circulated during the cooking. Instead of hanging a shank and having it drip brine, I put it in a net so it cooked with the brine in which made the ham moist. This way I gained 5 to 6% weight and produced a better quality smoked ham. Instead of handling them five times, the old-fashioned way, the hams were put up once and after eight hours they were taken out and left in the coolroom.

But there was one slight problem – so much energy was required to make this work. As electricity was expensive, I went to the Electricity Commission in North Sydney and asked for their help. They showed me how we could heat the room electrically. It was about forty square metres and we were hanging five hundred hams at a time. Three people from the Electricity Commission worked on this for about four days, but they couldn't deliver the goods. In the end they walked away and charged me nothing, as that was part of the deal we made.

Then I spoke to the gas company. They thought I was joking. I said, "No, I want you to come up with a way of doing this. Everyone will tell you what a good idea it is. You'll have every butcher shop in town calling for your work if you can do it for me." This seemed to win them over a little, so I decided to appeal to their competitive spirit. "The guys at the Electricity Commission couldn't get anywhere," I said. "Surely you'll be better than them." That really fired them up. They came up with the idea of installing a big gas jet on the side, which we were able to turn on and set. On the end was a fan and this fan was sucking in heat and then it would blow it on the stainless steel sheets on the wall – moving back and forth across the steel sheets to balance out the heat. The steel sheets would heat up and warm the room enough to smoke and cook the hams.

It would automatically switch itself off and the next day we would come back, take out the hams and be ready for the next batch.

It was such a triumph that I wanted to shout 'Eureka' through the streets of Naremburn like Archimedes himself. The labour costs were cut by 10% and it reduced the cost of this operation by 80% by smoking and cooking perfectly with no one even in the room, every six hours unloading and loading in my small smokehouse, five hundred hams at a time.

And the hams sold like hot cakes. If I had a smallgoods factory – we would have really raked in the money. In fact, one of the smallgoods factories that we deal with now – Belmore Smallgoods Factory – they said their father told them that he used my idea on their hams. They used to last longer. It was a new venture for the gas company – and it cost me nothing. I'd pretty much given them a free patent on a lucrative invention that they advertised to butcher shops country wide.

Chapter Five

In the space of two years, the strip of shops in Naremburn had a big increase in business. My booming business brought many people to the area. After the two years were up, I said to my solicitor, "Tell the landlord that I want to exercise my option and I will buy the property." However, the property owner of the Naremburn site had seen how much we had developed the business and how big it was. Back came the message, "I'm not selling." I tried to explain to her that she had no choice as she had signed the contract with the option clause in it. She still refused to sell. In the end I stopped paying rent and deposited £7,000 in the solicitor's trust account. Eventually, a lawyer explained the situation to her and the property was ours.

I now had in my mind Pablo's advice about investing in small properties, and an opportunity to do this came up in Naremburn. As I have already mentioned, our butcher shop was RTA affected when we bought it. Similarly, a lot of properties surrounding us had the same issue – the Roads and Traffic Authority reserved the right to resume the properties to build an expressway. When the expressway was going to be built was anyone's guess, and its impact on the remaining properties was also a big unknown. But every now and then a rumour would go around the suburb that construction was imminent and the RTA's lawyers were about to resume them.

I knew this because customers would come into the Naremburn butcher shop and say they were worried about what was going to happen with the RTA – they'd be offered compensation, but would it be enough to enable them to buy a decent place somewhere else? I remember one woman coming in and saying all of this and then being amazed when I offered to buy her house. "What do you want for it?" I asked.

"I don't know," she said, and then plucked a figure out of the air, and said, "£5,000. Sorry no, £5,500."

"Sounds good to me," I replied. Then I opened the till and gave her £550 deposit and said, "My solicitor will be in touch."

The word soon spread and in no time at all I had another RTA-affected property person in the shop. "You bought my sister's property," this woman told me. "I have the one next door to her. We inherited them from our father. Would you buy mine as well?" "Which one is it?" We walked out to the front of the shop and she pointed to it, "That one."

"Oh yes, that one. How much do you want for it?" I asked.

"You paid my sister £5,500. Mine is a little bit bigger and better than hers so I was thinking £6,000."

"Look, it may be better than hers, but if I pay you more, your sister is going to get upset. You don't want a fight in the family. I'll give you the same – £5,500."

"You want to come and have a look at it?"

"No," I responded and again pulled £550 from the till. "My solicitor will be in touch."

And so on; altogether I bought thirteen RTA-affected properties. The locals thought I was mad, and even my solicitor said, "Nick, the RTA are not fools. They know what you paid for these places and you will be lucky to get your money back." But time has proved that I was right. The way I looked at it, people always overestimate the speed at which the government will do something. If an expressway is planned to start construction in three years' time, the chances are that work will not start for ten or fifteen years, and sometimes never. Markets rise and fall, but over the long term, they go up.

By the time I had over a dozen properties, my solicitor suggested we contact the RTA and ask about their plans. He sent off a letter stating that Nick Andrews was his client and then listed the properties we owned, which were all RTA affected. The letter made it clear that I knew they were affected when I bought them and asked, "When are they going to be resumed?" and "How is he going to be compensated?"

The answer from the RTA was as follows: "These properties will be unlikely to be resumed before five years and when the time comes your client will be paid at the open market value as if they were not affected." After we received that letter, we kept buying more.

Eventually, the RTA resumed the properties some ten years later. They took ten of the ones I owned – properties which I had paid a very low price for. The RTA offered us 'corporate market value' as if the sites were not affected. In the end, the RTA didn't want all of the properties affected – they took a 250 square metre corner section of 316 Willoughby Road and paid $2,000 a square metre for it. Theo Karedis of Theo's Liquor wanted to put a store on the 1,000 square metres I had left on this site. He was shocked when I asked for $2 million, but changed his tune when I showed him the letter where the RTA had paid me $2,000 a square metre. We still own four properties in Naremburn.

Chapter Six

One of the other butchers in Willoughby Road was Ted. He was a Catholic who had something to do with the church in Naremburn because all his customers wouldn't go anywhere else, only to him. Perhaps he had a priest blessing the meat. He was there for a while, but lost more and more business and then left. I then bought that property as well.

Soon after this, I purchased a residential property in Lavender Bay with beautiful views of Sydney Harbour. It was occupied by a tenant protected by what they called 'fair rented'. Fair renting came in during World War II to help the families of servicemen manage their finances. Their rent was fixed by law, which meant that if you wanted them out you couldn't just raise the rent to do this. One day I said to the tenant, "Bob, the house is awful. You have no hot water, no refrigerator, no wardrobes, you haven't even got a bed." I offered him a lease somewhere else where his rent would still be set at £10 for the rest of his life. "If you live another thirty years," I pointed out, "the rent will be the same."

By this time Bob must have been in his eighties. He wasn't interested in my proposal. I wanted to renovate and subdivide the large spaces in the home that he wasn't using into flatettes. I offered to give him the best flatette on the property – it would be self-contained and fully renovated. And he would pay the same rent he was now paying – £10 a week – for the rest of his life. All he had to do was sign a 5A lease.

"If you sign the lease, I will repair and renovate your new room. I'll give you a new refrigerator, give you furniture, a bed – a king-sized mattress. I'll give you wardrobes and carpet on the floor. I will do the verandah for you so you can have a little table and have a coffee there. I will give you a sink so you can wash your plates because at the moment you carry the water from the bathroom to wash your plates. I will do all that for you – paint it, a new bathroom and you will pay no more. What do you say?"

"What's the catch?" he asked.

"There is no catch. What about if we go and see your lawyer?"

"Yes."

Bob was a stubborn old man, so I was surprised he agreed to this. When I went to pick him up, it took him an hour to put his boots on, because he didn't want to go to the lawyer. "Come on Bob. Come on." He was hesitant, but then agreed. "All right."

We went to the solicitor who drew up the agreement in the detail I had outlined. Bob signed the new lease. We renovated the property into six flatettes and gave the best flat to Bob, to live in for the same rent, He was happy, and I was happy.

About twelve months later, Bob told me he was going to see his sister. I think she lived in Adelaide. "I don't want to lose the lease," Bob explained. "I'll pay my rent to the agent and I'll come back in three months."

"Nobody will touch your lease. You pay, it is yours. If you are not in it, nobody knows, nobody cares if your payment is delayed while you are away. If you want to stay longer, Bob, don't worry.

If you are a couple of months behind I am not going to move you out. You have my word. Your lease is for life."

I never saw him again. He went away and we didn't hear from him. We waited six months – and didn't hear from him. I took the property off the fair rental control and the property jumped in value. I used it with other properties when I bought the large property in Miller Street, North Sydney, which today is occupied by the ANZ Bank.

The main difference between individual tenants and retail tenants is that the retail tenants will always pay their rent to protect their lease and goodwill. So that is another incentive why one would invest in commercial and retail property. If it is a residential property, the tenant only has to pick up their belongings, load up their car and say, "See you later." They can leave it damaged and filthy and the landlord has to spend money to fix it before they can re-let it. With shops, tenants will spend money on your property if they want to sell the good will of the business one day.

While it is true that my interest in real estate investment was prompted by the advice I received from Pablo in Greece, there was also another reason. One day I had a problem with my leg, standing up on the concrete or something, and the doctor told me to stay in bed for a couple of days. Having time off started me thinking. I asked myself this question: "What if something happened to me? How the hell do the butcher shops and everything I am buying run if I die tomorrow? My wife knows nothing about it." The answer to this question was to focus on buying more real estate. If I died, Maria would at least get the rent and have an income. There were a lot of new Australians and they all looked to buy retail businesses.

I know it's hard to believe, but no one wanted to buy real estate in those days. With a property there is only a small income because it is a long-term investment. I was wondering why they were so cheap. The first business I bought in Sydney that I paid £4,500 for was a butcher shop at 247 Parramatta Road. The business was worth £4,500 whereas the property at the time was worth £2,000. The real estate generated only £15 a week in rent, for example, but the butcher shop would make £300 a week. Because of that, real estate seemed to be a bad investment.

Everyone was going for a bigger cash flow in those days. So I started there. Mr McNamara sold me that shop. It was a good shop, and we were doing well. I bought another shop in Miranda, another in Paddington, one in Drummoyne and then went on from there. I started buying larger properties, Today, 90% of my fortune is in property. All this happened because of the good advice I picked up from Pablo, and my concern about Maria's future should I not be able to work. Income from real estate was my answer to financial security.

Chapter Seven

Business in Naremburn continued to boom and the complaints to the council about the lack of parking continued. I used to get on well with the council, up to a point, but I was told seriously that the business was too large and I should go to an industrial area because this was a neighbourhood area. I asked for time. They gave me a year and I managed to stretch this out to two years. Business was good because I was blessed to have many fantastic employees. I always paid my staff above the award wages – if the wages were set at £10 a week, I paid £15 plus a cut of the profits. The reason being that if they went elsewhere they wouldn't earn the same wages, therefore they'd work harder to look after the business. Therefore, I'd provide a better service and make more money. They used to say, "How are we doing this year Nick?"

No one called me Mr Andrews. "Are we going to have a slice of the cake?" I would say, "It depends on the size of the cake!"

But the pressure was coming from the council to reduce the business activity in Naremburn. For a long time I supplied meat to the shipping company A.W. Miller, but then they went into the meat business themselves and had their own butcher shops supplying the

Above: My parents on Nick's boat, having arrived from Greece.

Above: A day out on Sydney Harbour in 1981 on the boat of my good friend, Nick Peters, a shop assistant at the Paddington butcher shop.

export market. However, when one of their ships sank, A.W. Miller faced a lot of claims. The company had to pay compensation for lives and property lost and the company was going backwards.

John Nitties, a young fellow who used to work for me, suggested that we go and see Mr Oliver, who was the general manager of A.W. Miller. Their office was in the city, on the corner of Bridge Street and Loftus Street. Mr Oliver told us that he didn't need to buy meat from us because they had their own butcher shop at 150 Lyons Road, Drummoyne. "How much is it costing you for these cuts you are using – how much does it cost you per pound?" I asked. After he told me the price I said, "I'll supply you at the same price and give you 10% off."

Mr Oliver sat there stunned. "You're kidding me."

I could see that he was now interested and so I said, "Mr Oliver, let's be honest with one another. Answer me this: do you make money out of that butcher shop?"

He sat there for a while, and then he said, "No."

"Think about that," I went on. "I'll save you 10%, plus you save all the cost to run the butcher shop."

They were interested in selling and so I went to see the shop at Lyons Road. From the moment I drove into the staff car park, I knew there were huge problems there. Some of the most expensive cars on the market were parked there as well as a flash-looking speed boat on a trailer. I went inside and asked to speak to the manager. "I was asked by Mr Oliver to drop in and see you because we are looking at taking over the shop." The manager I spoke to wasn't very helpful. Curious about the cars I said casually, "Who owns all the cars out the back?"

"Me and the staff."

"They're very nice cars," I said. "Gee whiz, you are doing well. Did you fellas win the lottery or something?" The manager smiled, assuming I liked what I saw whereas I was horrified. Clearly, they were robbing A.W. Miller blind. There was no way at that time that men on butcher's wages could afford Mercedes and BMWs.

John and I went back to Mr Oliver and indicated to him that we were interested in buying the butcher shop. We said nothing about our suspicions about what was going on down there. We negotiated a deal to continue to supply A.W. Miller with meat 10% cheaper in return for buying the Lyons Road property and butcher shop.

When we took over the butcher shop at Drummoyne, I made the mistake of believing that I could change the way things were done. Life experience tells you this is not possible. When you have a situation where employees and even managers are involved in stealing from the company, the only solution is to get rid of them. Instead, I put John Nitties in as the new manager and tried to change the culture of that business. We, as in John and I, took over the buying of the meat. We told them how to cut it and also told them how much profit we expected to make. However, the former manager and the other staff there made life so difficult for us that we had a real battle on our hands. They did everything they could imagine to make life intolerable for John. He was even scared they might try to poison him – that was the extent of the hostility.

And there was a good reason for their hostility – as a group they had been robbing A.W. Miller blind – and now the party was over. At one point I contacted the fraud squad and explained the situation. "I have a problem here and beware they can cause damage and the purpose is that they have got a plot of dishonesty. What can we do? I think they are stealing and selling the meat for cash and the cash goes in their pockets." A detective from the fraud squad agreed to watch them. This detective went undercover as a person who fixes the phone lines. He was across the road and mucking around with screwdrivers but he was watching and telling me when trucks went in and out. He followed them and they were unloading meat in a butcher shop. After we obtained this evidence, I saw a lawyer and the detectives charged them. The lawyer said, “It is not going to be easy. You have to prove it in court. They will have their stories and excuses. Meanwhile, while you are spending time and money on this they are still working at your shop.” The lawyer had some smart advice – better to sack them – and then let them take you to court.

So we cleaned them all out. I didn’t mince my words. “I’m sacking you because you are bloody thieves!” I said. “I could have you all locked up in gaol.” I then told them we had some undercover men who had been out there for days on end recording everything they did. Naturally, I exaggerated how much information we had on them. I said, “I said once you are found guilty, how are you going to pay back all the money you stole from A.W. Miller?”

Everyone one of them was sacked. They never took legal action against us and we brought in our own crew. Almost overnight, the business started making a profit.

But the financial problems of A.W. Miller continued and they put some of their hotels up for sale. At that time I had a fellow working for me by the name of Nick. He was managing my shop at 10 Oxford Street in the early days. His father wanted me to buy a shop with him in Bexley, but for one reason or another we didn’t proceed on that. When I heard that A.W. Miller had their hotel in Eastwood, Sydney, on the block, I suggested to Nick that we buy it together. I had no idea about hotels and thought that Nick and his cousins could run it. “How much do they want for it?” he asked “Two million.”

“What! Two million dollars! How do I get that kind of money?” Nick wanted to know. “Don’t worry about it,” I replied. “We will go in together and make a deal with them.”

Back we went to see Mr Oliver, who ran A.W. Miller. I pointed to Nick and said, "Here is the man who can buy it – I can't buy it. He can take it over. He will buy it with his family." I explained to Mr Oliver that Nick didn't have the cash, so the family would form a consortium and that company would buy the hotel on call option to purchase.

"They will purchase an option for two years to buy it," I said, "and in the meantime they will pay you a deposit plus rent." I think Mr Oliver was desperate to sell the hotel and so he had no objection to any of this. A deal was done.

Then I made a big mistake. When the consortium was formed, I didn't put my name on it as I should have done. I don't know why this didn't happen – probably distracted with other things going on. Nick, who worked for me for a while, was a good friend of mine. He used to call me 'Captain' and once a week he would come to my office in Elizabeth Street and we'd have lunch. He and his family worked hard and as well as the hotel bought a lot of butcher shops in shopping centres. I heard they sold the hotel for big profits many years later, which for me was 'the one that got away'. That Nick and his family made so much money makes me feel pleased. I can't recall anyone being associated with me who didn't do well. I feel good because it is not always about 'the money', it is also about helping other good people get ahead and seeing what they do with their lives and continue learning.

Chapter Eight

In the end I ended up purchasing two butcher shops with the properties in Drummoyne – the one at 150 Lyons Road and another one three blocks further down on the corner. It was a meat export factory and we did our deliveries to the restaurants and hotels from there. I left the Naremburn shop in the hands of a manager. He only had one panel van instead of the seven or eight which we took to Drummoyne. The Willoughby Council were now happy.

I called the business in Drummoyne Greenland Meat Export. I thought the name had a nice ring to it. I was specialising in refrigerated meat and Greenland is a cold place. Also, the name sounds healthy, cool and cold – instead of sounding hot or something from the desert. It is unusual name I'll admit. People always asked me why it was called Greenlands. I used to buy livestock and do the kill at Goulburn. Then I used to pack it in Drummoyne and export it, or sell some to the restaurants and hotels we supplied. If our export sales didn't have enough margin, I'd switch to the local market. If the export price was good, I would put the price up on local sales, lose a few customers and stick to the export market when it had better profits. I have always played that game.

I always admired successful people, wondered how they were doing it and tried to learn from them by talking to them. One fellow who was a close friend to me was A.J. Bush. Alfred John Bush used to own about fifty butcher shops. Today, his son is friends with my son, Anthony. They go out and socialise together. I don't know if his father is still alive as we lost contact over the years. I used to always want to be like him.

I noticed when I increased the size of my business, I did spread myself thin. I couldn't offer the same service that I wanted to and I couldn't control the money 100%, and I noticed the best way was to stay smaller and put my profits into buying more real estate.

Greenland Meat was owned by me and two other fellows, John and Bill Halias, who used to run a restaurant in the city – they wanted to go into the meat business. I also gave them a small shareholding and we were doing all right for a little while. Bill worked with me in Trangie – he was a quiet sort of fellow. They were supposed to go out and talk to the customers and collect the money at all hours of the day, like I used to do. Now that I was married with young children, I wanted to be home more and get them to manage things.

We did well and we were making quite a lot of money from the restaurants we supplied in the city, but people get greedy. You give them 'x' and then they want that plus more. You give them a yard, and they want three yards. You give them three yards, they want a mile. Often, that's the way life is. These are the things you experience in life as well as business. But what can you do? If you want to finish up living peacefully without any headaches, then you may not end up with very much at all. My wife, Maria, doesn't care for business, she doesn't care about money. All she wants is to live and live peacefully – just like her father. Maria puts up the 'V' sign with her fingers, like Winston Churchill, and says, "All I want is peace! Peace and quiet!" That's what she wants.

I made an agreement with John and Bill that because I was running other businesses, I wasn't going to spend all my time over at Greenland, while they had to spend 100% of their time there and nowhere else. One day I went there and found John throwing meat trays on the floor. Personally, I found him to be a bit pretentious because he went through school in Greece, and thought he was above Bill. Neither Bill nor I ever had much of an education.

"Are you cranky mate?" I asked John. "What's the matter with you?"

"I'm working my bloody guts out and sharing the money with you blokes and you're taking most of the money." This was true – I owned most of the shares.

"But that was the deal, John. I have other businesses to look after and bought my other business to this one – when we didn't have a business. I also brought my customers from the Naremburn shop here. What are you complaining about?"

We argued and he had one complaint after another. Even though I supplied the capital and took all the risk, I was not given any credit for this. There was one word after another until I finally said, "Mate, do you want to split?"

Then they tried to take me to court to claim the hours they used to work and that they were entitled to more money. The solicitor did a good job because he said that if they wanted to expand anywhere else they'd have to get my permission, because I had control of the shares. I was my own boss. That stopped there, otherwise I would have finished up in an expensive court case. John was actually living in Drummoyne and a couple of months after that, he picked up the newspaper and as he was crossing the road he and another pedestrian were struck by a car. He died on the spot.

The other Drummoyne shop was vacant for a couple of years. Then I leased it to an Italian firm who spent half a million to renovate it and made it into a bakery and restaurant. I still own the site and only recently I was wondering how much their goodwill would be worth. My friend who dines there quite often lives one block away from it. He used to come to my place and play tennis every Saturday with a group of friends. I said to him, "Go in there and offer them $800,000 to buy the business."

My friend came back and told me the answer was 'no'; they'd been offered $1.5 million and wouldn't sell it. So, naturally, I knew how well they were doing and I increased the rent a bit higher as they could afford it.

That is the main thing when you are in business and you are self-made: you work in the business yourself and always keep an eye on the property you've bought. Before I put the rent up, I see how well the business is doing – if it is a fish shop, I see how much they sell, so I know straight away how much they are making, how many people working. If it is a butcher shop or a fish shop, each person should be taking $5,000 a week in sales each. So if you have ten employees, your takings should be $50,000 a week. If you take $50,000 and you are working on about 25% net, because they work on 50 or 60% gross, but 25% net, I know how much it makes. Then I say, well, I will take a little bit of that, so I will put the rent up. If they try to tell me they can't afford it, I put my formula down and I say, "Can you deny that? Show me your books – the proper books, not the ones you show to your accountant."

Chapter Nine

In 1969 I heard on the news that A.W. Anderson, a major meat exporter, had gone into receivership. As it happened, I knew the manager of the factory, Mr Paul Berner. One morning I saw him at the wholesale meat market in Homebush. Traditionally, all the meat buyers would purchase all the stock they wanted and then go to the cafe and have a bacon and eggs breakfast. I was aware that Paul had been brought out from Denmark to see what he could do to turn the business around. So when I saw him having breakfast, I went up to him and said, "Mate, I heard that Andersons has gone to the administrators."

He told me about all the problems they had been having and he did this in his very clear, very precise English – he might have been a Dane, but he spoke far better English than I did. "The problem is, Nick," he explained, "it costs us a lot of money to run the abattoirs." As well as that, the drought and a few other things had set the company back. Paul said the plan was to try to get out of debt with the administrators in charge. However, he pointed out, with the abattoirs and the Dulwich Hill factory losing a lot of money, the administrators may have no choice but to sell the business. He also informed me that the company didn't own the Dulwich Hill property – it was owned by the railway department. There was a long lease in place, with an option to extend it for another thirty years.

Then Paul asked if I was interested in buying the business. "Yes," I replied honestly, "but I don't know anything about export – the way you are doing it, selling overseas direct." I told him my experience of export was packing meat for brokers, who were locals, and then they on-sold it. He looked at me and said, "I think we should talk if you are interested."

"Okay. I am interested. Let's do that."

A.W. Anderson was a long-established company – it had been started by Alfred William Anderson in the 1940s – and after he died in 1956 various people ran it. It was an enormous enterprise which owned about four abattoirs all over the country and a meat-processing factory in Dulwich Hill.

Over one hundred people worked in the factory and on average the abattoirs slaughtered about 2,500 cattle per week. The problem was that they were losing money and the main cause of that was the company's abattoirs. Traditionally, abattoirs were very high-risk businesses. They were usually heavily unionised, expensive to run with high fixed costs, and prone to catastrophes such as drought, or floods, or disease. Right from the start I knew it would be a mistake to have anything to do with the abattoirs – if I was to buy the business, the official receivers would have to sell them off separately to someone else.

After giving it a lot of thought, I set up a meeting with Paul. Part of my reasoning was the fact that I actually love dealing with official receivers. I had found that in the past, if I talked to them man to man, they were good to deal with. Administrators don't like having to run companies – they prefer to pass on 'the mess' – at a price – to someone else. A lot of the time a company will go broke, but have assets such as real estate. So the banks sell the property and use that to get out of trouble. In this case, A.W. Anderson didn't own the property it operated from. The other advantage I had was that there were not too many buyers interested in taking it on. Les Holden in Trangie had taught me that once the profits stop, administrators will often sell the business at a heavily discounted price.

After a number of meetings, I offered the official receivers the $1.5 million purchase price they were asking for, but on a number of conditions. Firstly, I would pay a 10% deposit, with an option to buy or not to buy in twelve months' time. If I exercised the option to buy the business, I would then settle the sale. Or, the other option was that in twelve months' time I would simply walk away and lose my deposit. After a lot of umming and ahhing the official receivers agreed to my offer, except that I would have to pay them something every month. That seemed fair to me, and whatever I paid would come off the final price. The great advantage to me in this arrangement was that I had direct access to the cash flow of the business from the moment this agreement came into effect. Another part of the terms and conditions of sale with A.W. Anderson was that they would teach me how to do exports because I knew nothing about it. While they were still operating the business, A.W. Anderson employees working in the factory showed how to pack the meat for export to America, England and Japan. The main buyers were English – and it wasn't until much later that the Japanese became big buyers.

And so in 1970 I took over A.W. Anderson at 1 Hill Street, Dulwich Hill. The export manager was Dennis Carr. He showed us how to pack the meat into the cartons for export and various other facets of the export business. Dennis suggested that we print our own cartons under the name Andrews Meat Exports. I said to him, "Nobody overseas has ever heard of Andrews Meat Exports." I pointed out that A.W. Anderson had a good name overseas, and we should use that name when it came to exports. This had to be discussed with the official receivers and in the end the meat was put in boxes labelled 'A.W. Anderson's Meat, Australia packed by Andrews Meat Exports'.

I found Dennis Carr to be a very friendly person and extremely helpful. He had been working for A.W. Anderson ever since he was a kid. Over time we became friends and he showed me exactly what needed to be done exporting meat overseas. There was nothing worth knowing that he didn't know. Whenever one of the managers asked me questions I would say, "Don't ask me, ask Dennis."

After my first week of ownership I did my P&L. I did this every week in my businesses because when I was in Trangie I knew nothing about book-keeping until Les Holden, who was a Jewish gentleman, helped me out. Les taught me how to work out the profit and loss every week. Once, when the accountant was doing the books for the company I said to him, "You are about $34,000 short, mate."

"What do you mean?"

"It's not there. Your figures are out," I said.

The accountant was mystified. "How do you know?"

I am a great believer in double-checking. The accountant agreed to have another look at his figures and found it. When he wanted to know how I knew, I told him I did my own P&L. Even today, so many years later, I haven't changed. All my staff and assistants are working off computers because everyone works on computers. I don't have a computer on my desk. I still do my own P&L.

At the end of our first week, the Danish General Manager asked me how it had all gone. "Mate, no good," I replied. "I lost $800."

"Oh very good Nick, that's very good." "No, you didn't hear me – I lost $800."

Paul said, "I say 'very good' because we used to lose $14,000 a week. So that is very good Nick."

"I'm not in business to lose money Paul," I complained. "We had better improve, mate."

And improve we did. I was able to quickly see where there was waste, mismanagement and inefficiencies in the business and deal with it. There were over a hundred people working at Dulwich Hill of all nationalities – Greeks, Italians, Yugoslavs, Croatians. The thing I liked most about them was that they were hard workers, hungry for money. I offered them generous incentives and at a time when workers were happy with $500 a week, my men were regularly taking home $2,000 a week as they were paid per carcass quarter.

One of the reasons the business was so successful was partly because we prided ourselves on the quality of our meat. In Japan, for example, meat supplied by Andersons and Andrews Meat Exports was consistently bringing 2–2½% above average at the auctions. Dennis Carr taught us everything about how to pack, and how to keep the meat inspectors happy. We had our own inspectors looking for a hair, or a black spot, or just plain dirt. We never had a claim against us and this is how we developed such a good name. Efficient boning is important because if it's not done properly, too much of the product goes to waste for it to be profitable. There are sixteen main items in every beef carcass – chuck, blade, topside, sirloin, tenderloin, round, brisket and so on. With cattle, when you slaughter them, you lose about 40% in guts, skin and liquids. Then, after two days in the coolroom, all the pores are closed; you take the carcass into the factory to bone it and pack it. When you bone out, then you weigh the meat and you have still about 30% bones and fat. So from about 800 kilograms live, you lose through processing about half that weight. How much waste there was depended a lot on the skills of our workers and managers. I kept a close eye on this and enjoyed making the whole business more efficient and more profitable.

When you don't own a farm and run your own livestock, but want to sell a superior quality of meat, it becomes very important to have at least two good livestock buyers. That was their world – buying livestock – they knew virtually nothing about anything else. These livestock buyers knew just by looking at cattle in a yard everything there was to know about them – condition and quality of meat, how much product we would end up with after they had been processed – and things like that. These buyers also knew all the tricks of the trade. They could tell if one of the auctioneers had made the cattle drink before the auction to add water-weight to the selling price.

I paid the buyers $1.50 per head – that was it – nothing more. They drove their own cars and paid their own expenses. In those days it was a good job – $1.50 a head on 1,200 cattle a week is $1,800 a week. Wages in the country at the time were one third of that. They would go to the auctions and buy the cattle we needed. They would then arrange to send the stock to the abattoirs. My instructions to them were to buy 1,200 head every week until further notice. I'd tell them the price I wanted the carcasses landed at in Dulwich Hill and they had to work out how much they would buy the livestock for, how much they'd sell the hides for, how much they'd get for the offal and what the margin would be. It all had to come under budget.

I used to have a meeting with them every Saturday. I gave them a green accounts book with three columns – again using the same system I was taught by Les Holden from Trangie. We would discuss areas where there hadn't been enough rain, and what the impact would be on the cattle there. They knew that if they paid too much for the stock, I would complain. When I did this they'd reply, "We can't get them any cheaper Nick." "Well bloody try," I'd say. "Go and steal them if you have to. That is your job – I don't care what you do, don't come back with the same losses." But they were good men and they always came through with my request. While I might have put on the pressure, they managed to buy the meat cheaper for me and I never sacked anyone.

Every morning I used to turn my transistor radio on at eleven o'clock for the rural report on the ABC. They'd give details about the cattle and sheep sales results from all over Australia: how much they were selling for – steers, cows, calves, lambs – everything. By doing this I kept in touch with the market and knew when there were new developments and when there were threats. In the back of my mind, I kept reminding myself that taking over A.W. Anderson was a big thing for me. If I didn't manage it properly, if I made a mess of things, I knew I would regret it; that I had somehow let an opportunity slip through my fingers.

BOOK SEVEN

The Empire Grows

Chapter One

There is no doubt in my mind that the purchase of A.W. Anderson was what the Americans call a 'game changer' for me. That one deal changed everything. We as a business moved from one league into a different game altogether. The risks were greater, but the opportunities seemed unlimited.

As part of the takeover arrangements, I was responsible for the payment of all incoming accounts – paying for livestock, paying wages and so on. But the best part was that I was also paid each week with all the revenue that had come in. Every Friday I used to pick up from the AWA official receivers a cheque which was usually between $250,000 and $330,000. The accepted payment practice then was to pay for livestock every fourteen days, and other suppliers every twenty-one days. This meant that before I paid out a single cent, I usually had close to $1 million in the bank. And the P&L showed that we were averaging over $50,000 a week in profit.

During this time, the Japanese began to buy more and more of our meat. They had a government body in Japan, the Livestock Industry Promotion Corporation (LIPC), which controlled the meat import market. We had to sell to the LIPC, which would then auction the meat. The reason the Japanese did this was to make sure they controlled the price of meat coming in so that they protected their own farmers. If it was too cheap, their farmers would not be able to compete. Because of this, the prices paid by the Japanese were always high, and good for business.

The quality of our meat was so good that customers would often ask if we had our own abattoirs. When I told them we didn't own any abattoirs, they'd say, "Oh. You must have your own cattle farms?"

"No, we don't have any farms either." "Where do you buy your cattle?"

"At the auctions. In Newmarket in Melbourne, which is the biggest in Australia, they sometimes sell 20,000 cattle a day. Other markets might sell 4,000 or 5,000 cattle a day."

My gut feeling was that our clients were disappointed that we were not a very big company with our own farms and abattoirs. But my strategy made sense. Owning and running a farm is hard work and there are lots of risks. Not only that, I knew nothing about farming. Even if I had my own farm and killed about 1,200 cattle a week, the farm itself would have to carry 40,000 or 50,000 head of stock to produce that. And if there was a problem – such as a drought – then we'd have a farm with stock which would not be up to the standard expected by our customers and be able to fulfil our orders. By purchasing cattle at auction, we could pick and choose and look for the best product. One of the reasons that A.W. Anderson went bust was because of the cost blow-out at the abattoirs that they owned and operated. Sometimes, when A.W. Anderson had supply problems, they had to bring their cattle from one end of Australia to the other to keep their abattoirs operating. This often meant the stock were half-dead before they even reached their destination.

Above: One of the first delivery vans we owned being driven by Leo in 1955 – we then traded as Andrews Meat Company.

Above: Myself at the airport circa 1985.

Above: One of the exhibitions promoting our company, Andrews Meats.

Above: Two business associates I invited to my daughter Marietta's 21st birthday party in a Kings Cross hotel. I mentioned them in my speech as "the flying Dutchmen". I was negotiating beef exports with them to Holland and Greece.

Marietta

Also, always in the back of my mind was the Coles/Woolworths model. They didn't own anything, or manufacture anything. Their mentality was to let someone else worry about that and instead focus solely on the most profitable way to sell to their customers. In my time in the industry, I had seen a few public companies go under a few years after their board decided to 'vertically integrate'. Despite what they may say in public, there isn't that much fallout when a board makes such a bad decision – sometimes they don't even lose their board seat – and so the consequences aren't overly drastic. It's entirely different when it's your own money you're playing with. And so, I knew we had a good business.

My gut feeling was that sometimes we were pushed to the side because we were too small for the auctioneers. To fix this, I hired a professional photographer. Then I found out from the stock and station agents who had the best cattle and sent the photographer off to take photos of these beautiful animals. We then used these photographs in our advertising. Another thing I did was to purchase some second-hand trucks from Peter's Ice Cream. We repainted the trucks and had our name, Andrews Meat Exports, on each truck, alongside photographs of ships and photos of the stock being unloaded. Whilst I might not have been one of the big boys, I did promote us so that we always appeared bigger than we actually were. Buying A.W. Anderson was a big step forward for me and my company. Over time we developed a good name and our reputation became second to none.

Left: Marietta cutting the cake, with a little help from Mum and Dad, on her 21st birthday.

Previous page: Visiting my brother Bill (right) in 1974 and me (left) standing outside the house in Porovitsa where we were born and grew up in until I left for Australia in 1947.

At first we traded as Andrews Meat, and then Andrews Meat Exports, and Andrews Meat NSW, and Andrews Meat Co which later became known as Ampco. With A.W. Anderson I was very lucky. Its cash flow was very strong, and with their problem abattoirs no longer our concern, it consistently made a profit. At the end of the first twelve months, I was able to complete the purchase of that business.

Chapter Two

I used to walk from my office in Elizabeth Street, through Hyde Park and up to Kings Cross to the Hyde Hotel. That is where we had our Rotary Club meetings every Wednesday. At every meeting there was a guest speaker, and this encouraged me because I felt that as a young man in this country I had a lot to learn about life, about business, and the way of the world. Also, the guest speakers were interesting – one week it could be the commissioner of police – and the next week the mayor of Sydney. Just by listening to them I learnt about their work and their philosophies of life. The thing that attracted me to Rotary was that you could educate yourself, meet people and help those less fortunate people in the community. Over the years I used my home, or to be more exact, my tennis court, as a way of raising money for Rotary. We'd organise a tennis day and put on a free barbeque with free drinks. Those who came had to pay, and all of the money went to Rotary. They were great fun.

At our Rotary meetings I was like a giant sponge soaking up the stories of the members and learning as much as I could. There was only one thing that worried me. Each week a member was asked

Above: Helmos Award, 2005.

by the president to give a speech about his or her profession to the rest of the members. I was really nervous about being asked to do this because I found most of the speakers very entertaining and informative and could not imagine what I could say that would interest anyone. And so for a long time I managed to avoid being called on by the president to make a speech, but eventually my luck ran out. Finally, the president pulled me aside, put his hand on my shoulder and asked me to deliver next week's address.

Being a proud Greek man, I accepted this invitation to speak as if it was something I had been waiting to do. It was only after the president walked away that the smile disappeared from my face. I felt I was in a terrible situation. Really, all I was in life was a butcher. I had no experience in public speaking or addressing the public. What was I supposed to speak about which would interest these intelligent people? How to cut a rump steak? Not only that, I was very self-conscious of the fact that I spoke a form of broken English and that my schooling was interrupted about a fifth of the way through by World War II. The last thing I wanted to do was embarrass myself in front of these very interesting and influential people.

The president had suggested that I speak on the topic of the meat industry in Australia. As luck would have it, at that time I had a fellow working for me who was very clever. He was a Frenchman by the name of Bernard. Bernard was my export manager and he was very knowledgeable about things like meat and abattoirs. He had been a great help to me in the early days of the business. In fact, Bernard was one of those men who was good at everything – if you asked him something about cars, he could tell you the answer; if you asked him about art or history, he could talk about it for ages. He was brought up in the French school system. Bernard had something that I didn't have – a great education – and I had something that he didn't have – great business sense. Together we made a pretty good team.

In those days, the MLA (Meat & Livestock Association) had offices in North Sydney. After discussing my task of giving a speech to the Rotary Club, I suggested to Bernard that he go down to the MLA's head office and find out what they had available on the history of meat exporting from Australia. The great thing about Bernard was that he was a perfectionist. He went down to the MLA and asked them to give him all the books they had on the history of the industry. A couple of days later, he came back loaded up with notes, books and a projector.

When Bernard read to me the results of his research I became very excited. It was terrific. I got up and kissed him. I said to him, "Mate, this is amazing. No one in Rotary will ever know where this came from, because even I didn't know and I'm a butcher." Bernard admitted he didn't know about any of this either.

This is the rough outline of the beautiful speech Bernard worked up for me after his research at the MLA.

"After the English had been bringing convicts over to the penal colony of New South Wales for some time, and the population had been built up, they decided they would start bringing cattle over. Obviously, there were no cattle in this country before European settlement. There were ten breeds of cattle that were imported; the main ones being Jersey cows, English Longhorn, Aberdeen Angus, British White, Ayrshire, South Devon and Butler Galloway. After the cattle industry had been built up, the first abattoir started operations in 1824 on a harbour-side site in Mosman. Later this place became famous as the site for Taronga Zoo.

"After the slaughtermen killed the sheep and cattle, they used to hang their skins and hides on wire clotheslines strung out along

Balmoral Beach. They drove posts into the sand and the wire went through the posts all the way across the beach.

"Sometimes when I go for a stroll along Balmoral Beach, I think what this must have looked like. It's hard for us to image this happening today, but life was very different then. Firstly, only poor people lived on the beach or close to the water. The interest in living close to the water or on the harbour only started to happen in the 1950s. Back in the 1800s, people didn't go to the beach, and swimming – or public bathing as it was called – was outlawed. Where you see today all those magnificent homes and the grounds of the zoo were the yards and slaughtering houses of the abattoir. Imagine what would have happened if you had a great-grandfather who thought it might be a good idea to buy a few acres of land there. It would be worth a lot of money today.

"In those days there were mosquitos and other insects breeding in the waters, so they used to dry the skins before they packed them and exported them. The freezers were located in Manly and all the meat was cut in the A.W. Ingles butcher shop in George Street, opposite Town Hall. Back in those days, the butcher shops had columns outside with red rings around them to tell people that it was a butcher shop, a bit like you see with barber shops today.

"As you can well imagine, ships coming to Australia were heavily loaded. These big sailing ships carried convicts, free settlers, as well as food supplies. However, Australia didn't have any commodities to export, and that was a problem for the ship owners. Their ships were too light to be able to sail across the ocean properly. If they did this, they risked being smashed up in the ocean. The ships had to be weighed down with some form of ballast. In the beginning it was decided to use cobblestones to weigh them down. This is why many of the streets in London were paved using cobblestones which

Above: The Rotary Foundation Paul Harris Fellow Award I received in appreciation of tangible and significant assistance given for the furtherance of better understanding and friendly relations between peoples of the world.
Left: Making my Rotary speech on the History of the Meat Industry in Australia from the beginning of first delivery to England, which was tested by Queen Victoria.

came from Australia. This practice really bolstered that industry in Europe. When Australia was ready to start shipping meat though, they no longer needed cobblestones to weigh the ships down. They stocked the meat onto the ships bound for London, where the first meat from Australia was tasted by Queen Victoria."

Like any person giving a speech for the first time, I was quite nervous when I started but I soon concentrated on what I had to say and things settled down for me. When I made the speech, I brought with me one of the girls from my office and she was changing the film slides which illustrated my story. One of the Rotary members at Kings Cross was a very wealthy man who wasn't all that popular. His name was Ralph and he was the sort of person who kept to himself. If you didn't talk to him, he would walk past you without ever saying hello. I don't know what his occupation was, but he was a wealthy man. If he sat at the table for lunch, everyone would go to another table. Sometimes he waited for everyone to sit down and when he saw an empty chair he would slip into it. This fellow was sitting in the middle of the hall.

When I finished, there was polite applause from the audience. Everyone was so happy to hear all of this because they found it interesting and hadn't known much about the history of this industry before. I then said, "I have still a few minutes left for questions." Ralph raised his hand and asked, "Nick, I hope you don't mind. I'm going to ask you a personal question. You don't have to answer if you don't want to."

"It's all right Ralph, tell me."

"Where did you receive your education?"

Without thinking I replied, "Oxford University." There were a few shocked looks around the room. Then I added, "of Trangie; the Oxford University of Trangie." Everybody got up and clapped and cheered: "Good on you mate!"

Poor Ralph, he just looked around and walked straight out the door. I felt a bit small that I had embarrassed him like that. I shouldn't have said what I said. But I was pleased that my talk at the Rotary meeting had been so well received. I had done what was asked of me, and met the challenge without making excuses. For me Rotary was a chance to meet other businessmen, to learn something and to be involved in a charity which did so much behind the scenes.

Above: An award, "Food for Sport Supply Program", for supplying meat and fish for the Sydney Olympic Games, 2000.

Above: At Nick Greiner's home during his campaign to become NSW State Premier. We became close friends during our time as we were both members of Kings Cross Rotary.

Certificate of Appreciation

Mr N Andrews

Thank you for supporting the RFDS since 2001

Your ongoing commitment is enabling us to fly further, helping to close the gap between country and city healthcare.

With your support we will continue to bring the finest care to the furthest corners of Australia.

Greg Sam
Chief Executive Officer

Above: Royal Flying Doctors Certificate for Supporting the RFDS since 2001.

Chapter Three

I've spent almost a lifetime working in the meat industry, and in that time I have met and worked with many wonderful people as well as some wild characters. But, like any business, it does have its dark side. Sometimes, if you're not careful, things can go wrong. One of the things I didn't do was try and do everything myself. I saw others go down this road and end up broke.

Make no mistake about it, working in the meat industry is physically very demanding and I could probably count on the fingers of one hand the number of meat workers I thought were lazy. They worked hard, but some of them would take advantage of any weakness in your setup. It was very easy for a dishonest employee to pick up a box of meat and put it in the boot of his car. On a high-quality cut, a box of meat could be worth $500 – so it was very tempting. All they had to do was then take it to a restaurant and sell it for $300 cash.

We used to have the trucks come to the factory every day to pick up the fat and bones. All the fat and bones would be pushed to one side of the boning table and then dumped into a basket. All a meat worker had to do was make sure no one was looking and throw a strip fillet into the boning basket and put the bones on top. Then when the truck came to collect the fat and bones they'd dig the fillet up out of the basket and put it in their car. One time I caught some blokes in my factory doing this. They'd managed to hide a couple of sirloins each. They got the shock of their lives when I called the police. They were caught red-handed, but claimed they didn't know the sirloins had been 'accidentally' put in with the fat and bone. None of them were charged; all I wanted to do was send a message – that I would not tolerate theft – and it worked. After all, my father was a policeman for all of his life.

I used to have my own tricks up my sleeve for increasing productivity among the workers. This was something I had to do when our running costs were becoming too high. I'd call the manager, point to someone and say, "That fellow over there, go and pay him and sack him."

The manager would look at me amazed. "But that's Harry – he's our best slicer!"

"Sack him!" I'd say. "He might be good, but he's too expensive for us."

Gossip would quickly go around the factory that I had sacked Harry, a Greek and a good worker. Some would even remember that I was the best man at Harry's wedding. They couldn't believe it. People would think: "Jesus! If they are sacking him, where does my job stand?" And then I'd spread the word that our costs were too high and that we might have to start shedding more jobs.

Of course, I was not crazy enough to sack someone like Harry. I'd tell him to take a month off and then go and work for us at my other meat factory. "If anyone from here sees you there," I'd explain to Harry, "just say that Vic, the manager there, gave you a job against my orders." Straight away, after the 'sacking' of Harry, we would see productivity go through the roof at Dulwich Hill and the profits soar.

Chapter Four

For many years I had my office in Naremburn. In the mid-1970s, Herb Pearl from A.J. Cunningham – an American company – rang me and said he was coming to see me to arrange more business importing meat into America – if the price was right. I said, "Do you remember where my office is from the last time you were here?" He had come out to Australia about ten months earlier. He laughed and said, "How could I forget? Your office is on top of a garage, right?"

Which it was. My head office was a little building in the corner and the garage below us used to spray radiators. Herb Pearl was laughing. He thought this was funny, but I didn't think it was funny. This embarrassed me. For the first time it occurred to me that I didn't have a nice office to run my business from and to have a place to conduct my meetings. It so happened that around this time I had seen advertisements for a building for sale on Elizabeth Street, two doors down from the Ritz Hotel.

After I got off the phone from Herb Pearl, I drove into the city to see the agents, Raine & Horne, and purchased the building. It was seven stories high and not far from the Hellenic Club. People will not believe it when I tell them I paid $750,000 – for a seven-storey building in the heart of the Sydney CBD. Today, you would be lucky to find a one-bedroom unit at that price in the city. I then spent $250,000 renovating the top two floors which were to be my business headquarters. My office was plushly decorated and all the areas were fitted out by interior designers. We had a one-bedroom apartment there for guests, as well as a rooftop terrace. I spent the next fourteen years conducting business from this office.

And as for Herb Pearl? Well, I have never seen him since. Having a smart, beautiful office was not always good for business. A lot of people used to come down there, have a look around and think to themselves: "Nick is making too much money – he's trying to screw me over!" It's the same if you show off by buying a Rolls Royce and driving it in front of your customers. They think you're making too much money. It's only natural they would think: "How the hell am I going to get a fair deal out of him?" But if people see you driving around in a Holden Commodore, they say to themselves: "Well, he seems to be doing okay. I will help this fellow – he's a good guy. He's humble. He will appreciate it one day."

Four years later, in 1980, my daughter Marietta was working with me after she finished school. I was having a sandwich in the back office and I opened the back door to get some fresh air in as it was a bit hot. As I sat there I was looking down at a property in Castlereagh Street. I noticed it had a rusted roof – a sure sign that it was neglected, possibly not wanted. It was only a double-storey building. I said to myself, "One day it will make a good development." So I said to Marietta, "Go down and have a look and find out what the number is of that property. Take $15 with you and go to the City Council and find out who the owners are." She went down and she did all that. It belonged to the Uniting Churches. I rang them up and asked them if they were selling the property. By coincidence their governing committee had been actually talking about selling the building. They wanted $350,000. "Okay," I replied, "send me the contract. I'll buy it."

That same day, or a couple of days later, I was driving to my office in the city when I heard on the news that properties in the city were going up. The news item mentioned there had been a recession for a few years, but now properties were going up by as much as 30%. Unfortunately, the news item also mentioned Castlereagh Street. I say 'unfortunately' because I knew someone from the Uniting Churches would hear this and decide they wanted more for the property.

I had agreed to buy it for $350,000. But the contract had not arrived and no deposit had been paid. Experience taught me that often a man will honour a verbal agreement, but never a committee. Sure enough, they asked for a valuer to value the building and came back to me asking for $430,000. I didn't hesitate to buy it. After we took it over, we rented it out to a fitness studio.

A lot of people thought I made a bad deal because I paid too much for such a low rental. My strategy was not rental income at all, but something that I call 'marriage value'. If you have this one block of land with an old building on it, you won't be able to do much with it. It doesn't have a car park, so the council will not let you go very high if you redevelop. But, if you buy the block next door, and have two blocks side by side, you have 'marriage value'. Having two blocks virtually doubles the value of each block. Any developer looking at this would see we had one block on Elizabeth Street and backing on to that a block in Castlereagh Street. They could easily join the blocks and can justify building higher as well as going underground and building a car park.

I am a long-term investor. If you are the sort of person who is going to borrow the money – up to 60% of what it is worth – then to me this strategy is too risky. The bank will charge you more interest. My method is to try and keep my borrowings low – not more than 15 to 18% of my assets. This means that I have a lot of titles unencumbered. If one bank doesn't give me a fair go, I can go to another bank and show them my unencumbered titles and they welcome me with open arms. That is my advice to people who want to get ahead – buy small properties, don't borrow big sums of money, and look for marriage value.

Chapter Five

In 1976 I became aware that another meat company, K.N. Harris, was in the hands of official receivers. As you would know by now, this was news which sparked my interest. At that time, I was doing very well at A.W. Anderson and Australian meat was in high demand around the world – it was hard to understand how anyone could go broke. But there is always a story. A son of Mr Harris went and made a deal to supply fresh meat to some supermarkets in America. It was a deal which looked good on paper, but brought them undone. Somewhere in the fine print the American had inserted this clause which said that any shipped product which was past its use-by date was to be put back in the freezer for the exporter to take back to Australia. It sounds fair enough – the only problem being that it's illegal. By law any meat exported from Australia cannot be returned. You can only bring it back if it's marked for dog food, but not for human consumption. Apparently, some of these unscrupulous Americans manipulated this clause and K.N. Harris found themselves with large quantities of meat stored in freezers in America that nobody wanted.

Because of this situation, the business itself was now worthless. I was only interested in the property which was located at 40–44 Harris Street, Pyrmont. It was the last property down towards the harbour on Harris Street and in my opinion, very valuable real estate.

I indicated that I might be interested and went to talk to the official receivers in the boardroom of the Hellenic Club in town. We met there because my office in Elizabeth Street, was being renovated at the time. There was a solicitor and an accountant there, and I could tell from how they were behaving that they were starting to become nervous. I suspected there were few others interested and it always has to be remembered that these official receivers are often worried whether they will ever see their own fees paid. After a bit of discussion, I along with members of my family put in an offer similar to that which I had made for A.W. Anderson five years earlier. From memory, I made an offer on my terms and conditions – an option to buy in twelve months and rental payments up until then. Of course, they thought the offer was way too low and it took many meetings to justify the price I was offering them. In the end, they accepted our offer and we took over the property and business.

After we took over K.N. Harris, I did much the same as I had done at Dulwich Hill with A.W. Anderson – brought costs under control, lifted productivity and brought the business back to profitability. Work went on at K.N. Harris for the next ten years. Then, Premier Neville Wran came up with the idea of developing this area west of the city centre into the precinct it is today, Darling Harbour. Our site was near where the Star Casino now is. To develop this area, the government needed our site. The state government and Sydney City Council gave me a notice to vacate. They were going to resume the property as it was going to become part of their Darling Harbour development. Their offer was about the same price I had paid for the business and the property of K.N. Harris ten years earlier. In a meeting to discuss this, I said to an official from Sydney City Council, "Is that your best offer?"

"Yes."

"Has your mother got other smart kids like you?" I asked. He didn't like the sound of that and said nothing. But, we have to laugh sometimes! The pressure on me to accept their offer was great, but I refused.

Instead, I spoke to a QC from Mosman. He was more than helpful. Acting on his advice, we decided to lodge a DA (development application) with the council to enlarge the factory by putting freezers up in the car park in the rear. The land was about 2,500 square metres. It was a lot of land and more than enough to permit this under the existing council regulations. We submitted a DA to extend the factory with a large freezer which would reduce the traffic and trucks movements on Harris Street by 70%.

Experts were engaged to attest to this. We didn't have a blast freezer and we were packing for export as well as for the local market, supplying hotels and restaurants. When we used to pack we used to send at least three or four trucks a day to the freezers, which was Sydney Cold Stores in Harris Street near Broadway. The reason there were so many trucks was because the inspectors would not let us pack any more than three layers of boxes on top of each other in the truck.

Our DA argument was that if we had a large blast freezer, we could stack up to twenty tonnes at a time and would eliminate all this truck movement and extra labour and so on. Our proposal had a lot going for it and I was prepared to spend a lot of money with the experts to support it. This was all set out in the DA as if we were seriously going to do this. The reality was that we knew it was never going to happen as the news of the Darling Harbour project was all over the newspapers.

My QC explained to us that according to the law the council had forty days to respond to our DA. If I didn't receive refusal or approval, that meant that they hadn't dealt with my application within the specified forty days, and on day forty-one I could issue a summons demanding the council respond to my DA. From the day we lodged our DA, I was counting every day that passed until the day when we reached the magic number of forty. I could hardly believe my luck. Typically, the council had failed to stick to their own deadlines.

And so on day forty-one, I personally hand-delivered a summons to Sydney City Council for not acting within forty days to pass or reject our DA.

I rang my QC and told him the news: "Mate, they have got the summons." "Great!" he said. "Now leave it to me."

My QC was in the newspapers at that particular time for another reason. There was some domestic dispute between his daughter and her husband and she went home to her parents. The son-in-law knocked on the front door demanding to see his wife. My QC exchanged words with the son-in-law and then invited him to step on to the front lawn and sort it out like a man. Next minute there was a quick exchange of punches and the young bloke was on the lawn and my QC was standing over him. When I heard all about this I said, "You are a father with balls!"

"My little girl was crying inside and this fellow comes along and wants to take over my house," he explained.

"But your position as a QC," I said, "did you worry about the publicity?"

"No. I didn't think about it at that moment, not for a second. My mind went blank and all I wanted to do was punch him up because she was an unhappy girl. Nobody does this to my girl – I will shoot him if I have to!" My QC was an interesting character.

We finished up in the Land and Environment Court which was in the American Express building on the corner of George and King Streets. It was quite a big case and there was a lot of media attention. They knew they could not complete their Darling Harbour project without my land – and the delay was costing them a hell of a lot more money than it was going to cost them to pay me the extra amount I was asking for. At some stage the state government dropped out of the case – they didn't want to deal with it – and left it to the council. It took us two years and although it cost a lot of money in legal fees, we won. The council had to pay their own costs, win or lose, and so did I. There were three judges and they all passed a harsh judgement on Sydney City Council in our favour. The council was ordered to pay us four times higher than their original offer.

But before I accepted their offer, I said to the lawyers for the council, "I want the money now and I want a two-year lease, $10 a year and you pay all the outgoings for the factory because you are now the owner. I want a two-year lease so I can go and build another factory to relocate my business." They had little choice but to agree to my terms.

Chapter Six

When I lived in Trangie as a young man, it never ceased to amaze me that there were people who were almost starving, but still had enough money to be able to afford cigarettes. I couldn't believe what the hell they were smoking for. My uncle Sam never smoked and he was very strict about people smoking. In those early years just after the war ended, tobacco was restricted. You were only allowed to buy one pack of cigarettes a week, because the government had arranged it so that shops were supplied by quota. Our shop used to have tobacco, cigarettes and pipes locked up behind the counter.

Some customers would come in, but didn't have enough money to buy a full packet of cigarettes. So they used to ask me to break a packet and sell them just ten cigarettes. Later on, the cigarette companies started making packs of ten, but this was long after I left Trangie.

So there was the influence of my uncle and also my father. Even during the war he didn't smoke – and this was unusual for any man at that time and highly unusual for a Greek policeman. I used to think that war made heroes out of some, cowards out of many and smokers out of all of us. It stuck in my mind that cigarettes were a bad thing even though at the time most doctors smoked and didn't see any harm in it. However, I would serve customers who were long-time smokers and I'd notice that their teeth were going yellow.

After I came to Sydney at the age of twenty-one I spent a lot of my time in the company of butchers, and when they had their cup of tea at 'smoko' they would have a cigarette. They would light a cigarette, have a few puffs and then a customer would come in; so they'd leave it on the table and go and serve the customer. When they came back the cigarette would have burnt the table. I used to go crook on them to use an ash tray. Then they'd do that, but leave the ash tray full of old cigarettes and wouldn't clean it. It was something that I found filthy. However, as time went on it became harder and harder to resist the urge to smoke. When I did go crook at some of the butchers about this, they would offer me a cigarette from their pack as a way of getting me to calm down. "Nick, take a cigarette," they'd say. "Here, take it easy, have a smoke."

Sometimes I didn't want to embarrass them so I'd take it, smoke half of it and then put it out. I think you know how this story ends. This went on for a while, perhaps a year or more. I would be offered a cigarette by a friend or colleague and take another one. Then I started to worry that these people thought I was a bludger – that I was always taking their cigarettes – but never offering them one of mine. The solution to that was to buy my own packet of cigarettes. Now I could offer them a smoke.

The first pack I bought were called Rothmans. I remember the brand. Still, I was smoking only half and then throwing the rest away. Sometimes, I would only smoke two or three; and if I was perspiring heavily because of the heat, the packet would get wet

OPTOMETRY HOUSE 1924
OPTOMETRY HOUSE
Peters
ALEX HALE

and I'd throw it out. Even if it had eight or nine cigarettes left in it, I'd throw the lot into the garbage bin. Then I'd buy a new packet, to have one there just in case, but I never opened that one to smoke myself.

Slowly I started smoking and some ten years later I became addicted and was smoking between twenty and twenty-five a day. At one stage I started coughing and had a very sore throat. Maria sent me to our local doctor who referred me to a specialist. This doctor put me on a bed and put some tubes and wires down my throat with a torch. The next minute I coughed up what felt like half my lung and phlegm came out and went all over his face. "I am sorry doctor, I am sorry," I said apologetically.

"Don't worry, Nick. That is a good sign, don't worry."

Maria had to go off and do some shopping and we had arranged for her to pick me up at five. As I was the last patient of the day, the specialist said, "We're finished here." "What do you think doctor?" I asked.

"Everything is fine. What sort of work do you do?"

I told him my story. After listening for a while the doctor said, "That's very hard work. If I tell you not to smoke at all, it can cause you more problems than binge smoking. My advice is to not smoke the amount you are smoking. I am going to ask you as a doctor, to only smoke ten a day. If you can make it less, slowly, then your system doesn't miss it anymore, then give it away if you can. But to give it away altogether now, you are going to miss something and it will cause you more damage than smoking." He suggested that when I have a cigarette I should not smoke it right to the end; smoke three quarters and then toss it away because the nicotine

Left: The first office building I owned, at 247 Elizabeth Street, Sydney. My office was on the top two levels for fifteen years before moving it to Neutral Bay.

is at the back. His advice was to limit it to ten a day, and then to slowly wind it back.

I was satisfied with his advice. It meant that I could still have a cigarette. The doctor and I walked downstairs and we both stood there at the front of the building – he was waiting for his wife and I was waiting for mine. We stood there for a minute in an awkward silence. The doctor looked at his watch, then he looked at me. "The wife is not here yet mate. Let's have a cigarette."

With that he took a packet from his jacket and offered me one. Not long after this Maria arrived and she saw the doctor and me smoking together. "I can't believe what I'm seeing," she said. She looked at me very crossly and asked, "Did you give the doctor a cigarette?"

Above: In my Elizabeth Street office.

"No. He gave me one of his." Maria didn't know what to think.

When I saw that specialist, I had asked him about cigars. He said to me, "You can't cause too much damage because you can't smoke them too much – they're so short. They're a lot better than cigarettes." Because of that advice I switched to smoking little cigars. After that, I bought myself a pipe. I must say with a pipe I overdid it because with a pipe you have a couple of puffs and you put it down and it goes out, so you stack it and light it again, you puff it a couple of times and you put it down. This cycle goes on and on. This was going on at the office and at home.

However, at home I was not allowed to smoke inside, so I used to go out on the verandah to smoke, or downstairs to the billiards room. At home I have about eighty pipes. We have a cabinet which has all my pipes and all the toys I have picked up overseas when travelling. Another cabinet used to have all my guns, but you're not allowed to put them on display anymore. I took my guns out to the farm where they were all locked up.

I used to go to Hyde Park opposite my office and have a sandwich and a cigarette. One day a chap came up and said, "Can I sit on the bench?"

I said, "Yeah, no problem. Take a seat."

After a while this stranger asked, "How many cigarettes do you smoke a day?"

"About a packet – twenty."

"Twenty! In your life you are smoking away so many thousands of dollars." "I agree."

He then pointed at the buildings across from the park. "If you didn't smoke, you could own a property like that." Unfortunately, he was pointing at my property, the one where my office was located. I looked at him and asked, "Do you smoke?"

"No."

"Do you own a property like that?"

"No."

"Well, the property you're pointing to is mine."

"Oh, I am sorry." He almost died of embarrassment. For a while I wondered if this was someone who knew me and was playing games with me. But this fellow was a genuine stranger. He then stood up and walked away with his tail between his legs. I said, "No, don't walk away. Sit down. We will talk."

"No. I've made a blunder. I'll see you later."

He then kept walking and I never saw him again. What he had said was so true – it was just a pity it wasn't true in my case.

Times change, attitudes change, medical opinion changes and so does the law. The law became stricter on the issue of smoking around people. Sometimes the thought crossed my mind that one of the staff might sue me. I used to smoke a pipe fairly constantly. Then one day I ran out of tobacco and the shop I used to go to didn't have my brand. The tobacconist gave me another brand, but I didn't like it. This interrupted my smoking and little by little I began to enjoy the simple pleasure of breathing in fresh air. While I enjoy going outside on the verandah at the farm to read the paper and smoke a pipe, all these years later I am starting to get more enjoyment out of just breathing fresh air.

One of the things I did to relax was to go fishing with friends every year, sometimes twice a year, to the Great Barrier Reef off Queensland. On one of those trips I was fishing from a dinghy at low tide with a 70-pound line when something took my line and almost pulled me into the water. I was wearing gloves and they were smoking – then suddenly the line broke. We soon discovered what had been on the end of my line when this shark which was longer than our dinghy started circling us. I remember seeing it roll near the surface and this big eye check us out. My fishing companions and I quickly started the outboard and headed back to our boat.

The last time I went fishing we were caught in really bad weather with twenty-five metre waves. Everyone was scared and we all thought we were going to die. One of the fellows managed to get us into Gladstone Harbour. From there I caught a seaplane out and said to myself, "My fishing days are over."

Above: Once or twice a year I'd fly to Gladstone, Queensland with up to ten friends and hire a fishing boat. We'd take about eight hours to reach the Great Barrier Reef, where we'd fish for two weeks. In that time we caught between two and four tonne of fish (clean-weighed after filleting,) with the exception of Red Emperor. We would divide up our catch among ourselves and store it in freezers in Sydney.

Chapter Seven

I operated out of my office in Elizabeth Street for fourteen years. Then, in about 1987, developers made us a good offer and I moved my office to Mosman. At that time I thought I wanted to slow down and retire. We owned two houses on Stanton Road, and I moved the office into the guest house next door. Around this time, I transferred to my brothers the Dulwich Hill business so I could concentrate on development.

One of the valuable investments I had made was to purchase 116–118 Miller Street, North Sydney, in 1979. That year Australia experienced its first credit squeeze. Construction halted and cranes were left hanging idle across the city. This happened in the middle of my negotiations to buy 116–118 Miller Street, a property known as the 'Stramit Building', as it housed a company originating from Melbourne which sold ceiling tiles. The building was in bad shape and was in desperate need of renovation. It was located next door to the Northpoint Tower which is still there today. I made an unbelievably low offer. Three months later, after agreeing to several conditions and a slight increase, my offer was accepted.

Not long after that, I happened to be on a family holiday cruising the Greek islands on the ship *Stella Solaris*. One day I met a fellow called Marc Anthony, who was an entertainer. He was a trim, well-presented, likeable and approachable young man who said that he had worked at Caesars Palace in Las Vegas with the living legend of show business, Frank Sinatra.

Marc and I had a few discussions over breakfast and dinner and he told me that Frank Sinatra wanted to open a club in Sydney. The idea for this club would be to bring out entertainers focused on a particular ethnic group – they would bring out Greek entertainers for all the Greek immigrants – and then follow that up with bringing out Italian entertainers for the Italian immigrants and so on. I noticed that when Marc Anthony mentioned the name

Above: On our departure from the *Stella Solaris*, saying goodbye and thank you to the Captain. We became good friends and suppliers of meat to the cruise line for many years after.

'Frank Sinatra', he did it in a very matter-of-fact way – not like someone who was a name-dropper.

This club idea seemed perfect for my new North Sydney purchase as the economy was down and it was proving difficult to lease it. I told Marc about the building and that I thought it could be converted into a club fairly easily. There was also plenty of parking at night in the commercial building next door. When I told him this, Marc seemed very interested and said he would mention it to Frank when he spoke to him next. He said this all so calmly that it did make me wonder if he really knew Frank Sinatra.

One day we disembarked onto the island of Mykonos and Marc said to me that he was going to call Frank and tell him about my Sydney club premises. I sat there while Marc was talking on the phone all the while saying to myself, 'Is it really Frank Sinatra on the other end of the line?' Then, Marc turned to me and handed me the phone. I must admit I was very nervous and spoke to this person who sounded exactly like Frank Sinatra. Even so, I had to make sure it was him and thought of something I could ask him which only the real Frank Sinatra could answer.

The last time Frank Sinatra came to Sydney, the promoters put on his concert at a terrible boxing stadium at Rushcutters Bay which had low ceilings, poor lighting and virtually no seating, which meant thousands of people had to stand up all night. So, when I was on the phone I mentioned that I was in the audience the last time he was in Sydney and would never forget that when he came on stage he said to the crowd, "Pleased to meet you all tonight in this …" I paused just before the end of the sentence and Frank Sinatra finished it with "… in this garage." It was such

Left: With the singer Marc Anthony, after speaking to Frank Sinatra on an island day trip break from the *Stella Solaris* cruise.

a funny thing to say and when he said this I knew for certain I was speaking to the real Frank Sinatra.

He liked my idea and we were all very excited about the club and continued talking about it for months afterwards. However, the contract negotiations dragged on longer than expected and at the same time the economy changed for the better and I had people wanting to lease the Miller Street property. In the end, I could not wait any longer and was forced to make a decision to lease the building and forget about the club. It was unfortunate that nothing eventuated with Frank Sinatra, but it did leave me with great memories of talking with one of the most popular and influential musical artists of the twentieth century.

The Miller Street building turned out to be a very good investment. I used to get a lot of developers coming down to see me to try and buy it – eventually the ANZ Bank bought it and they still have it today.

Everybody who was interested in Miller Street – agents and architects and developers – all came to the guest house in Mosman. I was doing business in thongs and shorts with my German Shepherd dog coming in and sleeping there. Some of the time I was lying down watching sport on television. Maria would be next door and would buzz me to say lunch was ready. In the beginning I thought it was fantastic. But having all those businessmen coming and going to my own home became too much. Also, I felt lonely, I felt depressed, I wasn't happy. I thought, "This is no good."

I also owned a property at 161–163 Military Road, Neutral Bay, which I had bought years ago. It was two shops – a butcher's shop and a florist shop. My son Harry had just finished university

Left: Me riding a donkey in Santorini.

Above: The building at 119 Miller Street North Sydney – where we planned to open a nightclub with Frank Sinatra.

Above: Our current Neutral Bay office property on Military Road.

Above: At home with my favourite German Shephard dog, Tammy at the back of our home in Balmoral. I used to walk her to Balmoral Beach every morning.

and had a Bachelor of Construction Management degree. He was interested in project development. "Pull it down," I told him, "and rebuild." The tenants were not doing so well. We asked them if they wanted to break their leases, and they accepted.

This property was also RTA affected. They wanted to resume about three metres from the front and were offering $40,000 compensation per shop. I hired an evaluator, an old chap named Bruce Shore, who used to work for the RTA. He was retired and living in Gosford. I met Bruce and liked him immediately. I told him the RTA said they'd compensate me for the metres lost from the front of the property. I asked Bruce to revalue the properties, but on the basis that I pulled the whole lot down. Strangely enough, this would make life easier for the RTA. Rather than resuming this particular section and then having to do restitution work on a remaining building, we would clear the site – better for them, better for us. Bruce liked my idea and negotiated with the RTA. We accepted their offer.

Harry had told me he wanted to be the project manager and 161–163 Military Road was his first project. We had a few disagreements – he is strong minded – but what do they say? "The apple never falls far from the tree." Although we lost three metres of frontage, he pulled down what had been a cheaply made building and replaced it with two well-built shops downstairs and offices upstairs for our family business.

One block further down Military Road I also owned a large property with seven shops. When the National Australia Bank (NAB) next door was put up for sale, I went to the auction and bought it. I didn't care what I paid. My strategy was that I could beat anybody in terms of getting value because of my belief in 'marriage value'. The Neutral Bay property is called Andrews House.

In the years ahead I have successfully purchased very valuable properties in Tweed Heads, Surfers Paradise and in Brisbane. Along with purchasing properties overseas, which I still own with my family.

I have been very fortunate during domestic and international travels, checking in with the managers for my real-estate properties. It has allowed me to see a lot of the world, sometimes squeezing in a break, but most of all I have learnt a lot. For example, Greece has Roman Law and, in comparison, Australia uses the Anglo-Saxon law. I like to think I will never stop learning.

Chapter Eight

If I sell meat to a customer in America, I sell it to them under terms and conditions known as CIF – carriage, insurance and freight. That means I pay the lot. They give me so many cents to the American dollar and I have to take a cover with the bank to cover my risk with the Australian dollar. Most of the time I used to sell to local meat brokers, because I was too busy to go overseas all the time. Meat brokers are like financial brokers – they offer you a certain price for your goods.

The Japanese companies used to have representatives in Sydney who would ring me up and ask, "Nick, how much for chuck and blade?" I would give them a price. The Japanese fellow would then complain, "Awwww, too much!" It didn't matter how much I quoted him he would always say it was too much. He'd try and haggle and after a few attempts to get it lower he'd say, "All right. Send me two containers."

"Where do you want it?" I'd ask, and they would name a port in the United States or Japan.

One time, the meat market in America collapsed – I can't remember why. But because these importers had committed themselves to my business at a certain price, they were looking for any excuse to put a claim on the supply of meat going to America. For example, they would claim $100,000 because the meat we supplied had way more fat than we had guaranteed. We supplied the trimmings for hamburger meat to be 95% lean and they claimed it was 85%. Because there was more fat in it, they claimed they were entitled to a discount. I couldn't accept this because when we pack every day in the factory, we have a machine which tests this in front of our quality and assurance officer.

My son Anthony is an officer of HACCP, a quality assurance system. If you're exporting or have a restaurant, or even have a food business, you have to have HACCP in place. In a restaurant the inspectors might come through once a week or once a month. When you have an export business, it's checked every day.

Anyway, the Americans were complaining and we had big problems. I flew to the United States but didn't tell them I was coming. I hired this fellow from New York who was an inspector. I employed him full-time to be with me and flew him everywhere with me.

He was a Greek fellow but American born, and he had a big name as being a tough inspector. My plan was to visit twelve cities in seventeen days. I went to San Francisco first and then to Cleveland; from there to Boston and then to Detroit and then up to Chicago; I went everywhere there was a claim. I would book into the hotel, settle in, make myself comfortable, do my homework and then call the company and tell them I wanted a meeting to inspect the meat.

There is a machine which is used to test the meat. A handful of meat is put in, and because the meat is frozen they have an electric drill, which is about as thick as a person's thumb, and they drill down in the middle in two or three places and bring up a tube of meat – like they do in the mines with soil or rock core samples.

The machine then cooks the meat with gas, and registers what percentage fat it is. Once it registers it, the machine then prints out a report. It is quick and accurate.

Of course, the Americans were shocked to see me on their doorstep, but they could not refuse us because they were the ones claiming our meat did not meet the specifications. In some cases, they had four container-loads of meat – about sixty tonnes – and wanted to argue about which meat we tested. Test after test we did, and the result was 95% or higher.

One of these companies even tried to substitute other cartons of meat for ours. They brought these cartons out which were labelled Andrews Meat Exports. The test came back at 85%. Then I noticed that where the carton had been strapped, there were two marks – the carton had been opened – the meat replaced with inferior meat – and the carton re-strapped. What gave it away was the two strap marks.

The Americans were furious – in some places we went they started shouting and screaming at us. But we kept our cool. I offered to pay for their time and also reminded them that I had come all the way from Australia and that a lot of money was at stake. The arguments with these companies were far from over, but my visit did give me the upper hand when it came time to negotiate.

To settle the whole thing, we offered them 10% of their claim on the basis they had been a good customer in the past and to give them something that they could accept. After all, they were losing a lot of money.

Chapter Nine

With two factories, I had the capacity to take big orders. I was doing business all around the world and always on the lookout for new opportunities. In the 1980s, Mikael Gorbachev became the General Secretary of the Communist Party of the Soviet Union and promised things were going to be different. He talked about the new policies of '*glasnost*', which means 'open-ness', and '*perestroika*', which means 'restructuring'. By chance, I had a friend whose cousin was working in the Russian government. He heard rumours that the Russians were considering importing large quantities of meat as a way of overcoming the infamous food shortages that they put up with. While I was digesting this news about possible sales to the Russians, my friend's cousin hit me with a bombshell! He believed that they were looking at importing over 150,000 tonnes of meat – an order worth around $300 million!

When I heard about the size of the order the Russians were thinking of making, I knew that it was far too much for any one company in Australia to supply. The only way to deal with this was to form a consortium. My plan was to contact the four largest meat exporters and see if they were interested in joining me as joint venture partners.

The first company I contacted was A.J. Bush. They did a lot of exports and had quite a few shops. Also, Mr Bush happened to be a hero of mine. The second company was D.R. Johnson, which was run by Don Johnson who I knew and respected. The third company was actually a public company and there were difficulties communicating with them because of their board and so forth and so that did not happen. The fourth one I contacted was George Whittaker, who was a very colourful Englishman.

Whittaker had a cattle business in the Northern Territory. He was involved in a government program where the Aboriginals were encouraged to become involved in running cattle stations and operating abattoirs. I guess the idea was to turn these Aboriginals into businessmen. In my opinion this was never going to work. I have employed Aboriginals; I've played football with them and I've been friends with them. They are good people, fantastic people, but a lot of Aboriginals like to be free; they don't want worries, and they shy away from responsibility.

Sometimes, I think they are smarter than us and that their way of looking at life is better than ours. So it was not a surprise to a lot of people when the abattoir they owned and operated in Katherine lost money hand over fist and was run into the ground. George Whittaker took it over and not long after there was a disastrous fire and the abattoir went up in smoke. Luckily, it was insured for about $12 million. George went back to England, but then returned and was once more in the meat export industry. He was very smart and a good friend of mine. Also, he was a very good wheeler and dealer, which is what you needed for a consortium dealing with the Russians.

That was our consortium: Andrews Meat, A.J. Bush, D.R. Johnson and G. Whittaker. We held our first and all subsequent meetings at my Elizabeth Street office and I was elected chairman. The big questions discussed were how we were going to manage this consortium. We all put in a small stake of $1,000 to open a company to be called Austeuro Meat Exports Pty Ltd. The Russians wanted to send their own ships, and in those days the Russian ships were not containerised – the meat was packed in cartons and loaded into baskets which were then lowered into the ship's freezers.

The payment made by the Russians for every shipload would go to Austeuro, and each partner would be paid the percentage of their shipment. If A.J. Bush supplied 30% of the shipment, they would get 30% of the profit – the more you do, the more you get paid; the less you do, the less you get paid. Whatever expenses there were, they would be debited to Austeuro and Austeuro would then send the bills to individuals and those bills would be based on the percentage of profits or sales they were making. There was a feeling that the people in the room were all solid businesspeople and that this would work.

After that I caught a plane to Moscow. I must admit that I took with me a red briefcase as some sort of pretence that maybe they would think that I was sympathetic to communism. If they did their homework on me and all my business and real estate holdings, I wouldn't get anywhere. I went to see the Australian trade commissioner, who was beside himself with enthusiasm for this project, and a meeting was organised with some Russian officials. Greeks actually have a lot in common with the Russians. We are Orthodox Christians – as are Russians – and although there are lots of differences – the two religions are very similar.

And although the church was officially outlawed, Gorbachev was relaxing those laws as well. Russians also drink the same coffee as us – we call it Turkish coffee – and the Turks call it Greek coffee. My meeting with these officials seemed to go down well and it was agreed that five of them would come to Sydney to have meetings with our consortium.

I sourced an interpreter from Canberra who had a Russian background. As the meetings were scheduled to go for at least five days, I hired him for the week. When the Russians arrived, we arranged for them to be picked up and taken to a very nice hotel in North Sydney. I had deliberately kept them away from hotels in the CBD because I wanted to keep the Russians away from the likes of Dalgetys and Elders, the stock and station agents.

Then we spent a small fortune wining and dining the Russian delegation, and true to form they were dull, drab and humourless. We took them up the Centrepoint tower and while we were eating at the restaurant there, one of them noticed there was a revolving series of flags for all the different countries. He pointed out through the interpreter that he could not see a Russian flag. "Why don't they have Russian flags here? We are doing business with Australia?" Acting as casually as I could, I assured him that there was bound to be a Russian flag on the revolving wheel. I waited a while and then excused myself to go to the toilet. Instead, I hunted down the restaurant manager. As I was supplying meat to the restaurant, I knew the manager and asked him, "Haven't you got a Russian flag?"

"I think so," he replied. Then he looked in one of the store rooms and found not one, but a whole box of Russian flags. "Stick them all up," I said. "Or I am going to lose these Russians as a customer."

I went back to our table and continued eating. About five minutes later the Russians started pointing and gesturing at a Russian flag which had appeared on the carousel. Then there was a second, and then another and so on. They all laughed and everybody was happy. We also took our Russian friends out on a boat to show them the wonders of Sydney Harbour. This event almost backfired because they somehow assumed we were interested in buying boats and started talking about our consortium buying boats from Russia and trading boats for meat, rather than paying in cash. I quickly made it clear to them that we were meat men and knew nothing about anything else.

After five continuous days dealing with these Russians, we were all nervous wrecks. There was a lot of money at stake and they were very cautious, very stubborn and hard to read. But after so many days with them I wasn't convinced that all of the five Russians spoke no English. I concluded that one or two spoke English, but they pretended they couldn't to listen to our conversations, and also to give them time to think during negotiations. It's an old European trick. At one stage there was only the interpreter and one Russian in our boardroom. They were chatting away in Russian when then the interpreter went to the bathroom leaving just me and the Russian.

"What time does your plane leave tomorrow?" I asked. Instinctively, the Russian looked at his watch and I knew I had been right. He knew he had given the game away, but just sat there waiting for the interpreter to come back. I was furious with the interpreter, but because the deal was yet to be signed, could say nothing. He would have known that this Russian understood at least some English, but said nothing to us even though he was supposed to be working for us.

Finally, the deal was closed. Our price was accepted and we then confirmed the cost price with the abattoirs on every shipment of about 6,000 tonne lots. The sales were documented and it was agreed the Russians would take deliveries of the meat from various ports in Australia in their own vessels. This was a massive export deal and I was very proud of the fact that our consortium had remained unified and worked. But it would not last. At our last meeting with the Russians, I gave them some advice which they disregarded.

When we negotiated our deal – the prices were fixed only for the first shipment – nothing was fixed for the future. Because of that, I asked the Russians not to talk to other meat suppliers for the simple reason that this would be counterproductive and only drive prices up. This may sound self-serving, but wasn't. I explained to them that in Australia a lot of farmers are in debt to the large stock and station agents, such as Elders or Dalgetys. This means that these agents have considerable power over the farmers and they exercise this power by manipulating the prices paid for meat at auctions. For example, if it suited them, they might ask farmers to hold their stock back and not bring it to the auctions. This artificial shortage pushes the price up which is what they wanted – they get higher meat prices and also get a better commission on the sales. I knew that if these companies found out the Russians were looking for massive quantities of meat, they would try and manipulate the market by getting their farmers to hold their stock back to jack-up the price.

However, as I explained this to the Russians I could see that they did not believe me. And in some ways, I don't blame them. If you buy cars from a car dealer and the dealer tells you not to speak to any other suppliers, you assume he is telling you this so that he can charge you more and make more money for himself. But I was being honest with the Russians. We were able to negotiate a price which was reasonable and a price which made us a fair profit.

And what I predicted came to pass. After the first shipment, the Russians decided to go and see what better offers were around. They found the larger companies seemed to offer them meat at a far cheaper price than our consortium. The Russians were hooked. Then, suddenly, the price paid at auction went up 'unexpectedly', and at the end of the day the Russians paid far more for their meat than they ever did with us. Despite this, I was proud of our consortium and proud of the fact that we could work cooperatively and profitably for the Australian meat companies and the Russian buyers. After three years, each of the companies traded individually with the Russians, taking their own risks. Nobody lost any money and after it was all over we in the consortium were still firm friends.

Chapter Ten

I once heard that when Captain Cook's ship the *Endeavour* pulled into Botany Bay, there were about ninety sailors on board and one female goat. Sometimes I used to wonder if it was this goat which had mothered the masses of feral goats in this country. On a lot of farms in Australia, there are serious infestations of feral goats. And in my youth I used to go out with my friends shooting wild pigs, feral goats and kangaroos. In those days farmers were always happy if you wanted to come on to their properties and go shooting.

As I was always on the lookout for new business opportunities, I began to think if there was much of a market in goat's meat. Traditionally, in Australia, the consumers did not show any interest in goat's meat. But times and tastes change, and I started to look into this. Everyone was doing the cattle meat business. I thought that it was something new and I liked to have a go at something new – and it worked out. In my life I always liked to set a goal and get others to follow. I can't remember now how it happened, but somehow I was put in touch with a fellow called George who was a livestock buyer.

The word was that George was a 'goat expert' and after I began my association with him I learned that this was true. He knew everything there was to know about goats and after we met I employed him to look after this business. It was a simple enough plan – we had to arrange supply through the herding of feral goats – then find some suitable abattoirs.

Together with my son Anthony, George and I travelled through Perth, and up to Darwin, before coming back down to Katherine. From Katherine we went to Bourke, and then on to Cobar, Charleville and Pyramid Hill. After doing all this, we established a depot in Cobar where we kept 2,000 to 3,000 goats. We used to have a lady there who was an accountant and she would sign the invoices. We would pay and keep them there. George used to go up there and grade them out – young ones and older ones – and we used to feed them and then send them in trucks – six hundred at a time – to abattoirs in Pyramid Hill and Charleville.

It wasn't long before George had farmers ringing him from all over the country. He lived in rural New South Wales and would come to a meeting with me every Saturday in Sydney. It went very well, and in the beginning we depended on other people's abattoirs. But they were changing ownerships and becoming less reliable.

This was at a time when we were processing 150,000 goats a year. Because of this, we had plans to open our own abattoir in Cobar. If it went ahead, it would be the biggest abattoir in Australia doing goats.

We had architects and all the experts looking into it and were looking at spending about $16 million on it. The only thing that held me back was that Cobar is often short of water and the place has too many droughts. This meant there would be water shortages, and you can't run abattoirs without water.

I liked George and we got on. One time we found a 50,000-acre property about eight kilometres south of Cobar. We made a deal that for every goat George bought, it was taken to this property and let loose there. I remember we had to check the fence and to do this you had to drive for one full day. I drove around with the owner's son and checked the fence to see if the goats could get out. The owner's son sat in the car and made a note of where he needed to make repairs.

Meanwhile, George was paid handsomely for his efforts, and when he realised that we were making good money, he started to make little negative comments here and there about how I was getting rich at his expense. It's not good when this happens, and it is always easy in hindsight to be critical of someone making money – it's different when you put your money on the line and take the risk.

And not so long after this, we parted ways. That was the end of my involvement in the goat business. All up we had about six good years. I had to make a decision. If I stayed in the goat business, it would be worth a lot of money today – I believe there is currently $250 million per year in goat exports and goat meat has become so very popular and expensive. And it has to be admitted I had plenty of other things going on in my life to keep me out of mischief such as the real estate investments.

Chapter Eleven

In the early 1980s, bank loan interest rates went up massively. The mortgage rate for most people hit 16 or 17%. Because of my special relationship with the ANZ Bank, I was only paying about 14% interest. My position was better than some, but still not good. One way around this was to take out a loan in foreign currency – for example, Swiss Francs – and then you'd pay only 5.5% interest. It sounded like a tempting bargain, but there was a lot of risk. If the currency the loan was written in depreciated or appreciated compared to the Australian dollar, then it was possible to find that the amount you owed had halved or doubled. Because I knew the hazards, I was very careful.

As I was interested in foreign loans and currency trading, a meeting was arranged with Citibank. I went with a representative from an accounting firm – a tall fellow called Simon. On the other side of the table was David, a representative from Citibank. I asked him if I converted my Aussie dollars into Swiss Francs did he think I'd save money due to the low interest, or could the currency go against me and I'd end up losing money. David, the Citibank representative, waved his hands like I had it all wrong. "We do the trading for you," he explained. "You give us a power of attorney to deal on your behalf, and we look after the trading." As an example, he said that they would ring me up and tell me the Swiss franc was going down and suggest I sell and buy French francs or British pounds or US dollars. This was the sort of professional advice I was after. I asked David if he was doing this sort of thing already, and he said, "Of course."

"Show me," I said.

He frowned, then replied, "Let me speak to the boss."

A short time later he was back with his boss, whose name was Patrick, and we were introduced. There were about thirty computers in the foreign exchange trading office. The boss walked over to one of the computers and David sat down behind the screen. Patrick asked him to block out the name of the customer on the screen. He did this and we were all looking at a screen which to me looked very impressive. Remember, this was over thirty years ago.

On the screen were details of the amount invested, the deals made, the rates of those deals and the profits and losses. The one that was brought up on the screen showed that this client's losses were 10% and his profits were 90% on a large investment. In seven months he had made a sizeable profit. Of course, my eyes lit up when I saw that, so I was tempted to start, but my natural caution kicked in and I said, "This looks like what I am after. I'll open a small account to start with. And I'll give you power of attorney to deal. Whatever profits we make, 30% is yours."

We shook hands, there were smiles all round and now I was in the foreign currency trading business. Although it wasn't necessary, I offered David 30% of the profits, because I have always been a great believer in giving financial incentive to people. Within six months I was sitting on a nice profit. With his share of the profits, the Citibank representative told me he bought a unit in King's

Cross, and was even able to pay for the renovations. I increased my original investment.

At about the nine-month mark, David rang me. He was very apologetic and said he'd lost $200,000 on a deal which had not worked out as he had hoped. I joked with him that I should have put it in our deal that he had 30% of the profits and 30% of the losses. Anyway, as any investor knows, you can't win them all. And David was confident that he could get us back on top. We agreed to close that particular account and continue trading in other currencies.

Over this period, I developed a close working relationship with the man from Citibank. He used to come to my house on the weekend and play tennis. One day I asked him in casual conversation what he had done in life before going into banking. "My father had a bakery and I worked with him as a pastry cook." Like me, he came from humble beginnings, but I assumed after that start in life he would have studied commerce at university. "What education did you have to go into dealing with money?" I asked. "None really," he answered honestly, "I just finished school and went from working as a pastry chef to getting a job at Citibank."

A little stab of fear went through my heart. By this time my investment was significant. I realised that I'd given a former pastry chef my money to play with however he liked. True, I never received a formal education, but I had been dealing with money almost all my life, and relied heavily on common sense and intuition. But David had no education in finance whatsoever, and I was totally reliant upon him.

One day, I received a message from him that we were behind in a big way. I will never forget that moment. I was in my kitchen, which has a beautiful view all the way down Balmoral Beach. I was staring out the window looking down at the beach. Maria said something and I didn't answer. "What's the matter with you?" she asked. "Whenever I talk you don't answer back." I looked at her and then looked back at the beach. "I've lost a huge amount of money on the foreign exchange deals with Citibank." Maria looked at me. She was very angry. "This has been going on for too long and it just has to stop." I kept staring down the beach. "You've changed since you started doing this," she complained, "and changed a lot. Pay them and get out of there!!"

"What do you mean pay them and get out of there? I've got to get my money back." Maria would have none of it. "Forget that. Pay them whatever they need to close it and get out."

"That's not how it works," I replied. "I need to make back the money I've lost." "Get out!" she insisted.

"No, I've got the right fellow on the job and I'm sure he'll look after me."

I was a stayer – that was my business style – I wasn't the type to throw in the towel at the first bump in the road. So I stayed on and six months later, my losses were even worse. I went into Citibank to talk to the big boss, Patrick, about this debacle. I wasn't too happy with him because whenever I asked them to sell a currency, it would take them about three days to do it because the buyers were waiting for it to drop further. By then the currency would have dropped massively and I would have lost even more money.

I told Patrick I wanted out and also hinted at possible legal action. Whilst I had a letter saying that I had given them power of attorney, as an investor I was relying on their experience to handle this on a profitable basis. However, the letter I signed had been drafted by Citibank's solicitors and there were clauses in there which got them off the hook and said they didn't really have any responsibility. "How much are you going to give me before we finish up in the courts?" I asked.

Patrick explained that there was no point crying over spilt milk; what's done is done. When I said I would see a lawyer because of the vagueness of the letter I'd signed, it didn't seem to bother Patrick too much. By this time the Australian dollar was down to 55 cents US. At the end of the day when the dust had settled, I had to pay back a sum of money which I could have used to buy a CBD building.

Sometimes, a man should listen to his wife. All through those last days I couldn't sleep, couldn't think, couldn't do anything much but tear my hair out. Thank God I had other real estate investments which I could sell off if I needed to. On the same day that I had this difficult meeting with Patrick, we were both distracted by a man swearing his head off at the other end of the office. I said to him, "Who's that?" He said it was one of their Jewish customers, who had just had all his assets seized by the bank. At least I still had a lot of assets, I reminded myself.

As I walked into the lift, I hit the button for the ground floor, and the man who had been screaming and swearing walked into the lift. I said to him, "Mate, you sound pissed off." He looked at me, and quickly realised I wasn't from the bank and then continued his attack on them. "Those bastards," he complained, "I have assets worth $25 million and borrowed $20 million from them. Now they want a $5 million top up. Because $25 million in assets isn't good enough. 'Put in another $5 million cash!' they said. So I threw them the keys – threw them on the table and said – 'You finish the building!'"

This fellow explained that he was building units near the fish market at Pyrmont Bridge and the bank got into a panic and wanted more money as security even though they had all his assets as security. It was a ridiculous situation – the units were partially complete – and he had decided to call the bank's bluff by throwing them the keys to the construction site. He had told the bank to finish the project themselves, knowing full well that without his expertise, the bank would almost certainly lose a lot of money on the project. And that was how I met Harry Triguboff. Later, I heard on the grapevine that Citibank realised they wouldn't be able to finish the buildings without him and caved in. Every time I see Harry Triguboff, I remind him of this story and he laughs. Now he's worth billions.

The mistake I made was to trust the bank. In business you always need to have something that the banks need, otherwise they're happy to just throw your investment away. I went to see our lawyers and we put the bank on notice and commenced negotiations. I suggested they refund me half the losses and they said no. We prepared to go to court. At the time taking the banks to court was unheard of. The thing that went through my mind was that if I win, or lose, it'll be publicised in the newspapers. I thought about my children – none of the banks would trust them if they knew I had taken a bank to court. They would never be able to have businesses in the future. We went back to the banks and asked for their best offer. They said they'd renew the loan, for a further three years on 10% rather than 15% interest. We paid them out and closed the books on this affair.

Strangely, after all this, the boss from Citibank, Patrick, came to see me one weekend when we were having a barbecue. Patrick offered to work for me and said if I thought he was good enough he'd want to be a junior partner. While we were eating our steaks, he explained to me how I was duded – they were selling my position to another international bank. That way they could never really lose money in a deal – because they were on both sides of it. It was simply outrageous. A similar thing happened in the global financial crisis many years later when some of the New York banks were giving investment advice which was disastrous for the clients and hugely profitable for the bank.

Unfortunately, I couldn't see where I could use Patrick in my business. This story of my currency trading was a case of me not living up to my own motto: "Trusting is good, but checking is better."

Chapter Twelve

My youngest brother Bill grew up in Greece and was a lieutenant in the army. He always claimed to be the best-looking boy in our family. The only thing is, Bill's got big ears and I'd always joke with him, "Every time I look at you mate, it's just like a Sydney taxi coming down the hill with the doors open." He loved that joke.

At first Bill worked in one of my butcher shops and then worked in our meat-processing factory in Dulwich Hill as one of the workers. After a year, he became the manager of the Dulwich Hill factory. To me he was very good at managing staff – at that time there were about one hundred and twenty employees. One of his ideas was to form a football team. He had jerseys made with the Andrews Meat logo on the back. Then Bill organised another team from our other meat-processing factory at Pyrmont called Ampco. There were another hundred and twenty people there and he put Ampco on their jerseys – which stands for Andrews Meat Packing Company. On Sundays they played soccer at Balmoral Beach, Mosman.

Bill was himself a good soccer player. He became the trainer and the coach of one of the teams. The families of the workers used to fill the whole of Balmoral Beach oval. Then, after a couple of years, the council told them to stop playing because they were too noisy and they were leaving a lot of rubbish behind from their families' barbecues.

Bill managed Dulwich Hill for about four years. He lived not far from me and we were very close. We were tossing up for either me to go back to Greece to look after our parents, and for him to take over my position in the meat business in Sydney, or for him to go back to Greece again. At that time the internal problems in Greece were enormous. The country was on the brink of war with Turkey over Cyprus, and were effectively under a dictatorship. My two sons and daughter were growing older and were now in high school. Maria said to me, "Where are we going to take the kids? What future is there for us? What are we going to do in Greece?"

I listened to her and I said, "Let's stay in Australia." As it turned out, that was the last time I considered moving back to my old homeland. Australia was truly my home now.

A few years later, when my parents again came to Sydney for a holiday, I took Dad over to the Dulwich Hill factory. He looked a bit stunned and said to me, "I don't know son. I don't know. I don't know how you handle it."

"What do you mean?"

"Fortunately, you didn't take after me. I couldn't handle all this."

"Dad, if you had put yourself in from a little boy you would have done it even better," I said. "Anyone can do it, when you put yourself in. Don't put your hands up – do it, believe you can do it. Then, it can be done. If you are doing it successfully, it gives you encouragement. It is just like a fight – you win a fight, then you get better and if you get a couple of slaps you don't feel it, but if you feel beaten you say, 'I have lost.' If you believe you have lost, you have lost, and you become a loser."

In the end, Bill decided to go back to Greece and look after our parents. Bill and I went back to Greece where we started a new business as a meat broker, Andrews Meat Imports. I exported from Australia to Bill's company in Greece for many years.

Chapter Thirteen

I became involved in a very interesting project in the 1980s when Greece was making a determined effort to join the European Union (EU). As everyone now knows, but didn't then, there was a cooking of the country's books which was virtually deceptive conduct. I knew nothing of this of course. What came to my attention was an off-hand comment made by one of my relatives who was whingeing that the government had stopped all meat imports as a way of making their financial position more acceptable to the EU. At first I thought this was too ridiculous to believe; but, being a Greek, it occurred to me that they might try something like this. If you cut all your imports, then your export figures go through the roof.

There was a simple way for me to find out if this was true – and that was not to contact the government. Instead, I asked a girl in the Athens office to get on the phone to all the big freezer storage places and put to them this question: "We are expecting to bring some goods in from Argentina. How much room do you have in your freezer?"

The first company she contacted answered, "We have 4,500 tonnes." Then she followed up with, "What's the storage capacity of your freezer?"

"4,500 tonnes."

From this response it was obvious that their freezers were virtually empty. This girl went through the phone book speaking to all the commercial freezer places and it was always the same answer – yes – they had capacity for 5,000 tonnes, or 4,000 tonnes and so on. I knew immediately that virtually all the freezers in Greece were near empty.

This was a possible catastrophe for the country and for me the business opportunity of a lifetime. What the government had done to improve their import figures was to ban temporarily all imports including meat. All the freezers in Athens were empty. There was no meat, especially lamb. Had it occurred to anyone what the country's 16 million tourists were going to eat for the summer? The government had completely sacrificed all their imports to maintain the appearance of economic strength to be accepted into the EU. After all, the EU didn't want a country that was a third-world economy and a burden on all the other members.

This is where I operated best – sniffing out inconsistencies – and making the most of opportunities. By my calculations, there was in Athens only about 10% of the lamb they would need. It seemed obvious to me that I could not lose in this situation. People have to eat. All I had to do was bring in lamb and somehow legally get around the government's import restrictions. When I spoke to importers in Greece, they were all happy to buy lamb from me but explained that because of the importing bans, they couldn't pay. It seemed to me that we would have to come up with a payment scheme where the importers were given a couple of months' credit.

Exporting/importing anything can be a complicated process – especially if it involves an agricultural product such as lamb. Normally, a meat export licence is required from the Department of Agriculture and also the Ministry of Trade has to know what's happening. And there was the added complication of the Greek Government not wanting imports to show up on their books. Obviously, I wanted to sell the lamb – but I had to work out a way of getting it through at the other end. What we did in the end was book the commercial freezer space we required in Athens through my brother Bill's importing company. We stored the lamb there on consignment – the money was to be paid when the meat arrived in Athens and before it went through customs.

At first none of the banks in Australia were interested in this deal. It was too risky for them. So I started trying to persuade my manager at the ANZ Bank. I pointed out to him that I had assets to cover the risk, and that there was a lot of money to be made. The bank was convinced, and they brought into the deal a Swiss Bank as well. Now I had to find the meat.

At that time in the 1980s, Western Australia produced a lot of lamb and it was also the type of lamb that was popular in Greece. Apparently, it was a breed which the Western Australians had taken from New Zealand and the Greeks loved New Zealand lamb. The largest lamb exporter in Australia happened to be the Western Australia Lamb Marketing Board, which was run by the Western Australian Government. I flew to Perth with my brother Bill and we had meetings with these state government officials and the premier. They were very keen to do business – especially considering the volumes I was talking about – I was proposing to buy $12 million worth of lamb.

The manager of the Lamb Marketing Board was a fellow called Rob. He asked, "How do we know the Greeks will pay us?" It was

a very good question. I then explained to the board how desperate the Greeks would be for meat, and that I had devised a way for them to pay up front to secure the imports. In response to that Rob then said, "Excuse me, Mr Andrews. Can you and your brother leave the boardroom please for five minutes? We will call you."

While we were waiting outside, Bill asked, "Why did they send us out?"

"I will tell you why," I replied. "They are going to say something like, 'We hear what you are saying and it all sounds good, but can you give us a personal guarantee?'"

"Don't put your head in the oven for me," Bill warned.

About ten minutes later we were called back to the boardroom. The premier said, "Nick, you're dealing with them and you understand them. You're Greek yourself. We don't have a problem with anything you've proposed, but can you give us a personal guarantee?" I could see from the looks on all the faces around the boardroom table that they believed this was a deal breaker.

"I can do better than that," I said. Then I leaned forwards, pointed to a phone and asked, "Can I use your phone?" They all looked shocked and so without waiting for an answer I rang the ANZ Bank in George Street, Sydney. I looked up to the board members sitting around the table and explained, "I'm calling my bank manager at the ANZ."

When the bank manager answered the phone, I explained where I was and that the WA Lamb Marketing Board had asked for a personal guarantee. "You have the title details for my property in Queensland," I said. "Can you telex through to the WA Lamb Marketing Board a bank guarantee for $12 million, please."

Left: Showing Rob from the WA Lamb Marketing Board the sights of Athens during our legendary trade deal in the 1980s.

A few minutes later a secretary walked into the board meeting carrying a telex confirming a bank guarantee on the deal. "What now?" the premier asked. Rob cleared his throat and said, "I'll organise the lamb and …" Before he finished I interrupted, "Rob, things have changed now." He looked a bit confused. I continued, "From today on, I'm in charge."

"What do you mean you're in charge?"

"I am flying to Athens at 5.00 pm tomorrow and you're going to be on that plane with me."

Rob quickly chimed in, "No, no, I'm busy. I've got to run half a dozen abattoirs here." "Mate, these are my conditions. You have to come to Greece. I want the people we're dealing with in Greece to see that they're dealing with the Western Australian Government. I don't want any mistakes, any misunderstandings. This is a massive deal for all of us. You're coming, or the deal is off." The other directors of the board didn't hesitate and the next day Rob was with me on a plane to Athens.

Poor Rob never knew what hit him. We stayed in the best hotel, the Hotel Grande Bretagne opposite the Parliament House. I hired a 500 series Mercedes with an English-speaking driver. I said to Rob, "This is your car, this is your driver." Then I said to the driver, "Take him wherever he wishes to go in Athens."

"Thank you very much," he said. With Rob, I didn't know what interested him, so I told the driver to give him a tour of the Parthenon, a few museums and to show him some of the countryside. Rob had never been to Greece and he just loved the place. Then it was down to business and closing the deal with the buyers.

A meeting was arranged with the buyers at our hotel and a secretary was hired to run the meeting. There were about nine buyers in all. The terms of payment were 30% now – that is due by 11.00 am tomorrow – and 70% of the payment when the ship arrives in Piraeus. The money had to be paid before the order was unloaded and before it went through customs. I knew that legally once the meat goes through customs, you lose control – it's no longer yours. The buyers were looking at each other – they would have paid all this money – but they would have no meat until it came through customs. I understood some had mortgaged their homes, their grandmothers, to be in on this deal. This is where your name and reputation matters, and when they did their checking up on me they learned that I was as good as my word. They all accepted the deal.

When I said farewell to Rob from the WA Lamb Marketing Board at the Hotel Grande Bretagne, he gave me a big hug. While I think he had finally come to the conclusion that I was a person he could trust, I didn't feel the same about him. He seemed to me to be a bit sneaky – but I reassured myself that he was a government official and nothing could go wrong from that end.

Chapter Fourteen

In the meantime, I had hired a cargo ship from Japan with a 6,000-tonne capacity at a cost of $900,000. It sailed from Japan to Perth, picked up the cargo of 6,000 tonne of lamb, and then sailed for the Greek port of Piraeus. All went well. Bill was there to meet the ship when it arrived and he handled it from there on.

Only one of the buyers didn't put up his final payment of 70%. When the ship was being unloaded, he was supposed to pay before the lamb went through customs. It didn't happen so I executed a deed to transfer the ownership of that part of the shipment to my brother Bill, who was in Greece with me doing the deal. I said to Bill, "This will go in your name in the freezer."

As I had rightly guessed, this shocked the businessman who hadn't paid me. "I am expecting the money," he explained. "I'm only about twelve days in arrears. I will pay you."

"No," I said, "the lamb is now ours. If you are going to pay, you will have to pay 5% more each and every day it stays there. We

Left: Business associate Saki Tsernos and his family visiting us from Greece.

will give you thirty days and if you don't pay up we will sell it and keep your 30% deposit." I went on to tell him that we would then sell the lamb for 70% of the market value, or the best we could get. If we sold it for 110% of market value, we would give him the difference. And if we lost, we would put our 5% on top. He came up with the money the next day.

I am told that this sale was the largest ever sale of lamb under that government's terms and conditions at that period in time. The importers doubled their profits on this deal. Shops now had lamb to sell to the restaurants for the tourists that year. I was very proud of this shipment – it left behind many good memories to everyone who was involved and especially to my brother Bill. He has two sons, Harry and Gregory, and they are in their meat importing business in Athens now. Also, it made my father very happy because he kept asking me to help Bill progress in business, and finally I was able to involve Bill in this deal. When Maria and I visit in Greece, even now, some of these importers can't do enough for us. Even over thirty years later they are still talking about our "perfect score".

One of the importers, Saki Tsernos, became a good friend and we did a lot of business together. One time at Athens airport he gave me a bank cheque for $1 million in my name. He said, "When you go to Australia, invest this cash for me, whatever you think is the best." I had to ring up my accountant. "Christ! I'm responsible for this, I brought the money from Greece. What can we do?" I invested this money in two or three different places when the interest rates were very high. Saki got all his money back and more – he averaged out around 14% interest. It goes to show you the trust that those importers had for us after that deal. A few years later, Saki came to Australia and stayed at my place with his family.

But you can't trust everyone. Rob from the WA Lamb Marketing Board decided to do another lamb sale to Greece the following year, but this time without me. He clearly had no loyalty and believed that this was his opportunity to make a fortune. He copied everything I did, except he made one very crucial error. When he chartered the ship, he didn't make it what is known as "a free liner" – a ship which is fully chartered. When you charter the entire ship, the ship owners can't claim there are other priority ports they need to go to. Worse, Rob didn't even take the precaution of paying insurance. Then, the month his ship arrived it was very busy and he was sabotaged by the Greeks. They made them anchor the ship off Piraeus for two months, and charged him $7.5 million in demurrage fees. That was the end of Rob – he was sacked for incompetence by the Lamb Marketing Board. If only he had had some sense of loyalty, he could have asked if I wanted to be in on the deal that year. But he was headstrong and ignored my experience, and it cost him dearly in the long run.

I always say if there is a will, there is a way. Nothing is impossible. Life is 10% how you make it and 90% how you take it. If you worry about little things and you aren't laughing, you are defeated, you are down. Even if you lose, you laugh. You see the big gamblers when they play cards and they don't have the right card, they are still laughing. Someone will ask him, "Why are you laughing mate? You lost."

The gambler would reply, "If I stop laughing, I'm going to start crying!"

Above: Our home in Balmoral.

Above: After building two houses down the coast in Akrata eight kilometres away, one was resumed by an expressway; the other, my brother Bill and his family live in. I purchased Vigla House twenty years ago. It's seven hundred metres from the beach and Maria and I, our family and friends use it on our holidays.

Chapter Fifteen

One day one of my suppliers to my retail butcher shops rang up to say there'd been an accident – one of their trucks had flipped over on its way from Coonamble. One of the girls had put this fellow through to me and said his name was Bill Scott – not an unusual name, but a name I was unlikely to forget. As this man spoke to me, I could tell that he was a young man. He was very apologetic and explained he had made arrangements to have the meat transferred to another truck, but the delivery would be late. Thankfully, the driver was uninjured.

When he had finished talking I asked, "It is Bill Scott, isn't it?"

"That's right."

"You wouldn't be any relation to Bill Scott who had the butcher shop in Trangie?"

"That's my father," he replied. "I'm Bill Scott junior."

"Oh right," I said. "So the Bill Scott who had the butcher shop in Trangie is your father?"

"Yes," said Bill junior, adding, "He's sitting here alongside of me."

I could not believe it. I did some quick sums in my head and calculated that the Bill Scott I knew must be in his nineties. I said to his son, “Can you put him on?”

“Sure.”

“Hi Bill, how are you going?” I asked.

“Good. Who am I talking to?” Bill wanted to know.

With a chuckle I said, “I’m the rascal from Trangie.” “Who?”

“The rascal from Trangie,” I repeated. “You used to call me a rascal, mate. I was across the road from you in Trangie. I had the Trocadero Cafe.”

“You don’t mean Nick?” I swear he was going to say, “Nick the Greek”, but stopped himself.

“That’s right. It’s Nick.”

“But my son told me he was talking to Nick Andrews.”

“I changed my name,” I explained.

“Really? You changed your name?”

“Wouldn’t you?” I joked, “If your name was Androutsopoulos? I changed it to Andrews.”

“Ah,” he said.

“Because I had to spell it out to people all the time.”

He said, “Jesus Christ! How are you Nick?”

“Fantastic.” It turned out we had been dealing with his son’s company for years and the connection had never been made. “Bill? Are you there?” Then I realised that he had handed the phone back to his son. “Is everything all right?” I asked.

Bill junior said, “He can’t talk – he’s crying.” I asked if he wanted me to call back another time, but his son said he would be all right – he just needed a moment – he’d been overcome by his emotions.

Bill’s son told me that his father was not very healthy, that he had problems with his eyes, but he went to the office every day to see how his son was going. After a while we continued our conversation and Bill told me that over the years he had heard about this fellow Nick Andrews making a name for himself in the meat industry, but never imagined it was me. He said that he remembered how much I loved shooting and suggested that I come out to their property and stay with them and do a bit of shooting. I accepted his invitation and drove to his place in Coonamble with Anthony, my eldest son.

Meeting Bill Scott after all those years was one of the most emotional moments of my life. When we drove up, out stepped this frail old man. We shook hands and hugged and cried. He invited us into the house. There was a lot of catching up to do. Bill said that after he left Trangie, he went to Dubbo where he picked up work at a butcher shop in the main street. At the time he had two boys going to Scot's College in Sydney – one was almost eighteen and the other about fourteen. He couldn't afford the fees, and so they left school and went into the workforce. Eventually, Bill was able to get enough money together to buy a butcher shop in Coonamble. They built a small slaughterhouse out the back and did pretty well.

Bill could only talk for about an hour and then he'd have to go and have a lie down. His boys were tremendous – they looked after me like I was their uncle.

Yet, all the while I kept thinking that I was the one who sent him broke all those years ago. However, I reminded myself that it never was, and never has been my wish, to send anyone broke.

My business philosophy has always been that there's more than enough opportunities out there for everyone to do well. Bill had been the musician, and I was the dancer. Whatever music he played, I danced. He put the price up, and so did I; he put the price down and so did I. Now, here we were all these years later. And of course, he wanted to know my story and what had happened to me after I left Trangie. My son and I stayed with the Scotts for three days. We ate until we thought we would burst and we also managed to get in a bit of shooting.

When we said our goodbyes, it occurred to me then that I probably wouldn't see Bill again. Life has so many twists and turns, but it did please me that there was no bitterness there. He would have been pleased that his sons turned out to be men he could be proud of.

BOOK EIGHT

My Family

CS-964

Chapter One

In his famous book, 'Zorba the Greek', Nikos Kazantzakis says, "I felt once more how simple and frugal a thing is happiness: a glass of wine, a roast chestnut, a wretched little brazier, the sound of the sea. Nothing else." To that I would add the greatest word I know: family. My greatest happiness comes not from making real estate deals, making a killing on an export deal or negotiating a better interest rate from the banks. No, my happiness comes from seeing, hearing, feeling my family. They are the only thing that matters to me – they are all in my head and in my heart when I wake up in the morning – and they're still there when I go to sleep at night. And like any family, we argue with one another, and feel upset and disappointed and are sometimes angry with each other. But that doesn't matter, because deep down we all know that

Left: Photographed in 1984, I had this van for over a decade which we used on family holidays, picnics, skiing at Thredbo and on shooting trips with friends out west as far as Nyngan, New South Wales. When my parents visited from Greece we used it to show them the Australian countryside. When they were tired, we would stop alongside a nice river for them to have a nap, before we continued on.

we have this unbreakable bond with each other; that no matter what, we will always be there for one another. And every day I give thanks to whoever is in charge of the universe that my family has been blessed with good fortune.

My father once said to me when I was a child, "I am holding you responsible. As the oldest child in the family, this is a big thing I am asking. You have to carry out the parent task with your younger brothers." That made me very proud and at the same time, made me feel responsible, not to disappoint them. They were only a few words, but I remember them to this day and I will remember them until the day I die.

In all, I brought my parents out to Australia four times. The first visit was in about 1964 or 1965. They stayed with Maria and me for about six months and then spent a month with my younger brother Peter, and then a month with my other younger brother John. My parents were proud of their three sons in Australia and proud of Bill in Greece and our achievements, and even though they loved Australia, they always wanted to go back home to Greece. I used to take my father to the Greek Club, and my brothers and I entertained him as much as we could with parties and barbeques at our homes. Maria did an exceptional job organising the good times with all of us and helping the other family members. As well, there were a lot of grandchildren for them to fuss over. However, my father missed his club and my mother missed her friends in Greece.

In the early eighties, the house next door to mine in Mosman was listed for sale. It occurred to me that this could be a good place for my parents and friends to stay in when they came here. The way I saw it, they could be next door yet not feel they were under pressure to be with us for lunch or dinner. They could relax and do what they liked and this would make it more relaxing all round. So I bought the house next door, pulled it down and built a new one. We put a tennis court out the back of it and these days refer to it as our guest house. By doing that, it has turned out to be a very valuable investment. The house was enough to entice my parents back to Australia. They stayed there and were very happy. But, as time went on, they were getting on in years, and travel was becoming too tiring for them.

They went back to Greece and my mother died in 1994 and my father two years later. It was sad, but not tragic to see them go. Both of them had lived into their nineties and lived productive lives. In the early years, many times, we thought my father would die any second at the hands of the guerrillas. Also, my parents lived to see that whatever wisdom they imparted on their children had the right effect. It was my good fortune to have them put me on the right path as a boy. They were very proud of me and it made me feel good that I had done things which made them proud. Many times they said to me, "You are a leader. You are the one who will act like a parent to your brothers and other family members." Sometimes, I think Maria felt that my parents put too much pressure on me, but it wasn't like that for me. They gave me a challenge, and I accepted it. Being able to make them proud was something that drove me to succeed in life.

My father was very wise. He often used to say, "Remember, family is family. When you have your differences, put them aside and look for a better day, because one day, if something happens to one of you, I won't be around and you will only have each other to help – and family will help. People outside, they are friends, but when you really need them to stick around, you don't expect them to sacrifice their lives for someone else because they probably have their own problems with their own family issues." This is a message that has stayed with me all my life – family is family – do what you can to try and be together – love and support one another.

Above: In the dining room of our home in Mosman with my parents and a large family gathering.

Above: Family dinner at the Bathers Pavillion, Balmoral Beach, when my parents visited Australia.

Above and next page: The Welcome Wall inscription for our family.

The WELCOME WALL
MORE THAN SIX MILLION PEOPLE
HAVE CROSSED THE SEAS
TO SETTLE IN AUSTRALIA.
THEY HAVE COME FROM
MOST COUNTRIES ON EARTH
TO THE LANDS OF THE CADIGAL,
THE BURRABURRAGAL
AND BEYOND
THE WELCOME WALL
AT THE AUSTRALIAN NATIONAL
MARITIME MUSEUM STANDS AS
A SYMBOL OF OUR GREAT
DIVERSITY AND OUR UNITY.
AUSTRALIAN
NATIONAL MARITIME
MUSEUM
PRINCIPAL SPONSO
'yes'
OPTUS

LINCOLN (HALL) Florence Elizabeth Edyth
ARMSTRONG L G, (JOULE) D P and family
IOSIFIDIS Konstantinos and Katerina
VALLA Ferruccio Mark
ANDREWS Nicholas H, Maria and family
TTOOULIS Michael
PAYNE Terence John
NOVAK Miroslav (Mike)
JOHNSON Ronald George
BELECKY Franz
HENDRY James
SANDER Lewis and Klementine
PISANO (IORFINO) Maria Rosa
PISANO Tommaso

Panel 33, Column 2, Line 19

Arrived in Australia 1947 & 1954

Above: The four Andrews brothers, taken after I brought all of my brothers to Australia. Bill was the last to arrive – he came in 1972. Front left to right: Myself and Peter. Back left to right: John and Bill.

Chapter Two

Traditionally, Greeks like to have a son for their first child, not a daughter – a daughter means that the parents will have to pay a dowry to their son-in-law when she marries. It's a custom that no longer exists as the ladies nowadays are well educated, independent and have equality in the workplace, and some women are even better placed – even though I never received a dowry when I married Maria. The other difference with having a daughter is that you are responsible for them until they get married. Because of this, Greek families are expected to be disappointed when they are told their first child is a daughter. Not me. I can tell you that from the time my daughter was born, I wished I had another half a dozen like her.

Marietta was our first child, and because of that she has always been number one. Actually, her first name is Maria: Maria Marietta Andrews. My mother was Maria, and my wife is also Maria. We named her after my mother, so we gave her two names, Maria Marietta, but everybody calls her Marietta.

When my mother and father first came out to Australia, we were then living in Kirribilli. Mum, who couldn't speak English, used to

take Marietta down to the park opposite our unit. She would sit down on the bench while the young five-year-old Marietta stood there and tapped the bench with a stick as she tried to teach my mum English. "Listen, when I'm talking to you!" she'd say to her grandmother. "Say: 'I love you.'"

My mother would try and say the words. "You're not saying it right." Marietta would be determined and try again, "Listen to me!" she would say. We enjoyed the stories that evolved from Marietta's English lessons to her grandparents.

When she was born in 1961, I was obviously very busy. I took Maria to the hospital, but then had to go back to work. Later that day the doctor rang me and said, "Congratulations. You have a beautiful daughter!"

"Thank you doctor," I replied.

Although it is not a good excuse these days, but because I was busy, and because it was late, and because I didn't go straight away, all the florists were shut. There were no flowers at all. When I reached the hospital, I was relieved to see that the florist there was still open. But there were not many flowers left and I was so desperate I asked the florist to put together all these flowers he had thrown out into a rough bouquet. I was a bit embarrassed in the lift seeing the beautiful bouquets other people were bringing, so I hid in the back.

When I went into Maria, I handed her the flowers and gave her a kiss. Then I saw this unbelievably beautiful baby. Unfortunately, Maria is still talking about those flowers even today. "If it was a boy," Maria had said, "you would have given me better flowers." Marietta went to Wenona School and did well in school. She was

Left: The night of Marietta's engagement party.

always very popular, and I can remember many of her friends at the house.

She studied Business Administration at college and started working for me at my head office in Elizabeth Street where we had the 6th and 7th floors. Marietta worked in our administration and accounting departments, learning the running of every department well. Then, after a few years, she moved into the meat export section where she organised the export documentation, production of stock and container-loads of meat to be shipped with various shipping lines around the world weekly, and coordinated with our factories that processed the orders. She also accompanied me on a few business trips to Japan and Europe to assist me. Later, she went on to work on our property portfolio, of which she is still involved with various projects and meetings, amongst managing her own family interests. I have been very proud and pleased to have her in the office.

Marietta loves to organise the family social calendar, where we always have a clan gathering when it's one of our birthdays. We usually make a large booking at a nice restaurant in Sydney where we all sing 'Happy birthday' and have a chance to catch up on each other's news. Now, as Maria and I have gotten older, we don't always have family celebrations at our home as much as we did in the old days. However, we have also had many wonderful memories for Christmas Day and Easter Sunday at George and Marietta's home where we all love to gather.

For my 80th birthday, she organised for all sixteen of us to fly to Ayers Rock, or Uluru as it's now called, for a long weekend where we had so many adventures. I think back on this weekend as a highlight of my life. We awoke at dawn to see the desert awakening and had a wonderful viewpoint of the Red Centre, an Australian spiritual heartland. The first night they had planned a special party in the hotel where we ate splendid local treats and every member of the family had a special tribute or speech to say to me to mark the occasion. The next day, we all boarded helicopters and flew above the whole area to see the wonder of the rock in the desert.

One afternoon we all shared a camel in twos and went along the red sand in a trail while the local guide told us stories of the Never Never land. We had a private gastronomic dining experience that was first-class silver service on a dune overlooking the red rock, where we drank champagne while a local played the didgeridoo and my family wished me a very happy 80th birthday. Later, we drank brandy in crystal glasses around a campfire while our guide told us stories about the stars above.

We also have weekends where all sixteen of us go to the farm together, again usually for Maria's and my birthdays which are only four days apart. We renovated a second farmhouse called Nardoo, which together with Woodlands house means we have eight bedrooms for us all to stay in. It is times like these that I reflect and think of what I have gone through in my life and where my life has brought me to today, to be able to enjoy these times of peace with my children and grandchildren.

In 1985, Marietta married the love of her life George Peter Manettas, whom she had met briefly as a young girl of thirteen, then again at nineteen years of age. He came from a good family that we knew. He is the son of Katie Manettas and another pioneer of his industry, Peter Manettas AM who made a big name for himself in the food and hospitality seafood industry. His career spanned seven decades. Firstly at P. Manettas and Co, a food distribution company supplying seafood and a myriad of other lines to hotels, restaurants, ships, airlines etc. His company then floated on the public stock exchange in 1988, then to be named Manettas Ltd. It is in this company that George learned his trade.

He is a born trader and is well known and recognised as a leader in his industry. In fact, Tourism Australia awarded him "National Tourism Legend" for hospitality in Australia.

We have a lot in common George and me, as he too pursued and achieved obtaining the best clients in Australia and Asia Pacific for supply of seafood and other products. Over the years we have worked together on many successful ventures in food and property. He is a good family man and together Marietta and George had three extraordinary children: Peter, Katherine and Nicola, who was named after me. Both girls have been given Maria as their middle name after my wife, Maria.

Peter went to Mosman Prep then onto Cranbrook School, achieved a Bachelor of Business degree majoring in marketing and now is a director in our cruise ship food distribution sector. The girls attended Queenwood School for Girls. Then Katherine achieved a Bachelor of Design in Interior and Spatial Design degree, and Nicola achieved a Bachelor of Design degree, majoring in fashion marketing. Later, both the girls found their passion working in property sales and management and have now gone on to open their own business in residential property renovations and styling, called Niketi.

Above and next page: My 80th birthday celebrations at Ayers Rock, now known as Uluru.

VH-PHL

Chapter Three

Because I never had an education of any sort, I wanted my children to have a decent one. I remember reading a book which said that Kerry Packer's father went to Cranbrook when it first opened and that James, his son, who is two years older than my son Anthony, also went to this school. That impressed me. Around this time, when Maria and I were looking at schools, there were a couple of businessmen I dealt with who also sent their sons to Cranbrook. Everyone spoke very highly about the school, and I figured that if it was good enough for Kerry Packer, it was good enough to me. So Anthony and Harry completed their high school education there.

We named Anthony after Maria's father. It wasn't exactly necessary, but when you don't do it, some old Greek men can become a bit cranky. And at each family reunion they might be heard asking, "Hey, why didn't you call him after me? I'll pass away and somebody has to carry the name on." Anthony is an unbelievable and good-hearted boy. When he was born, it was fantastic. I am in the property as well as the business, so when he left school he didn't want to go to university. Instead, he went

Above: Maria with Harry, our third child, 1969.

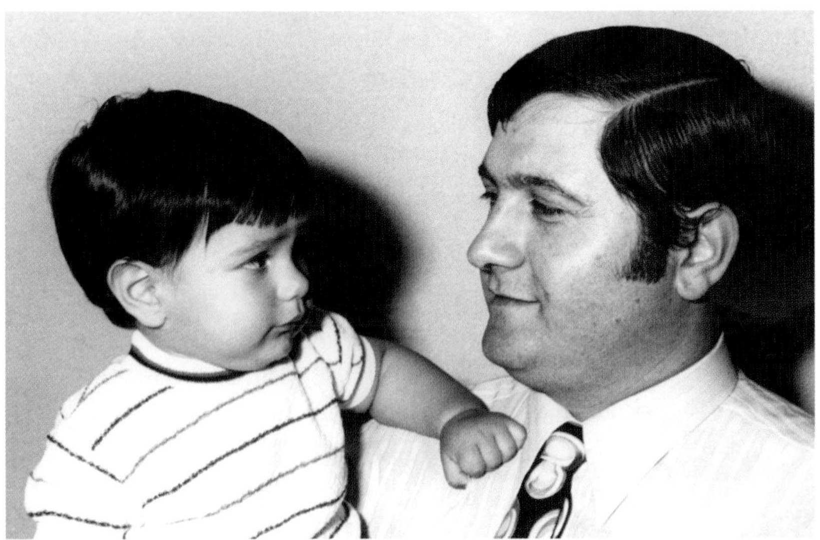

Above: Me with Harry in 1970 in our new home in Balmoral.

and obtained his licence as a builder. It took him five years to do that. He worked as an apprentice with a building company called Tecton, which is from the Greek word *techni* meaning 'technology'. Anthony also liked working in the meat business as well. We had the factory at Dulwich Hill, so after he finished his building course, he worked there. He saw to it that the operation ran smoothly and later became the quality assurance inspection officer for the group. These days, Anthony is working with me in the cruise ship business. Clients are always impressed when they see a member of the family who has a hands-on role checking the quality of our product.

As well, he enjoys helping me run our olive grove, 'Woodlands' and oil brand, 'Woodlands Olive Oil'. We also produce other lines like infused oils, tapenades and table olives at our property in the Hunter Valley.

Anthony married, but unfortunately after ten years that ended in divorce. He came away from that with two beautiful sons: Damien, and his brother Nick, who was named after me. They both went to Mosman Prep and their high school was Scots College. Both boys are very keen on the topics of health and fitness, and spend their time exploring everything to do with health. They have progressed to become personal trainers and pursue these interests. Anthony has now remarried. He met his wife Chantal a few years ago and has found happiness again. She works as receptionist at a well-known real estate agency.

My son Harry has done well. At first he wanted to be a barrister. But then, a chance encounter made him move in another direction. One day Marietta and her husband George invited Harry to their home at the Connaught building in the city for lunch. Also there was this young fellow from America, about the same age as Harry. He just happened to live next door to Marietta and George. This fellow told them about the work he was doing on a development at Darling Harbour. As a project manager, he was being paid something like $2,000 a week. Everyone was interested in what he had to say and as he had the keys to the site, he suggested they go with him to check out the project. Down to Darling Harbour they went and spent most of the day there – not a soul was around. After this, Harry said to me, “That is what I want to do, be a project manager.” This fellow from America had made him realise this was something he could do and be very good at.

Harry went on to complete a Bachelor of Commerce at the University of New South Wales. When he left university, his first project was my offices here at Neutral Bay. There was a florist shop and a butcher shop downstairs. Harry came up with a plan and demolished the building and built a new one. Since then, Harry

Above: My son, Anthony Andrews, as the Quality Assurance Officer inspecting goods before deliveries.

has become invaluable to our family's property investments and an asset to my other businesses in food import and exports.

Harry married his childhood sweetheart Alexandra Vass, which made him very happy. She is daughter of Nick and Marion Vass, a successful self-made couple who also value family. Sixty years ago they created Vass Electrical Industries, a company that designs, manufactures and supplies high-quality busway power distribution solutions for clients all around the world. Over the years, we have enjoyed a few overseas trips with them. Alex always supported Harry in achieving their goals while bringing up their family. In later years when the children grew up, she became a life and business coach, which suited her personality. She has always created happiness with her vivacious character and enjoys helping people.

Harry and Alex have three exceptional children: Stephanie, Nick, also named after me, and William. Stephanie attended Queenwood School for Girls and then achieved a Bachelor of Commerce, majoring in commercial law marketing, and now works at KPMG in the consumer brand and marketing advisory division. Nick and William went to Mosman Prep and after that went to high school at Shore School. Nick is now studying a Bachelor of Commerce and a Bachelor of Law at the University of Sydney, majoring in finance, and works part-time at KPMG. William is the last of the grandchildren and is still at Shore School in his final HSC year. He is a platoon commander in the Shore Australian Army Cadet regiment.

Maria and I have enjoyed watching all our grandchildren grow to be very special, intelligent individuals, with each one having something unique to offer the world they live in. It amazes us to see this new generation of young ones that all think quite differently and probably all aspire to different goals and ambitions. But all share the common desire to be part of our bonded family, to love and be loved. Maria and I don't always agree with what they all get up to, but times have changed and life is very different now to the world of traditions and boundaries that we grew up in. Nevertheless, we are very proud of each and every one of them, and look forward to seeing what they will do with their lives in time.

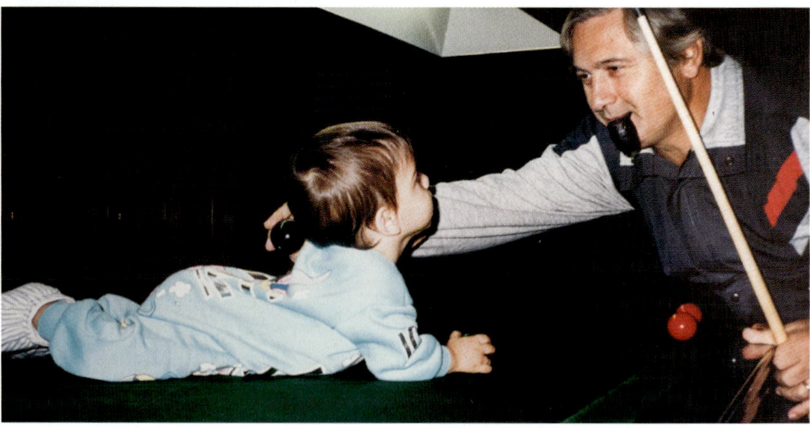

Above: Peter, my grandson, helping me play snooker at home in Balmoral.
Right: With my youngest grandson, William Andrews, Harry and Alex's youngest son, in the park at Balmoral.

Above: Anthony celebrating his birthday with his wife Chantal, his sister Marietta, and his two sons, Damian and Nick.

Above: Harry and Alex with our granddaughter, Stephanie, at her graduation in 2017.

Above: Nicholas Andrews – Harry's son at his Shore High School Cadet Parade 2017.

Above: Our dear friend and visitor from Akrata, Harry Railis arriving in Sydney on his 104th birthday.

Above: Taken from our home in Akrata with our friend and neighbour, Vasilli.

Chapter Four

In 1970 we purchased our current home in Stanton Road, which is on Balmoral Beach. Sometimes, I think it is the most beautiful place in the world. We are right on the beach and have wonderful views of Sydney Harbour. And the people who live in this part of Sydney are kind, friendly and welcoming. Maria and I are very happy here and we can't imagine we would ever want to live anywhere else. It is a very special community.

Every second day I walk down to the beach and go about halfway along – to where the Bather's Pavilion is located. Then, I turn around and walk back up to Stanton Road which takes me about twenty minutes. After that, I have a shower, have my breakfast and admire the beautiful view we have straight between the heads. It is a stunning sight.

In 1990, Paul Francis from Balmoral started the Humpty Dumpty Foundation. I became a sponsor to help raise money for this worthy cause. They raise money through a now-famous event called the Balmoral Burn. This is a run, or a walk, depending on your level of fitness, up Awaba Street from the beach to the top of the hill. It's not all that far, about 400 metres, but it is very steep and a challenge no matter how fit you are. The record is about one and a half minutes. I think if I had to walk up it, it might take me twenty minutes. Of course, the point of the Balmoral Burn is to have everyone participate so that the Humpty Dumpty Foundation can raise money for hospitals. They look after over two hundred hospitals and have donated millions of dollars to them.

As part of the event, they have an annual dinner for the foundation for about five hundred people on Balmoral Beach itself. The organisers bring in big tractors which level out the sand on the beach. Then, they erect an enormous marquee that fits all the guests. When you walk in you would just think you are walking into one of Sydney's finest restaurant venues, rather than being seated under a tent on the beach. As a sponsor, each year I attend the Balmoral Burn dinner.

Often the prime minister or the treasurer will be at the function, as well as other distinguished people. I buy a table for ten guests every year. They raise money from the guest price and they also run an auction. This money is used to buy life-saving equipment for hospitals and over $3.5 million is raised altogether from this event at Balmoral every year. Last year there was this fellow who told us his life story. They showed photos of when he was born – they didn't expect him to live, he was so tiny. But they used one of these breathing machines and he survived. He went on to become a professional singer.

Opposite, top left: With my grandsons visiting at home. Front left to right: Peter Manettas, Nick Andrews. Back left to right: Nick Harry Andrews, Nick Anthony Andrews, Damian Anthony Andrews, William Harry Andrews.
Top right and bottom: The Humpty Dumpty Foundation Balmoral Burn, with our grandson, Peter, handing the relay baton to William. Teams take position for the race up the very steep Awaba Street hill – approximately 450 metres uphill!

Above: William, Nick, Peter and Damian before the Burn. The winner is not yet determined.

Above: Our son Harry with three of our grandchildren, Stephanie, Nicola and Peter, celebrating crossing the finish line.

We had seen him sing on television and there he was standing just beside us. When I looked at him, I couldn't believe he was the same person they showed in the photos of this fragile, little baby. One of these machines had saved his life, and it was up for auction. His story really encouraged Maria and I to bid for it. Maria did the bidding and donated $6,000 for a machine which saves prematurely born babies who can't breathe properly. It is such a good cause and it makes me proud to think that it happens in the community where I live.

My family also loves Surfers Paradise. I love Surfers so much and that is why I made a lot of investments there. The Golden Gate was one of the first big high-rise building in Surfers. We bought a nice unit there on the thirty-second floor forty years ago. There is only one floor above it which is penthouses and swimming pools. There are four swimming pools on the roof and other ones down in the garden. It is a beautiful place. When the kids were young, we used to have a lot of fun up there. I used to go up there with the family in the school holidays. I'd stay with them Saturday, Sunday, Monday and Tuesday – four days. Wednesday morning I would fly to Sydney – Wednesday, Thursday, Friday – three days in the office and then Friday night fly back up there. It was always a special time with the family and one I shall never forget. We still use it today.

Chapter Five

Sometime after I arrived in Sydney from Trangie in 1954, I had the pleasure of meeting a gentleman by the name of John Kuvelis. He was a much older man – well it didn't take much to be older than me – I was only twenty-one – but John Kuvelis was my idol. He owned many of the cinemas in both the city and in the country; although in those days we called them 'picture shows'. Even today there is a very well-known cinema complex on George Street in the city – this was once owned by John. Remarkably, he came from the same town in Greece that I did: Akrata. So when we met and discovered this connection, from then on we had a special bond.

John Kuvelis was responsible for the building of the Hellenic Club in Elizabeth Street. It was an impressive building – about 1,400 cubic metres and seven stories high. His committee also purchased an adjoining block in Castlereagh Street. From my earliest days in Sydney, I was a member of the Hellenic Club, although no one called it that – to us it was always the 'Greek Club'. And over the years the impressive building that John constructed became older, more tired and shabbier by the day. The kitchen was an antique, the toilets stank, more often than not the lifts didn't work and there was no car park.

The board of the club asked me to join them in planning the development of the Elizabeth Street and Castlereagh Street sites, which backed onto each other to create one large building. The proposal was that the developer would sell 60% of the completed building and the other 40% of the completed building remained the property of the Hellenic Club. After sixty-eight years, the ownership of the entire building would revert back to the 100% Hellenic Club's property. I was both honoured and wary. To be involved in this I would have to join the board, and this meant going through the ordeal of trying to get a boardroom of Greeks to reach agreement on something. Friends of mine urged me to take it on, claiming that without me a new building would never happen. "The Greeks can't get their heads together, they are always fighting," my friends complained. When they said this, I reminded myself that we almost lost to the Trojans all those years ago because of infighting! You never see the Greeks working as a group, like the Jewish or the British. You put Greeks together and before long they want to start fighting each other. Everybody wants to be the boss. There is a Greek saying: "When you hear too many roosters cry every morning, it takes longer for the day to break."

So when I joined the board of the Hellenic Club, I went in with my eyes open. I was appointed the leader of the building committee. I knew there would be obstacles and people with their own agendas, but I could cope with this. As someone who had done well in this country, I believed I had an obligation to make a contribution to the community, to give back.

There were three of us on the building committee: John Cominos, a chemist; and a young economist, whose name I have forgotten. I don't think he knew what the hell he was talking about – he had just graduated from university – but I was okay with that – the club liked to give young fellows a go. Our job was to come up with a proposal to develop the site. The plan we came up with was to enlarge the current building to twenty-two stories. The ground floor would be leased to shops, coffee shops and bars. The next few floors would be leased as commercial office space. The club itself was to be greatly expanded and its facilities upgraded. When special guests, such as the president of Greece, or other important people came to Sydney, we would have a smart reception hall where they could have receptions and make speeches. The top floor was to be a restaurant and bar. The floors in between would become residential units with views overlooking Hyde Park. As well as this, we would also build a new underground car park.

As the club had no money, there were only two options: either the club would have to take out a massive loan for the project; or we could bring in a developer who would fund everything in return for a long-term commercial lease. I knew the board of the club would never consider taking out a loan, and I agreed with this strategy. It was too risky and the club could face an interest bill which they'd never be able to repay.

My committee realised that the only way to make this happen was to agree to lease the total land, owned by the club, to a developer for sixty-eight years. After that period of time, ownership reverted to the club. But in the meantime, this arrangement would put the club on a very sound financial footing – it would bring in rent for the lower floors as well as the restaurant and by our calculations, if this were to happen, the Hellenic Club itself would today be sitting on about $12 million net profit. As well as being in a good financial position, we would have a new club, and a bigger club, with better amenities and facilities, and best of all, at absolutely no cost to its members.

We spoke to a number of developers and made it very clear to them that it was a non-negotiable condition that they pay all the expenses for the DA, and of course pay for every cent of the construction cost. One developer became convinced that it was a good project. He said to me, "Nick, do you think it will go through after a vote of the members?"

"They can't be that stupid, mate." I replied. "They're Greeks, they like to argue, but they're not stupid. We will have new lifts, a car park, new club rooms – who is going to knock that back?" In the end, this developer spent a quarter of a million dollars on the DA – this is what it costs to draw up plans, liaise with council and government bodies, and so forth.

According to the club's constitution, our proposal had to be passed by 75% of the members to get the go-ahead. From memory there were about 600 members, and I believe many of them had a background similar to mine – they came out to this country, they started a business, did well and were now Australians proud of their Greek heritage. However, I had a conversation with one member which made me realise that we had a fight on our hands to get the approval of the members.

This member, who was about sixty years old, was talking to me one day and he told me he was buying an off-the-plan unit at the Hellenic Club for $1.1 million. He was very happy with the price because this unit was probably worth $1,450,000 or more elsewhere in Sydney. It sounded like a bargain until I told him he was not buying, but leasing the unit for sixty-eight years. By contrast, the units which were to be constructed on our site would be freehold title – not leased. I said to him, "Why wouldn't you pay more for a unit which was yours forever?"

"No. I have leasehold for sixty-eight years. Do you think I'm going to live another sixty-eight years?"

"You're only thinking about yourself," I said.

"Who else will I think of? Who is going to pay it? My sons and my daughters or my grandsons? Stuff them. They can go and find their own homes." I have never forgotten that conversation and I must admit it rattled me. It wasn't like he didn't have the money – but sometime later, admittedly a long time down the track, his entire investment would be lost when the lease expired. Our proposal couldn't have been more different – but this man was retired and thinking only of himself. I was still working, as I do today, and thinking of one thing and one thing only: family.

Our proposal was relatively simple. The club did not have to fund anything, but it had to surrender the land to a developer for sixty-eight years. The developers would get the money they invested back by selling the residential units they built. In the meantime, the club would get an income stream from renting the lower floors as well as the restaurant. After that sixty-eight years, ownership would once more revert to the club. My committee took our proposal to the board and they agreed it should go to a vote of the members. A general meeting was called and it disappointed me to see that very few of our young members were there. People stood up and asked lots of questions, many of which I thought were pretty dumb questions. "Why should we lease it for sixty-eight years? This is our club. We built it ourselves!" Very patiently I would point out that the developer was paying for the building of a new complex and they were needed to be able to recoup their investment by having those income streams for those sixty-eight years. After that, ownership would revert to the club.

The first vote came in at about 60% which was disappointing. Then, I learned that one of our 'supporters' was in fact encouraging members to vote against us. There was a bit of a whispering campaign that Nick Andrews was pushing for this because he was going to make a fortune out of it. “Now you can understand how he became a millionaire,” they would complain. Not only was I not going to make a cent out of this, I had actually contributed a lot of my own time for absolutely no remuneration whatsoever. But I think it’s easier to believe that people are only in it for themselves. I wanted it to give something back to the Greek community and especially the younger generation to come. In the end, we could not get 75% of the members to give us the green light. It just broke my heart. Since then of course, real estate values in Sydney have sky-rocketed, but time has stood still at the Hellenic Club. If you go there today, you will see that it remains an old and sick establishment slowly falling into ruin.

Chapter Six

When I lived in Trangie all those years ago, I became friends with farmers and often went out shooting feral pests on their properties. At one stage I bought a farm and some sheep with the local bank manager, Keith Duncan. Things didn't turn out very well because of the drought and we both lost a lot of money. His wife used to bring his lunch out to the property when we were working there and put it under a tree. He would put his hat on so that people didn't see him feeding the sheep on the railway line. In the end, after I left Trangie, I walked away from this investment and left it to him. By then there were about 500 head of sheep left and they looked like they were just about ready to die. A few years later I heard that it eventually rained and my bank manager friend made a few bob.

Decades later, I was about to drive out of my garage when a car pulled up out the front. A young woman in high heels climbed out and I could see her struggling to lift a box which must have weighed over twenty kilograms. "Hang on," I called out. "I will help you. What is this?"

"It's for Mrs Andrews."

"I am her husband, Nick Andrews."

"Nice to meet you."

I realised this was the girl from Amway, because Maria bought all our soap and stuff from them, and they home delivered. I said, "Maria's in the garden. I'll call her. She will be up shortly." I invited her into the house and carried the box in for her. She came in and was very grateful. I was leaving for the office, but didn't want to leave her on her own in the kitchen. So I sat down and talked to her while we waited for Maria. For some reason I said to this young woman, "Where did this firm you work for come from?"

"My father started it."

"Oh. How did he do that? Did he work for a company like that?"

She said, "No, he was a banker."

"Really? Where? In the city."

"No, in a small town. You would never have heard of it."

"I'm just curious," I explained.

"It's a place in the middle of nowhere called Trangie."

In disbelief I said, "Where?"

"Trangie," she repeated. I was speechless. She saw this meant something to me. I looked at her, took a good guess at her age and asked, "You have a sister, haven't you?"

She smiled. "Yes."

"Are you twins?"

"No, but there's only a year between us. I'm the youngest. How would you know that?"

I said to her, "Do you remember a cafe opposite the bank?" This was the CBC Bank, which is non-existent now.

"Yeah," she replied, trying to remember the name, "the … the …"

"The Trocadero," I said.

"That's it! I remember it very well."

"Do you remember the fellow there who used to work there? A boy?"

"Oh yes. He was very cheeky. He used to undo the bow in my hair. One day I started crying so he gave me lollies."

I started laughing. "What was his name?" I could see that she was going through this in her head. "I don't know. But my father would know. He liked him a lot and used to eat there all the time." Then just as I was about to say something, she said, "Nick! It was Nick. Nick the Greek!"

I looked at her and said, "I am Nick the Greek. That cheeky boy was me."

"Oh my God!" She ran up and hugged me and kissed me. I said, "If Maria walks in she will think what the hell is going on here!" Then I told this young woman who I was and about my business after I came to Sydney. She said, "I am having a surprise party for Dad on his 70th birthday. You must come!" It was at this place in Willoughby Road.

On the day of his party, his daughter explained to me what I had to do and so when I arrived I rang the internal phone. She then told him that he had to guess who this was coming to his party. The daughter had said to me that I had to ask him a question, something that he would remember, but not something obvious. I knew if I said something like, "Do you remember the young bloke in the cafe across the road from the bank?" that would be too easy.

When I got to the party I called the internal phone and they put Keith on. "Hello?" I heard him say.

"I asked you for a loan and you said, 'How old are you?' I said, 'Seventeen.' You said, 'You're too young. Come back when you're twenty-one.' 'But I need the money now.' After a few words you said to come and talk to you and then you gave me an overdraft of £1,000."

Keith said, "Come in Nick." The door opened, I went in and saw Keith for the first time in about thirty years. We hugged each other. I was so happy to see him. For a seventy year old he looked in good shape. He told me he had built a steel boat and had plans to travel around the world in it.

Chapter Seven

After Maria and I married, we had three children – this was in the early sixties. As time went on we invested in the most essential things: home, car, business and finally in 1990, a farm in the Hunter Valley. When I bought the farm, in the back of my mind I was thinking of the people who survived during the war years thanks to the food from my family's farm. Professional people like my uncle, the lawyer, used to come from the city down to the village and out to the mountains to get their food. Sometimes, grapes and other fruits were in season. If it was winter, there were walnuts and chestnuts and we would light a fire in our house each night.

In Athens during the war, money was worth nothing. You could throw bank notes in the streets and no one would bother picking them up due to severe inflation caused by the German occupation. It stuck in my mind how those people appreciated having somebody in the village who could provide food for them. And the people with the food were all poor – they were not rich, they didn't have cars, they had nothing more than donkeys and horses. My mother used to get together with other women and they would spend their time cooking, baking things and looking after the children. The men used to go into the club, to talk politics – who would be the next prime minister – how were they going to get more money – or a bigger pension, nobody was willing to work, and nobody was paying taxes. It still happens now.

I thought Australia was like a big garden with no fence – if Indonesia wants to come here, they can walk straight in – who's going to stop them? In the Second World War they called in the Americans and they stopped the Japanese. Otherwise, they would have taken over Australia. The Americans have their own problems now. I don't think they would bother to come to help us out. This makes me think that a person should always own a piece of land; somewhere you can grow food, have a couple of goats and maybe some cows. If you have a couple of lambs, you can shear them and have wool and make a jumper so you aren't cold in the winter. So this is why we bought a farm in the Hunter Valley which is called 'Woodlands'.

A man called Geoff looks after the farm. He is a terrific fellow. We have orange trees, pomegranates and 6,000 olive trees. Geoff sells everything – he sells the olive oil, the fruit and the vegetables. After one of our seasons, there were lots of leftover oranges that we just didn't need. I said to him, "Mate, take all the oranges. Do what you like. Take them. They're all yours."

"Are you sure?" He was counting and counting and filling the whole truck up, so he could sell them all. They had a beautiful flavour.

About half of the property is set aside for the growing of olives. This is mainly because of that time when my mother saved those two starving boys in the war with the spoonfuls of olive oil. My father had olives which he passed onto me. I still have three hundred olive trees on my property in Greece that are three hundred years old. There is one olive tree in my village which is believed to be 1,100 years old. It is in the restaurant and its trunk would be about three metres across. All the tourists go there. This famous tree has a large hole in it and the kids climb inside it and hide.

Olives are part of a Greek person's blood – probably in the same way that Australians have this obsession with 'the bush' – hardly any Australians live in the bush, but that's how Australians think of themselves – as being connected to the bush. Having a farm with olive trees gives me a connection to my past, and that's important to me. Ideally, I would like to go to the farm every weekend, but that's not always possible.

I am a member of the Helmos Club and they do a lot of activities. They have a ball once a year in Sydney, and every year on St Nicholas' Day, 6 December, they put on a big party at the club. All the Nicholases go there and everybody wishes them a happy name day. You have a couple of drinks, talk and laugh and misbehave. One time, the president of the Helmos Club asked me if it was possible to bring the members to our farm. I agreed. He hired these double-decker buses and over two hundred and fifty people turned up.

We partied as only Greeks know how. There was delicious food coming out of a big wooden oven, and being in the meat business I was able to supply the best meat available. And the chef cooked fish for anybody who didn't eat meat. An orchestra played Greek music and there was a lot of dancing. At the end of the night when everybody was happy, they started breaking plates in the Greek tradition.

Everyone has seen this in movies and it is such a tradition that Greek restaurants and cafes buy cheap and easy-to-break plates, for just such occasions. You buy a stack of these cheap plates, and then when people have had too much to drink, they get excited, pick up one of these cheap china plates and go boom, boom, boom!

Unfortunately, at the party on our farm, I felt I had thought of everything, but not this. We didn't have cheap plates and it's impossible to explain this to guests who are having the time of their lives that they are smashing all your best crockery. The guests even moved on from the nice plates and broke the cups and saucers as well. They broke all of our plates and for a long time afterwards Maria didn't have any plates in the house. I presume they thought we had remembered to buy the breakable plates and didn't realise they were destroying the very crockery from our house. Still, everyone had a nice time and at the end I gave them all a bottle of Hunter Valley wine and a bottle of olive oil each to take home. They are still talking about it. I think they raised enough money to put air conditioning in the club on Canterbury Road.

Above: Buying the Hunter Valley Farms has become Maria's and my pride and joy. It is always a special time when our family join us up there.

Above: The wood-fired oven at our olive oil farm in the Hunter Valley where we quite often roast full suckling pigs and full lambs for our guests.

Chapter Eight

Friends, family and business colleagues know that I love talking to people and I love a good story. I can't help myself and I have always been like this. I never have any trouble striking up a conversation with someone. And I love telling stories about my experiences. I think it's part of being a Greek. But I also know that not everyone wants to hear my stories. Sometimes, I have been telling a story and I notice the person listening looks at their watch, or yawns, or just looks bored. One time on a drive from Sydney to the farm in the Hunter Valley, I was telling a story to a passenger friend. I was so engrossed in the story, I missed the Hunter Valley exit, and ended up in Newcastle. Because of this, I was given the nickname: 'Mr Smoothy'.

We have a tennis court at our house in Mosman, and friends used to come over for a game and afterwards we'd have a couple of drinks and a chat. One time we were playing tennis and there was a little girl, the granddaughter of one of my mates, who was sitting there on her own watching us play tennis. She must have been about seven years old and looking a bit lost. I said, "Listen, it is no good watching tennis here. Go inside and ask Mrs Andrews to let you watch TV in the house."

"Okay," she agreed.

"Go around the side, knock on the door and she will let you in."

Off she went and then I heard this child tap on the door and say, "Hi, Mrs Smoothy. Mr Smoothy said I can come in and watch TV."

Where she heard it from, I do not know. But that is how I learned that I had been given the nickname Mr Smoothy. I wasn't upset in the slightest. I thought it was funny, but it did make me feel old. What else made me feel old was when my hair started to go grey. Although what kept me positive about that was one of my friends who was balding who said to me, "I wouldn't care if my hair went blue – as long as it stayed on."

Another nickname I have is: 'The Judge'. I earned this name because of what happened once downstairs at the Diethnes restaurant, which is a very popular Greek restaurant. There was about ten of us in our group and we'd all had quite a bit to drink. As I worked in an office, I wore a tie and so did the others; although when we went to dinner with friends, we wouldn't wear a tie. However, one of the blokes always wore a tie – he wouldn't take it off. One evening during our dinner, John, one of the men from our table, stood up and disappeared. He came back with some scissors which he tried to hide. He stood behind this bloke with the tie and started talking to him and being very friendly. Then, out came the scissors. He cut this fellow's tie off and put it in his pocket without him even noticing! The man sitting next to him was too drunk to notice. John, the man with the scissors, then snuck off to the bathroom and pinned this chopped off bit of tie to his shirt. When he came back, he sat down opposite the fellow whose tie was now half its normal size.

This man then looked at the tie John had pinned to his shirt and complained, "I went out and bought a bloody new tie and it just happens to be exactly like yours."

"It looks exactly like yours," said John, "because it is yours." The other fellow looked at John, trying to make sense of this, and then looked down and noticed that his tie had been chopped off. He was furious and wanted an apology – wanted a fight, wanted this, and wanted that.

I could see it was getting a bit tricky. I stood up and announced, "Listen, we are Greeks. That is where democracy started. We should know better. We should be more civilised than Australian men. Instead, you blokes are mucking around and abusing each other. This is a restaurant – quiet please! We are now going to hold court and listen to the evidence. We will see if he has done wrong and how much it will cost him if he has to pay a fine."

Someone threw a towel at me and said, "You be the judge." So I put it on top of my head, like a barrister's wig. We then went into session and heard the evidence from the various people – it was typical silly stuff – but we had a lot of fun. All the restaurant was listening. And after that, they started calling me The Judge.

Above: After playing tennis at my home in Mosman with friends.

Above: Celebrating my 70th birthday with friends at a restaurant in the city.
Left: Maria and I dancing and being encouraged and clapped on by friends to dance the night away!

Chapter Nine

It really stuck in my mind all those years ago when Mr McKay told me in Trangie that if any man worked hard enough, he could someday drive his own Rolls Royce. I have told the story of what happened when he asked his widow to sell me his Rolls Royce after his death. The first opportunity I had to buy a Rolls Royce was in 1974. I still have it – it has done less than 100,000 miles. Then, I couldn't help myself and bought a second Rolls Royce ten years ago. One I call 'The Old Lady' and the new one 'The Young Lady'. When you look at the car registration, it doesn't actually say what year the car was made in, so if anybody asks I always say, "Ladies don't like to be asked how old they are." They are the most beautiful cars and do turn people's heads.

The leather still smells new after all this time. The Rolls Royces are kept in the garage and serviced properly. I took my children to their weddings in them. About five years ago I drove one of my little granddaughters, Stephanie, in one of my Rolls Royce's to her hockey game. She said, "Can I sit in the back?"

"You can sit in the back," I replied. She was looking in the mirror and pretending she was the queen. I was watching her. Then I asked, "You like the Rolls Royce? You like my car?"

"I love it! You took my father to the church when my mother and father got married." "Yes."

"Can you take me when I get married in the same one?"

"Maybe," I said. "But you had better hurry up and get married because I might not be around. I will hang on to it, and I promise you, if I'm around, I'll drive you to your wedding."

I have always been mad about cars. I have about six cars including the Rolls Royces and a Porsche. In the past I have owned a Hudson, a Daimler, a Chrysler, a Studebaker and a Buick. Cars were my toys and they still are. Having cars gives me a lot of pleasure and I can justify this on the basis that I'm not a gambler or someone who wastes money. And it is true that cars are on the whole a very bad investment – you almost always lose money the moment you take ownership of the vehicle. Despite this, I wouldn't have it any other way. I love showing off a car and being its proud owner.

Many years ago, when I was a single man I found girls liked going out with a man who had a smart-looking car. This didn't happen in Trangie, but when I arrived in Sydney things were different. The girls loved having a boyfriend who could drive them to and from dances. Those days are long gone and today most of my driving is to travel to and from the office, or up to the farm in the Hunter Valley. Even so, the enjoyment I get out of driving one of my Rolls Royces has never been lost.

Above: Riding in one of my Rolls Royces back from a business lunch with Royal Carribean Cruise Lines. Peter, my oldest grandson, took a photo of us, and put this dear message on social media, "Waking up each day and being able to work with my mentor, inspiration and best friend is something I don't take for granted. Papou, thank you for constantly challenging my thoughts and teaching me the fundamentals of life. Everyday is a new lesson!"

Above: I always had a passion to own a Rolls Royce. I did manage to buy one in 1974 and since then have driven each of our three children to church on their wedding days. It will be available for my grandchildren when their time comes.

Chapter Ten

I'm now eighty-five years old and it seems to me that I am in the prime of my life. I still go to work every day, and I like to think that my experience of life and business will be passed on to another generation. It is strange how one's memory works, but those dangerous years during the war are almost as vivid in my mind now as they were then. That was a time when we considered ourselves lucky every day my father came home alive. Somehow, we survived those terrible times, and then they made that courageous decision to send me away to the end of the world in the hope of a better life. My parents gave me that chance and I vowed that I would never let them down – that I would return to Greece a success. Things didn't quite go according to plan, but I know they were both proud of me and my achievements. My father told me repeatedly they were proud of me, and moreover, that I also helped my younger brothers to succeed.

My grandmother Sophia never remarried. I have a photo of her with my daughter, Marietta, when she was two years old. They are in the garden cutting lettuce. Sophia lived in the house I built for my parents in Greece. It was a big block of land – a couple of

Above: Family photo, 1974.

Above: Family photo, 1979

thousand square metres. They had a fowl yard in the back and a couple of goats, and she used to look after the chooks and her garden. In the photo, my little daughter was inside the garden and you can hardly see her head from above the plants. My grandmother is bending over holding different vegetables on her arm. I took that photo in 1963.

In her later years Sophia developed cancer, but nobody was aware of it. It was only when Maria and I went over there in 1963. Maria happened to go through the laundry and found unusual stains on her clothes. She told my father, who told my mother, who called the doctor. The doctor checked her out, but it was too far gone. If that could have been removed, she would have had more years. Grandmother Sophia died at the age of ninety-six.

Also, I need to mention my uncle Sam, who sponsored me to come to Australia and looked after me when I was a thirteen year old peeling potatoes at the back of the Trocadero Cafe. I was in a strange country on my own. Uncle Sam was the nearest thing I had to a father figure – to be honest he was far from perfect, but I did learn much from him – and can never forget his wonderful sense of humour. He and his wife Maria looked after me and I am thankful for that. They were good family people.

Whilst it is true that we have been blessed with good health and good fortune, I was the lucky one who happened to be up a ladder in front of the Annandale shop when this most beautiful young woman walked past. I was transfixed from that moment. She proved to be the best wife that any man could find. I've spoken here about how important my family has been to me, but I must again say none of my achievements would have mattered at all were it not for Maria. She has been with me and by my side for almost sixty years. We have been through thick and thin together. Marriage is not easy, business is not easy, and life itself can throw at you some disasters every now and then. And yet through it all, there has been Maria – quiet, unassuming, never complaining, always cheerful and with a smile on her face – and ready and willing to be there at a moment of crisis.

I was a typical male in the Greek tradition – I went to work while Maria provided a home and raised our children. But nothing I did in business would have been possible without her being there to support me, and to give me encouragement and advice when I most needed it.

Greece, the country of my birth, is always in the news now, for all the wrong reasons. Many times in my life I considered moving back to Greece, but that would not have been a good move. It's going to be a long time before prosperity returns to Greece. This

Above: Outside the house in Porovitsa where I was born.

does strike me as being a strange situation, because I've never heard of a person leaving Greece and immigrating to another country who did not do well.

And as a boy in the village of Porovitsa, I learned from my parents all the things that set me on the right path in life – work hard, be honest, keep your word – and make us proud.

I've never forgotten the moment when my father and I were standing on Vigla Hill looking down on the beach at Akrata. My only dream as a boy was to make enough money in Australia to be able to buy my father a pushbike. But my father had more faith in me, more than I could ever have imagined. "When you grow up Nick, I would love to have a house down there so I don't have to walk up this damned hill, because you know I am getting old."

Above: Family photo in the ruins of our old Porovitsa house, thirty-two years after I left.

Above: A family ski holiday.

Above: Family ski holidays in our mobile home.

Above: Innsbruck, Austria.

Above: Family holiday to Turkey, 1982.

I promised him I would help him do that; a promise I was able to keep. And who knows, maybe I'll follow his example and one day find myself on the beach at Akrata. And just as I did, maybe a young Greek man full of energy and ideas will see me at the beach and decide it may be worthwhile listening to the advice of this old man. Where would I begin? What else could I say to him, but: "Trusting is good, checking is better."

The End

Left: My family – April 2018 – all sixteen of us at my home!